Margaret Oliphant

For my mother, Patricia Sanders,
And in memory of her mother,
Mary Hill (1890–1960)

Margaret Oliphant

Valerie Sanders

Professor of English, the University of Hull.

EER
Edward Everett Root, Publishers, Brighton, 2020.

EER
Edward Everett Root, Publishers, Co. Ltd.,
30 New Road, Brighton, Sussex, BN1 1BN, England.
Full details of our overseas agents are given on our website.
www.eerpublishing.com

edwardeverettroot@yahoo.co.uk

Valerie Sanders, *Margaret Oliphant.*

Key Popular Women Writers series, Volume 1.

First published in Great Britain in 2020.

ISBN: 978-1-912224-90-6 Paperback
ISBN: 978-1-912224-91-3 Hardback
ISBN: 978-1-912224-92-0 eBook

Cover designed by Pageset Limited, High Wycombe, Buckinghamshire.

Series editors:
Janine Hatter and Helena Ifill.

This innovative new series delivers original and transformative, peer reviewed, feminist research into the work of leading women writers who were widely read in their time, but who have been under-represented in the canon.

The series offers critical, historical and aesthetic contributions to current literary and theoretical work. Each volume concentrates on one writer.

The first five titles are available:

- *Geraldine Jewsbury* by Abigail Burnham Bloom.
- *Florence Marryat* by Catherine Pope.
- *Margaret Oliphant* by Valerie Sanders.
- *Mrs. Henry Wood* by Mariaconcetta Costantini.
- *Frances Trollope* by Carolyn Lambert.

These will be followed by volumes on:

- *Mary Braddon*
- *Rhoda Broughton*
- *Daphne Du Maurier*
- *Ouida*
- *Mary Shelley*
- *Marie Corelli*
- *Charlotte Riddell*
- *Edith Wharton*

We welcome suggestions for other titles.

The series volumes interrogate the ways in which women writers, their creative processes and published material can be considered feminist, and explore how recent developments in feminist theory can enrich our understanding of popular women writer's lives and literature.

The authors rethink established popular writers and their works, and rediscover and re-evaluate authors who have been largely neglected – often since their initial burst of success in their own historical period. This neglect is often due to the exclusivity and insular nature of the canon which has its roots in the Victorian critical drive to perpetuate a division between high and low culture.

In response, our definition of the "popular" is broadly interpreted to encompass women writers who were read by large sections of the public, and who wrote for the mass publishing market. The series therefore challenges this arbitrary divide, creating a new and dynamic dialogue regarding the canon's expansion by introducing readers to previously under-researched women writers who were nevertheless prolific, known and influential.

Studying the work of these authors can tell us much about women's writing, creativity and publishing practice, and about how popular fiction intervened in pressing political, social and cultural issues surrounding gender, history and women's roles in society.

This is an important and timely series that is inspired by, interrogates, and speaks to a new wave of feminism, new definitions of sex and gender, and new considerations of inter-sectionality. It also reflects growing interest in popular fiction, as well as a feminist desire to broaden and diversify the literary canon.

Ultimately the series sheds light on women writers whose work deserves greater recognition, facilitates and inspires further research, and paves the way for introducing these key women writers into the canon and modern-day studies.

The editors

DR. JANINE HATTER is an Early Career Researcher based at the University of Hull. With Nickianne Moody she has edited the volume *Fashion and Material Culture in Victorian Fiction and Periodicals,* already published by *EER.* Her research interests centre on nineteenth-century literature, art and culture, with particular emphasis on popular fiction. She has published on Mary Braddon, Bram Stoker, the theatre and identity, and Victorian women's life writing, as well as on her wider research interests of nineteenth to twenty-first century Science Fiction and the Gothic. She has also co-edited special issues for *Revenant, Supernatural Studies, Nineteenth-Century Gender Studies, Femspec* and the *Wilkie Collins Journal.* Janine is conference co-organiser for the Victorian Popular Fiction Association, and co-founded the Mary Elizabeth Braddon Association.

DR. HELENA IFILL is a Lecturer in English Studies at the University of Aberdeen where she is the Director of the Centre for the Novel. Her research focuses on the interactions between Victorian popular fiction, (pseudo)science and medicine. She is the Secretary of the Victorian Popular Fiction Association and a co-organiser of the Association's annual conference. As well as her monograph, *Creating Character: Theories of Nature and Nurture in Victorian Sensation Fiction* (2018), she has published work on Charlotte Riddell, Florence Marryat, Wilkie Collins, Bram Stoker, and Victorian mesmerism. She has also co-edited special issues for *Nineteenth-Century Gender Studies* and the *Wilkie Collins Journal.*

The author

VALERIE SANDERS is Professor of English at the University of Hull. Her interest in Margaret Oliphant began with *Eve's Renegades: Victorian Anti-Feminist Women Novelists* (Macmillan,1996), and she has since contributed four edited volumes to the Pickering and Chatto Masters project, *Selected Works of Margaret Oliphant,* including a scholarly edition of *Hester* (1883). Other edited work includes two volumes of *Records of Girlhood* (Ashgate, 2000 and 2012), anthologies of nineteenth-century women's childhoods, and she has also published widely on Harriet Martineau, most recently a co-edited essay collection, with Gaby Weiner, *Harriet Martineau and the Birth of Disciplines* (Routledge, 2016). Her monographs include *The Brother-Sister Culture in Nineteenth-Century Literature: From Austen to Woolf* (Palgrave Macmillan, 2002), and *The Tragi-Comedy of Victorian Fatherhood* (CUP, 2009).

Contents

Acknowledgements

My thanks are due first to John Spiers for inviting me to write on Margaret Oliphant for this series, and to the series editors, Janine Hatter and Helena Ifill, for their ever helpful and prompt assistance. Like other Oliphant scholars I have benefited hugely from the resurgence of interest in her writing, enhanced by the Pickering Masters *Selected Works of Margaret Oliphant* co-edited by Elisabeth Jay and Joanne Shattock. Their own work, both within and beyond this project, has been a valuable source of wisdom and inspiration, and it has been a pleasure working with them. I am also grateful to Jane Thomas, Sue Brown, and Andrew Hewitt for advice and suggestions, and to Emma Butcher, Katherine Howey, and the audience who attended my Oliphant presentation at the University of Leicester's Victorian Studies Centre in February 2018 for their excellent questions. These sent me away with fresh ideas at a point in the project when external input was especially welcome. Thank you too to the peer reviewers of the sample chapters and full text who responded with exactly the right balance of encouragement and guidance.

Quotations from Margaret Oliphant's correspondence with the Blackwood Publishing House are reproduced by permission of the National Library of Scotland.

Introduction: Margaret Oliphant: "One of those difficult cases for criticism"

"Mrs. Oliphant writes so fast that it is almost impossible
to keep pace with her. All she produces is readable; only
a little of it is memorable"

(Henley, 1884: 5).

How should Margaret Oliphant's vast oeuvre be read in the twenty-first century? As mass-produced "long, loose, vivid yarns," as Henry James called them (1984b: 1411), or a meaningful critical commentary on the lives of men and women in the second half of the nineteenth century? Of course there are many approaches apart from these, but W.E. Henley's observation of 1884 neatly captures what made her popular in her day, and then caused her to disappear for half a century. Her work is "readable," but not "memorable." There is too much of it, and yet (we might add), it is hard to know what she really thinks women should do with their lives. At face value, she seems like an archetypal Victorian writer, a slave to the three-volume novel with its repetitive, eked-out plots, misunderstandings, sudden cataclysms, and endlessly-postponed resolutions; yet her outspokenness about men, her resentment of the marriage plot, and her focus on characters who

1

upturn complacent societies, point to other aspects of Oliphant which make her more attractive to modern readers. If the purpose of this "Key Popular Women Writers" series is to find new ways of discussing authors in light of recent critical developments, a fruitful way of beginning is to question whether Oliphant was, in fact, archetypically "Victorian," or whether, in her later work, especially, she was challenging the social assumptions of her time, and revising her previously conservative responses to women's domestic responsibilities.

Oliphant seems contradictory, both because of her supposed anti-feminism, articulated through positive images of women and denigrating characterisations of men, and her "self-cancellation," as one might call it, alongside her self-promotion. Perhaps her self-protective, hesitant strategies (such as agreeing she should have written less) are little different from those of her female contemporaries, who were quick to apologize for work likely to be disparaged by the literary establishment, but for Oliphant they became a way of life. As Henry James observed soon after her death, she was "one of those difficult cases for criticism" (1984: 1411). My own approach in this volume will be to focus broadly on her self-appointed function as simultaneously insider and outsider, a "critic of the age," both on literary and social matters. If the aim of this study is to re-evaluate Oliphant's significance in the debates about gender during her time and beyond, much of what she says is sharp and surprising. She is wittier than George Eliot or Charlotte Brontë, and more subtle than the "sensation" writers whose work she so deplored. A self-confessed anti-theorist, she nevertheless theorises the nature of men and women, concluding that men are less competent than women, and women themselves socially and domestically undervalued, but doubts whether the status quo will ever change.

As a writer who was popular in the nineteenth century, but largely overlooked until the late twentieth, she was often compared with her contemporaries, not least by those contemporaries

themselves, but in ways that sound equivocal. When Charlotte
Brontë recommended Oliphant's first novel, *Passages in the Life of
Mrs Margaret Maitland* (1849), as suitable reading for an elderly
lady — "Margaret Maitland is a good book — I doubt not — and
will just suit your Mother" (2000: 727), her mid-sentence pause
—"I doubt not"— implies that she herself had not read it. Her
opinion was largely based on hearsay, and indeed the reviews agreed
it was an inoffensive and pleasant read.[1] It would be interesting
to know whether Brontë noticed a reviewer's apology in *Tait's
Edinburgh Magazine* for being so carried away by the "fascinating
Mrs. Margaret Maitland," that no space had been left for "a review
of Currer Bell's new work, 'Shirley.'" (*Tait,* 1849: 766). George
Eliot, eleven years later, was similarly offhand about Oliphant's
Chronicles of Carlingford. While purporting to respect them, she
assured *her* friend, Sara Hennell, that she was *not* the author of
this Trollopian saga: "They are written by Mrs. Oliphant, author
of 'Margaret Maitland' etc.etc.etc." (Haight, 1954–78: IV, 25).
To her publisher, John Blackwood, however, she conceded that
although she had "not read the last number of the Chronicles of
Carlingford, not having much time for extra reading," she had
read "the previous number, and thought the scene between the
Rector and his deaf mother delightful" (Haight, 1954–78: VIII,
292). This was Oliphant's short Carlingford novella, *The Rector,*
serialised with *The Doctor's Family* in *Blackwood's Edinburgh
Magazine* (1861–2), of which Eliot had clearly read the first
number featuring Mr. Proctor's attempt, in "despairing calmness,"
to convey an impression of his new parishioners to his deaf mother.
When Mrs. Proctor fails to hear that Mr. Wodehouse is the
churchwarden, and her son exclaims, "He's an ass!", confident that
his mother will not hear, she responds with satisfaction that this is
exactly her own opinion, and her son's "conciseness" in expressing
his views is exceptionally pleasing (Oliphant 1986b: 12). As Eliot
had already written scenes, in *Adam Bede* (1859), between her
own bachelor Rector, Mr. Irwine, and his dominant mother, she

3

was likely to appreciate this kind of middle-class clerical comedy. Oliphant's version, however, carries more complex nuances. Mrs. Proctor may be exasperating, but at heart she is much younger and sharper than her solemn son, a Fellow of All Souls, and he, in turn, is reconciled to his new post in the country largely because his mother is there in her armchair, making his bachelor Rectory feel like home.

Oliphant began her writing career with old ladies, retained her interest in them throughout her career, and repeatedly brought them to the forefront of her novels. Many of them, such as Aunt Leonora in *The Perpetual Curate* (1864), have the power to change lives and careers, by virtue of the ways in which preferment and estate ownership were managed during the period. For much of this novel Frank Wentworth's aunt toys, King Lear-like, with a clerical "living" she has the power to bestow on whomsoever she nominates, according to which candidate best accords with her religious principles. While we think of men at this time as the chief managers of ecclesiastical appointments, Oliphant reveals the vulnerability of legal arrangements to unexpected shifts in family structures, unforeseen deaths, and new opportunities for women. A striking example is Catherine Vernon in *Hester* (1883), who becomes head of the family bank when her predecessor defaults in disgrace. When history repeats itself and a second male heir to the firm engages in malpractice likely to destroy the business, Catherine reappears, reliable as ever, to restore the bank's credit and save it from collapse. In a more frivolous setting, Lucilla in *Miss Marjoribanks* (1866), becomes the "Queen of Carlingford," through her social "Thursday nights," attempting to influence the candidature of the local Parliamentary election. Oliphant's characteristic irony ensures we are never quite certain whether she is broadly satirizing nineteenth century political structures under Queen Victoria, or just the individuals of its small-town communities. No one is safe from her ambivalent gaze and dry humour, both of which are more extensive and unnerving than

Jane Austen's, though characterized by a similar double-edged scrutiny from the narrator.

Austen, Oliphant and George Eliot all examine the shifting balances of success and failure in the everyday lives of their characters. All three deal primarily with the ordinary humdrum lives of people living in tight-knit communities, where new people arrive and upset tradition. As Laurie Langbauer has noted, however, Oliphant "is not so much interested in portraying the everyday as in investigating the construction of it." Often eschewing neat endings (as for instance in *Hester*, where the eponymous heroine is left unmarried), she prefers to leave some questions open, theorizing the everyday as "a shifting, complex realm" (Langbauer, 1999: 69). It may be too simplistic an assumption to suggest that Oliphant's own life experiences gave her good reason to think like this, but perhaps the most striking thing about her *Autobiography* (1899) is the way she constructs her narrative as alternating between long stretches of steady routine and abrupt disasters over which she had no control. Alternately downplaying her own importance, and telling a story of determined survival against the odds, she conducted her professional life as a continuous attempt to stabilize her dwindling family of dependent men, and prepare them for the future careers they never achieved. Deirdre D'Albertis, however, sees her life and work as "complementary rather than competing realms," and feels there has been too much critical emphasis on her need to write in order to support her fatherless sons (1997: 817). Either way, like the Brontës, Oliphant's reputation is difficult to separate from the extraordinary life that shaped her career, and while its key events are perhaps better known now than previously (thanks to Elisabeth Jay's comprehensive *Literary Life* (1995)), they are worth briefly summarizing at the start of this reappraisal of her achievements.

Oliphant's Life

"Mrs. Oliphant" was born Margaret Oliphant Wilson in Wallyford, Midlothian on 4 April 1828, the youngest child and only surviving daughter of Francis Wilson (c. 1788–1858) and his wife Margaret (née Oliphant) (c.1789–1854). Names here are incestuous and difficult to follow, in that mother and daughter were both at one time called Margaret Oliphant, and when in 1852 the author married her first cousin, Francis Wilson Oliphant (1818–59), she became an Oliphant twice over, hence her initials of "M.O.W.O," which she sometimes used to sign off articles. The designation "Mrs." as with "Mrs." Gaskell, "Mrs." Browning, and "Mrs." Humphry Ward, marks her out from the Brontës, George Eliot, Charlotte Yonge and Harriet Martineau, as a Victorian novelist who had achieved the normalizing status of married woman, and therefore might be expected to win the critics' approval. Unlike Gaskell, Ward or Browning, however, Oliphant was a widow for nearly all her adult life, bar the seven years of her marriage. Both the Wilsons and the Oliphants were blighted by poor health and early death: just as three of her own siblings died in infancy, Oliphant herself lost three babies within their first year of life. Her only daughter Maggie (1853–64) died of gastric fever in Rome at the age of ten, while her two sons Cyril (1856–90) and Francis Romano ("Cecco") (1859–94) seem to have inherited their father's tubercular constitution, and survived only to their early thirties. Her nephew Frank (1854–79), whom she took to live with her when his father's banking career collapsed, fared no better, dying of typhoid in India at the age of twenty-five. Two nieces, Madge and Denny, survived long enough to provide some companionship in Oliphant's old age, but for her the family unit, to which she devoted all her earnings, proved desperately fragile, even by nineteenth-century standards. Oliphant was thus left a wife without a husband and a mother without children, still writing stoically, to within the last few days of her life.

Oliphant's living arrangements were also unstable, and dictated by a succession of family tragedies. Though she was born in Scotland and spent her first ten years there, she grew up in Liverpool, lived as a wife in London and Rome, and as a mother of Eton boys, decided to live close to hand in Windsor. She herself had little formal education other than at home — there is no record of her going to school — though her range of subjects as a *Blackwood's* reviewer demonstrates her knowledge of European languages and culture as well as her ability to read quickly and widely. When she returned home to England in February 1860, after being widowed in Rome, trailing two small children and a new baby, Oliphant in effect had to restart her life, deciding afresh where to live and how to earn a living. From this point onwards her writing was her mainstay, as she balanced her commitments as a regular contributor to *Blackwood's Edinburgh Magazine* (which she had approached for work in 1854) with the development of her career as a novelist. At any one time she might be reading for a *Blackwood's* review, alongside writing at least one, sometimes two novels, in the three-volume format of the time. This was quite apart from the historical, biographical, or literary works she produced at various points in her career. To take one example of an extreme, but not wholly atypical, year, in 1883 Oliphant published the novels *The Ladies Lindores, Hester*, and *It Was a Lover and His Lass*, while also serialising *The Wizard's Son* in *Macmillan's Magazine* (1882–4) and a story, 'The Lady's Walk' (1882–83) in *Longman's Magazine*. She also published a volume on Sheridan for the *English Men of Letters* series (1883). Despite — or because of her sheer stamina in producing this amount of material — Oliphant's relationship with the Blackwood's firm, while cordial, was never something she could entirely take for granted. On several occasions she had to ask for an advance or additional work to make ends meet. In 1882, for example, she wondered jokingly if William Blackwood knew of "any rich person," or "amiable millionaire," from whom she could request a loan, to be repaid by "fifty pounds a quarter." "I could invent one so easily in a novel," she sighed, "but it is harder work in real life."[2] Nor was she above inquiring whether there might be any work for her sons, as Cyril was otherwise likely to be a "briefless barrister."[3]

Nevertheless, as Gaye Tuchman and Nina Fortin have demonstrated, Oliphant earned a steady income from her writing and was not solely dependent on the goodwill of the Blackwood firm. In addition to what she received from Blackwood's, they estimate that "Macmillan paid Mrs. Oliphant at least £10,125 from 1870 to 1891," which averages out at £500 a year: less than a comparable "second rank" Macmillan male novelist, F. Marion Crawford (Tuchman with Fortin 1989:173). Although John Blackwood ranked her with George Eliot as "[p]robably the two cleverest women in the world" (Finkelstein 2010: 33), she was not paid on the same scale as Eliot, and her works were less profitable to the firm. David Finkelstein's research on the Blackwood archive shows that while Oliphant's profitability declined when the Carlingford Chronicles of the 1860s concluded, the Eliot titles remained a steady earner until the end of the century, "accounting for 51.2 percent of the major income generated" (2010: 34). As for sales, Finkelstein provides extensive statistics on print runs, volume costs, and profits of Oliphant's novels, showing that on average Blackwood's printed 1–2,000 copies of her novels, many of them in three volumes, selling most of the print run, and achieving profits of £500–£800 on her most popular, such as *Miss Marjoribanks*, *The Perpetual Curate*, and *Salem Chapel* (2010: 167–8). Elisabeth Jay records that she was paid £1,500 for *The Perpetual Curate*, but corrects the impression given by Tuchman and Fortin's aggregate figures which overlook the decline in earnings Oliphant was able to command once she passed the peak of her fame (1995: 282).

If Oliphant was sometimes disappointed with her offers and profits, her letters to the Blackwood's firm nevertheless provided an outlet for her to think aloud about literature and reviewing, suggest and plan articles, and make authoritative comments on the literary scene. She welcomed visitors to her house in Windsor, spent what she earned, worked long hours, and took a keen interest in the activities of her "young people." Her friends included couples and families, such as Thomas and Jane Carlyle, and Principal John Tulloch of St Andrews, and his wife Jane; there was also a delicate possibility of romance and remarriage with the Reverend Robert Herbert Story, but nothing came of it, and her personal life remained as blameless, heroic and pressurised as it had always been, with periods at home interspersed with foreign, mainly European, travel. Her work extended to the writing of male biographies (Edward Irving, Principal Tulloch, the Count de Montalembert, Laurence Oliphant, Thomas Chalmers), and in her final year, a chapter on "The Sisters Brontë" for a collection on *Women Novelists of Queen Victoria's Reign* (1897). While there was every sign that she was coping well as widowed mother and breadwinner, the relentless family bereavements, from the loss of her babies, parents, husband, and daughter, culminated in the deaths of her two adult sons, Cyril in 1890 and Cecco in 1894. Comparison with Charlotte Brontë's situation as one by one her siblings were taken from her, seems apposite here: only Oliphant was, in a sense, far more grown up and worldly than any of the Brontës, as she herself recognized. As she put it in her *Autobiography*, she had "learned to take perhaps more a man's view of mortal affairs, — to feel that the love between men and women, the marrying and giving in marriage, occupy in fact so small a portion of either existence or thought" (Oliphant 1990: 10). Her life experiences were broader, and her novels reflect a more extensive knowledge of nineteenth-century British social structures, from the Dissenting clergy and shopkeepers of her Carlingford series to the Scottish landowning gentry of *The Wizard's Son* (1884). Like Gaskell's communities in *Cranford* and *Wives and Daughters*, her middle-class families know people with titles, and when they go to London, key acquaintances can admit them to the edges, at least, of the "Season," with its dinner-parties and boat trips. At the other end of the scale, she has tenants afraid of being turned out of their cottages, and the respectable poor clinging to the last shreds of their respectability. Notwithstanding her public disapproval of sensation writing, many of her novels include people surviving on the very fringes of decent society, concealing disastrous liaisons. Oliphant's carefully stratified social structures, so like Trollope's in many ways, are also very much her own, while her multiplot novels, like George Eliot's, explore entangled communities in which the well-intentioned find themselves pulled down by the thoughtless, offhand behaviour of their insensitive friends and family.

Another comparison can be made with Queen Victoria, whose near-neighbour she became at Windsor. Both were widowed early in life and never remarried, and both had sons who disappointed them. An admirer of Oliphant's novels, the Queen occasionally invited her to tea, and wanted her to review *Leaves from the Journal of Our Life in the Highlands* (1868), published the year of their first meeting. Gail Turley Houston has defined the relationship between the two as amicable, though it could never be entirely straightforward. The Queen liked to consider herself a fellow author with Oliphant, without (in her subject's view) having the necessary credentials, while Oliphant, as a fellow widow, felt that the Queen should take greater comfort from her "large happy affectionate family of children," and resume her duties: "*We* have to do it, with very little solace, and I don't see that anybody is particularly sorry for us," she grumbled, perhaps unconsciously adopting the royal "we," or else speaking for widows in general (Houston, 1999: 148). When it came to reviewing *Leaves* for *Blackwood's* in February 1868, Oliphant praised its happy picture of a family at leisure, with the Queen at its centre, "an individual mind and heart," holding things together (1868: 243). But when more *Leaves* appeared in 1884 she could hardly contain her impatience with the Queen's second instalment of "such rubbish," especially her naiveté in writing affectionately of her highland servant John Brown, already suspected of being too closely involved with her. "It is her innocence I suppose," Oliphant conceded, "but one should not be so innocent at her age."[4] Her novella, "The

Mystery of Mrs. Blencarrow" (1889), which narrates the apparent discovery of the eponymous widow's secret marriage to her steward, "Brown," sails dangerously close to the wind, but in other respects Oliphant responded to the Queen's notice with diplomatic compliance. Whatever this entailed, the *Pall Mall Gazette* claimed in its obituary that Oliphant had enjoyed "friendly relations with her Majesty, of whom she was a great favourite, and who, it is said, had every one of Mrs. Oliphant's books read aloud to her."[5] Oliphant posthumously published *Queen Victoria: A Personal Sketch* (1900), determined to survive until after the Queen's official Diamond Jubilee celebrations. *Blackwood's,* meanwhile, marked her passing with an initial brief notice recalling that "in high and lofty example of perfect womanliness Mrs. Oliphant has been to the England of letters what the Queen has been to our society as a whole" (Lobban, 1897: 162).

The Queen was by no means Oliphant's only high-profile admirer. Gladstone read her non-fiction (*The Makers of Venice*, 1887, and *Jerusalem*, 1891); Joseph Conrad thought she was "a better artist" than George Eliot; Tennyson that she was "nearly always worth reading"; Stevenson that since *The Pilgrim's Progress* there had been nothing as good as *A Beleaguered City* (1879), and J.M. Barrie that her short stories were her best work.[6] While Emma Darwin records spending three shillings on an Oliphant novel, "An English Squire" (probably *A Country Gentleman and His Family*, 1886), and admiring her "very clever description of the feelings of a widow on losing a dull husband she did not much care for" (Litchfield 2010: II, 374), her husband Charles cited examples from *Miss Marjoribanks* and *The Brownlows* (1868) in his *Expression of the Emotions in Man and Animals* (1872), twice referring to her as an "excellent observer" (Darwin 1872: 80; 270). Jane Carlyle, who became a personal friend, commended *Salem Chapel* as being by "one of the best Novelists of the day," and passed on her husband's endorsement of Oliphant's biography of Edward Irving (1862) as "worth whole cart-loads of Mulochs

[sic for Dinah Mulock] and Brontës and THINGS of that sort"
(2010: 82; 88).[7]

When she died in 1897, Oliphant's life and achievements were
widely noticed in the periodicals, predominantly with respect,
tempered by what by then had become familiar lines of criticism.
That she wrote too much was always the obvious thing to say
about her. Her near-contemporary and fellow-novelist Charlotte
Yonge, admitted that Oliphant always puzzled her, "partly because
she can rise so much higher than what I suppose are 'pot-boilers,'
half of which I have never read" (Coleridge, 1903: 342). That
she wrote to support her children at least explained the prolific
output of mixed quality, and that no breath of scandal could
be associated with her was always another point in her favour.
Irish journalist Stephen Gwynn (1864–1950), in the *Edinburgh
Review*'s overview of her achievements, commenting on her
"fragmentary Autobiography," judged that the end of all her hard
work had been "failure," though not totally so: while the history
and biography were dismissed as so much hackwork, the fiction,
at least, stood up to scrutiny (1899: 27). Here again, though,
the reviewers were hesitant. If her fiction was better than might
have been expected, why had it never achieved the heights of her
contemporaries? Why was there no "single memorable Work," as
D'Albertis puts it (1997: 813), though many decent near-misses?
While Henry James wondered whether she was "capable of finer
things" but was ultimately "jaded and demoralized by incessant
production" (1984a: 29), Gwynn, in the *Edinburgh* spoke for
almost every other reviewer of the time, and for countless others
since, in asking: "What is it that sets the dividing line between
her and George Eliot or Charlotte Brontë?" (1899: 36). While the
answer lay for many in the difference between writing fewer than
a dozen novels and nearly a hundred, Oliphant's contemporaries,
and indeed Oliphant herself, in her more reflective moments,
prefigured early twenty-first-century critics in searching for
additional explanations.

Pierre Bourdieu's theory of the literary field may prove helpful in interpreting the unwillingness of critics, then and now, to see past Oliphant's prolific productivity as the most notable thing about her. In his explanation of Bourdieu's theory, John R.W. Speller argues that the value of a literary field's "capital" is tied to its autonomy: in other words, its value is defined or enhanced by "writers' ability to resist or ignore external (especially religious, political, and commercial) demands," and maintain its own values (2011: 48). At the same time, while, according to Bourdieu, literature has the potential to challenge, or even overturn the prejudices and preconceptions associated with particular social classes, his theories also "appear to present a society in which there is little room for resistance and change" (Speller 2011:22). This tension between the possibility of change and the upholding of the status quo, is further tightened by Bourdieu's division of the literary field into two subgroups: the "heteronomous" writers of bestsellers, and the "pure" or "autonomous" writers (Speller, 2011: 51). Bourdieu sees the bestselling authors as being susceptible to external influences, while the "autonomous" "respect no judgement other than those of their peers," and may be suspicious of commercial success (Speller, 2011:51). If we try to place Oliphant in one or other of these camps, she better suits the "heteronomous," in being, if not exactly a bestseller, at least not an exclusive purist or aesthete. Yet while acting as gatekeeper of literary standards via her reviews for *Blackwood's* and other heavyweight periodicals (as discussed in the next chapter), she provided peer evaluation of the "autonomous" writers of her day, including Henry James and Thomas Hardy. In similar vein, her novels toy with the sensationalism and romance of popular fiction, while objecting to both these trends, just as her tone is both middlebrow and ironic, even occasionally philosophical. In other words, while by no means unique in her heterogeneity, she left her contemporaries wondering why work that was often so good so often fell short.

One theory, proposed by Stephen Gwynn in the *Edinburgh* overview of 1899, was that Oliphant's devoted motherhood made it harder for her to feel passionately absorbed in her fictional people. Oliphant was, nevertheless, claimed Gwynn, a happy person by nature, and her life was "the tragedy of happiness" (1899: 28). What the reviewer seemed to mean was that Oliphant was meant to have a happy life, but it repeatedly went wrong, pushing her novels into the shade as so much necessary pot-boiling. For *Blackwood's* John Hay Lobban (1871–1939), by contrast, Oliphant "belonged to the race of literary giants to whom literature is an absorbing passion, and to whom its exercise brings a subtle and unfailing joy" (1897: 161). Whether or not she derived "joy" exactly from her creations is debatable. Evidence from her *Autobiography* suggests that her work was a steadying, even soothing, presence in her life, reliably waiting for her to resume it whenever a family tragedy suspended her routines. Occasionally, she admits, she did take pleasure "in a little bit of fine writing," which was done only when she "got moved" by her subject: "and began to feel my heart beat, and perhaps a little water in my eyes, and ever more really satisfied by some little conscious felicity of words than by anything else" (Oliphant, 1990:103–4). Experiencing her writing through her body, Oliphant captures for a moment how it feels to be both moved and excited by words, rather than by the human tragedy which dogged her life. Whatever else happened, there were always characters' life-crises to resolve and deadlines to be met, but unlike Harriet Martineau, whose *Autobiography* (1877) and letters recall a real joy in the creation of fictional characters —"I go into such places & have such companions!" she exclaimed over writing her *Illustrations of Political Economy* (1832–4) (Logan, 2007: 1, 125) — Oliphant never seems to have felt that her imaginary people were any substitute for the loss of her own real children.

That Oliphant was viewed and excused primarily as a mother worked both to her advantage and as a barrier to a more thoughtful and extensive evaluation of her achievements. Leslie Stephen's opinion was that she passed up her chance to write a novel like *Adam Bede* "because she wished to send her sons to Eton." This, for Stephen (who had met her, but declined to give Cecco any work on the *Dictionary of National Biography*), made perfect sense for a parent, but was less commendable in a serious artist, and he cited Oliphant to highlight Robert Southey's position in never doubting the "possibility of combining the professional author with the inspired prophet" (1899: 741). Far from trying to defend herself against the charge of being a mother first and an author second (let alone, an "inspired prophet"), Oliphant freely endorsed this Victorian interpretation of what we now call the "work-life balance." Throughout her *Autobiography*, she expresses incomprehension, and some slight contempt, of authors such as George Eliot and John Addington Symonds, who take themselves and their writing so seriously that they need to explain and discuss it, as if it really mattered. Instead of talking about her novels, therefore, she strays off into motherly anecdotes of her children when they were quaint and small, and loomed larger in her life than her latest set of characters. As Laurie Langbauer has argued, Oliphant must be held at least partly responsible for the denigration of her own reputation. In submitting that Oliphant's place in literary history has remained "unrankable" and "undecidable," Langbauer recounts that, herself "an arbiter of culture" through her extensive reviewing of her contemporaries, Oliphant contributed in no small measure to her own dismissal from the first rank of Victorian novelists. As Langbauer suggests, this is most evident in her *Autobiography*, where Oliphant "both insists on her minor status and implies that her work has been underestimated nonetheless" (1999: 72; 70). Why she might want to do this is, like everything else about Oliphant, not entirely easy to explain. For Langbauer, her commitment to the "commonplace," the unheroic small duties of the everyday, helps explain the downplaying of her own achievements, while other statements of Oliphant's own indicate that she flinched from modes of introspection which might unsettle her self-belief and productive output. "I always avoid considering formally what my own mind is worth," she says in one of many startling confessions in her *Autobiography* (1990: 14). Another is "I feel that my carelessness of asserting my claim is very much against me with everybody," something she attributes to a mixture of pride and "Scotch shyness" (1990: 15). Add to this her habitual irony and detachment from her characters, and we have an author who seems simultaneously to anticipate criticism and deflect it, by implying she is immune to it. Her apparently natural-sounding confiding of her grief in the *Autobiography* is, however, as many commentators have noted, anything but straightforward, and as a piece of accurate self-appraisal, further confounds the vexed question of her enduring importance to the history of nineteenth-century popular women's writing.

The "Tragedy of Happiness": The *Autobiography*

Oliphant was used to shaping lives, however difficult she found it to shape her own. Not only was she a biographer of men, an historian of autobiography, and an analyst of royal reigns; she also structured many of her novels around the lives of individuals, families and communities. Many have titles which sound like auto/biography, and draw attention to specific phases of a lifespan, or else its sense of locale, such as *Harry Muir: A Story of Scottish Life* (1853), *Agnes Hopetoun's Schools and Holidays: The Experiences of a Little Girl* (1859), *Effie Ogilvy: The Story of a Young Life* (1886), *Lady Car: The Sequel of a Life* (1889), and *Jeanne d'Arc: Her Life and Death* (1896). Others explicitly use the language of life writing, such as *The Days of My Life: An Autobiography* (1857), which John Stock Clarke describes as "a first-person narrative by a self-tormenting, almost masochistic woman, whose neurotic, self-deceiving pride drives her to extraordinary lengths" (1986: 3). In her account of her own life, Oliphant is too ironic and self-deprecating to torment herself with self-deceiving pride, but there is nevertheless a jolting oscillation in her history between fragile, fleeting episodes of personal fulfilment, and the irruption of a grief at first too devastating to share with the general public. Somewhere between the two extremes of experience she has to locate her self-estimate as a novelist, as this is what might be expected of the autobiography of a writer. The beating heart, so often mentioned in her novels when a crisis looms in the lives of her characters, is referenced here when her career shows signs of taking off. "My heart had come up with a great bound from all the strain of previous trouble and hard labour and the valley of the shadow of death" (1990: 104), she recalls at a point when her life with the children and her burgeoning career, seemed at last to have stabilized. "Poor heart of mine," she says at the start of her manuscript, "— it has had a good deal to go through one time and another —" (1990: 3).

Elisabeth Jay's discussion of the *Autobiography* in terms of "Arranging the Narrative" and "Alternative Readings" draws attention both to the more assertive ways in which Oliphant presented herself to her critics, and to the interventions of Annie Coghill, her cousin and first editor, who reordered the manuscript source to construct a chronological sequence which made greater sense to the reader (1995: 24; 34).[8] The manuscript, however, begins with false starts, cryptic, half-decipherable entries, and, in Jay's edition, an *in medias res* apology which assumes the reader is already familiar with what she is discussing: "To return to the idea with which I started that it was better when I steadily made up my mind in Edinburgh to enter without any props upon my natural lonely life —I am not so sure that it was a good idea after all" (1990: 3). Even if this was not the way she intended to begin her autobiography, it says much about the difficulty of interpreting Oliphant's interpretation of herself and her purpose in writing. The backwards-facing sentence structure which "returns" before it has even begun, enacts self-doubt, even as it tries to assert the dignity of determining upon a "natural lonely life." Writing now with hindsight of better times to come, she says philosophically: "It was bitter at the time, but it is not bitter to look back upon" (1990: 3); but no sooner has she reassured herself and her putative reader (her sons, initially), than the first disaster strikes, and her only surviving daughter Maggie dies, the tragedy marked in her narrative by the stark heading "Rome 1864" (1990: 4).

Oliphant's *Autobiography* simultaneously teases the reader with how much she knew of what was to come, and how much the reader can be expected to know. Comparing herself with a "giant" (Alcyoneus, son of Earth and Sky in Greek mythology), who "recovered strength every time he touched the earth" (1990: 4), she views her life in terms of falls and fresh starts which have been "good" for her. "Since then," she begins another cryptic thought, "but never mind what has come and gone since" (4). Experience, she claims, was good for her: but was it? "And now perhaps commences a graver era," she announces, "more guarded and cautious than the past — if experience ever teaches — which, however, I have already concluded it does not" (4). At the end of the book, but only half way through the chronological account of her life, she longs for the bodily touch of the last child to leave her, her Cecco, who gave her his arm whenever they went out: "I seem to feel it now — the dear, thin, but firm arm" (154). While Cecco was her prop, and she his ("consulting me about everything," 153), she could not retain him, and with the return to his death — already discussed much earlier in the text — she makes her final backwards turn and lets her narrative collapse into the silence of loneliness. When Oliphant writes "I cannot write any more" (the last words of her *Autobiography*), her childlessness at the end of her life articulates the waste of effort which now deprives her of the one thing that kept her going through every previous loss.

Women's Lives and Anti/Feminism
To trace these patterns of hesitancy and self-cancellation through the full text would in itself fill a book, and yet through it all

Oliphant is asserting herself as someone who has different values from her more widely acclaimed contemporaries. Both intensely private as a text, and then forced to "go public," as her sons died, the *Autobiography* is quintessentially a *woman's* life, written from the perspective of someone who does not feel part of the establishment, even as she functioned as one of *Blackwood's* most authoritative reviewers. The debate about Oliphant's alleged anti-feminism has moved on from the arguments of the 1990s as critical interest in her writing has more extensively examined both the chronology of her changing opinions and their inconsistencies, supported by closer study of the novels. If we mean by "anti-feminism" (an anachronistic term in Oliphant's lifetime) an ideological objection to the advocacy of women's rights, often combined with a belief in women's "natural" preference for a nurturing domestic life, Oliphant, like many of her contemporaries, flipped back and forth, changing her mind on specific issues, and believed most women "toiled away in total indifference to all theory" (1879: 206). As Merryn Williams noted in 1986, Oliphant's views, always "more complicated than simple anti-feminism," changed around the time of writing her article on J. S. Mill, "The Great Unrepresented" (1866) (1986: 106–7). This particular article, triggered by Mill's efforts to promote discussion of the women's vote, nevertheless embodies all the characteristic ironies of her contradictory position. Beginning with the loud, provocative announcement, "The present writer has the disadvantage of being a woman," the article immediately unsettles the reader's confidence in the author's reliability as a guide through the rights and wrongs of the suffrage debate (Oliphant, 1866: 367). Is she genuinely angry, or is this just pointed irony? Any hope of settling into a stable understanding with the reviewer is soon dispelled as Oliphant continues disrupting the case for the women's vote with alternating arguments for and against their moral and political entitlement. If British women are essentially "at liberty to do most things which are good and honest" (Oliphant 1866: 367), and not yet amassing to demand the vote, she sees no great justification for change; indeed, the superiority of women to men makes the vote irrelevant to their needs. Unlike her most stridently anti-feminist contemporary, Eliza Lynn Linton, Oliphant largely sees women as more capable than men: more sensible, practical and, above all, reliable, anchored by their sense of responsibility to their children. As for widows and older single women, those she describes as "respectable, but no longer charming" (Oliphant, 1866: 370). "Logic," she reasons, demands that the "penalties of sex should be abolished" (Oliphant, 1866: 371), yet she declines Mill's efforts on her behalf, and makes no claims to argue logically. This kind of wry humour, so characteristic of her style of argument, and playing to the notion that women are poor logicians, shelters her from direct responsibility for "unfeminine" views, while frustrating readers who want to know what she really thinks about the key issues of the day. Three years later, however, in "Mill on the Subjection of Women" (1869), she concedes that the suffrage might help the more "exceptional" of her sex (1869b: 590). By 1880, in "The Grievances of Women," an article signed with her initials, she was declaring it "highly absurd" that she should not have a vote, if she wanted one (1880: 708).

Nor is Oliphant's position necessarily any more straightforward in her fiction. As Tamara S. Wagner puts it, in her introduction to an essay collection on *Antifeminism and the Victorian Novel*, there is in Oliphant's writing a "shifting dividing line between the feminist and the antifeminist elements," which Wagner sees as only one of several "false" dichotomies in criticism of her oeuvre. Other "competing elements" include her use of "sensation" fiction subplots in her novels, while publicly excoriating the fashion for this kind of novel, and her ambiguous image of the home as both "unhomely" and an idealised domestic space (Wagner, 2009:12). Oliphant, in other words, seems to be having it both ways, not just when it comes to women's lives, but also on broader matters relating to literature, genre and social attitudes. Alternatively, she

INTRODUCTION

takes neither side, as Charlotte Yonge observed of her supernatural tale, "A Beleaguered City" (1879), having also "heard it observed of her other works" that she seemed "to sit outside and look at enthusiasm (often on the seamy side) and not share in it" (Coleridge, 1903: 342). More recently, summarising an essay by Amy Robinson, Wagner characterises Oliphant's humour in *Miss Marjoribanks* (1866) as operating "as a narrative tool to expose the complexities of Oliphant's position, proving that there is no litmus test for determining whether her predominantly ironic representation of marriage as a career is more suitably labelled feminist or antifeminist" (Wagner, 2009: 12).

Bowing both to the expectations of the readers and critics of her day, Oliphant seldom fails to include not just one, but several marriage plots and subplots in her fiction; but as will become clear in subsequent chapters, the theme provides opportunities for surprisingly direct social criticism, the most extreme case being "A Story of a Wedding Tour" (1894), whose heroine, Janey, appalled by the physicality of her loveless marriage of convenience, rejoices in her liberation from her ugly snoring husband, when after a short break at a station, their train departs without him. There is something anticipatory of Katherine Mansfield about this short story, not just in its juxtaposition of an older, sexually threatening man, with a naive young woman on a train journey, as in Mansfield's story, "The Little Governess" (1915). Here, the focus on Janey's sense of excitement, of being on an adventure, prefigures the introspective focus of modernism's "moments of being," as Virginia Woolf termed these experiences of heightened insight.[9] Janey's "fearful joy in thus being alone [...] Now how wonderful it all was" speaks volumes, yet by the end of the story, following another chance incident involving a train, she feels symbolically, at least, guilty of murdering her husband (Oliphant 2013c: 258; 261). This once again seems typical of Oliphant's habit — like those of many of her nineteenth-century contemporaries — of breaking the "feminist" trust she has initially established with her readers; but perhaps the existence of this trust is no more than the modern reader's wishful thinking, an attempt to recuperate Oliphant, and salvage the half of her writing which best accords with our own rejection of Victorian habits of thinking on gender issues. This cherry-picking habit is in itself partly the result of twentieth-century publishing decisions, driven by a need to make sense of Oliphant's massive output and create a manageable canon of her most deserving novels.

The Oliphant Canon

When we talk about Oliphant's fiction, the first challenge is to define which of her novels (over ninety altogether) deserve to be still in print and read. No mainstream nineteenth-century novelist produced this quantity of published work, and at any one time in the twentieth and twenty-first centuries, there have been only a few titles available in modern reprints. Canon formation often has its roots in the success of early sales, but with any Victorian novelist it is difficult to know exactly who bought their three-volume novels (at around 31/6s the set for one of the chunkier Carlingford novels in the 1860s), as opposed to borrowing them, a volume at a time, from a circulating library. Evidence suggests Oliphant fared well with library borrowings. Simon Eliot's sampling of 83 public library catalogues for 1883–92 shows that holdings for Oliphant were 1,255, putting her ahead of Wilkie Collins at 1,159, but trailing some way behind Mary Elizabeth Braddon at 2,254 volumes (Eliot and Rose 1992: 349). *Miss Marjoribanks*, to take an example of perhaps the best-known Oliphant novel today, and one that has attracted the widest critical interest, was regularly republished in the nineteenth century. First serialised in *Blackwood's Magazine* (February 1865–May 1866), it was then published by Blackwood's in three volumes. American and European editions followed (Boston 1866, New York 1867, Tauchnitz 1869), with further reissues in the 1880s and 90s, and then a shift to special editions in series (*Collected Chronicles of*

Carlingford, 1894; Collins' Pocket Classics, 1908). Because she was so prolific, magazines that carried publishers' advertisements were able to promote several Oliphant novels at a time, using the tagline, "by the author of —," sometimes endorsed by a critical "soundbite." Under "The New Novels," for example, *The Spectator* in December 1866 advertised "*Madonna Mary* by Mrs. Oliphant. Author of *Agnes* &c," with the tagline: "From first to last *Madonna Mary* is written with evenness and vigour, and overflows with the best qualities of its writer's fancy and humour" — a quotation in fact from its rival paper, *The Athenaeum* (*Spectator* 8 December 1866: 1379). Nearly thirty years later, *The Athenaeum* was promoting the latest volumes in "*Blackwood's New Series of Three-and-Sixpenny Novels*" which included four Carlingford novels, *Miss Marjoribanks, The Perpetual Curate, Salem Chapel* and *The Doctor's Family*, "By Mrs. Oliphant" (*Athenaeum,* 29 September 1894: 430).

Oliphant's stock, however, fell with the advent of modernism, and like many "minor" Victorian novelists, she had to wait until the second half of the twentieth century for a revival of interest. In his aptly named bibliography charting Oliphant's *Rise, Decline and Recovery of a Reputation,* John Stock Clarke includes a subsection grimly titled: "The extinction of Mrs. Oliphant, 1904–1948" (Clarke online 354). Q. D. Leavis was instrumental in resuscitating her with edited reissues of the *Autobiography* and *Miss Marjoribanks* in the 1960s and 70s, introducing the novel and its heroine as a "triumphant intermediary" between Jane Austen's Emma and George Eliot's Dorothea Brooke of *Middlemarch*, with Oliphant herself as "the missing link" between the two canonical women writers (Leavis, 1989: III, 135). What Leavis highlights is everything about both novel and author that is *anti*-Victorian, starting with the eponymous heroine, and culminating in the ironic witty prose which underpins the whole. She specifically admires Oliphant's targeting of conventional Victorian sentimental pieties, which Lucilla herself ironically apes, while the other women take them seriously. Underlying all, however, is a current of "seriousness," which is "what makes this novel as much a valuable criticism of mid-nineteenth-century provincial society as George Eliot's" (Leavis 1989: III, 153). As for the *Autobiography*, edited by Leavis in 1974, this had remained "unavailable," as Leavis noted, since its first publication in 1899, "suggesting that the immediate public interest having been exhausted, Mrs. Oliphant then passed into oblivion" (Leavis 1989: III, 159).[10]

In discussing *Miss Marjoribanks* Leavis also points to the need for an Oliphant canon. No one, she believes, can have read all the novels — though Clarke, who evidently has, maintains this is necessary for "any truly balanced judgment of Oliphant's work" (Clarke online: 36) — so while *Miss Marjoribanks* is to Leavis the only "outstanding" one (Leavis 1989: 139), *Kirsteen* (1890) is also recommended, and is indeed one of the still relatively few Oliphant texts available in a modern reprint.[11] At key moments in her publication "afterlife" Oliphant has been helped by publishers and individual enthusiasts promoting their favourite texts. J. M. Barrie, for example, took up the cause of "A Widow's Tale" in 1898, as well as giving the address when a plaque in her memory was unveiled in St. Giles's Cathedral, Edinburgh.[12] By and large, though, apart from some reissues under the "Novels of Faith and Doubt" imprint,[13] Oliphant's fiction would have remained largely unknown in the twentieth century without the Virago Press, who reprinted the best of the Carlingford novels in their distinctive green artwork covers, prefaced by Penelope Fitzgerald (*The Rector and The Doctor's Family*, 1986, *Salem Chapel* 1986, *The Perpetual Curate* 1987, *Miss Marjoribanks,*1988, and *Phoebe, Junior* 1989), with *Hester* (1984d) edited by Jenny Uglow, and subsequently, for Oxford World's Classics, by Philip Davis and Brian Nellist (2009). Fitzgerald even thought *The Doctor's Family* (1863) was "wonderfully suited for TV," though nothing came of this suggestion (Lee 2013: 337). Alan Sutton Publishing meanwhile republished *The Curate in Charge* (1987), introduced by Merryn

Williams, while Broadview took Oliphant into the twenty-first century with scholarly editions of the *Autobiography,* edited by Elisabeth Jay (2002), *Phoebe, Junior* (2002), by Elizabeth Langland, and *Queen Eleanor and Fair Rosamond* (2019) by Pamela Perkins. Canongate Classics, edited by Jenni Calder, helped revive interest in the supernatural tales, headed by *A Beleaguered City* (2000). These, indeed, seem the latest fashion in Oliphant studies, promoted by spooky front cover illustrations of skulls and candles, as in *The Collected Supernatural and Weird Fiction of Mrs Oliphant* published by Leonaur in 2014. George Levine, meanwhile, insisting generally on the power of Oliphant's writing, applauds "the devastatingly dark narrative" of the realist social narrative, *A Country Gentleman and His Family* (1886) (Levine, 2016: 238).

Oliphant's fortunes have further profited from the twenty-first century's advances in internet technology and on-demand printing, with many of her obscurer titles now surfacing via Amazon. In 2014, Joan Richardson founded the online *Margaret Oliphant Fiction Collection* which provides summaries of all the novels and short stories, with helpful symbols identifying those in print and considered the best. "In recent years," says the site, "Mrs Oliphant has been rediscovered and is once more acknowledged as one of the great Victorian writers" (http://www.oliphantfiction.com/ [18 May 2018]). Nevertheless, it remains the case that critical interest has continued to cluster around the Carlingford novels, some of which are also reproduced in Pickering and Chatto's scholarly edition of the *Selected Works of Margaret Oliphant* (2011–2017) under General Editors Joanne Shattock and Elisabeth Jay. For the purposes of this book I have chosen to continue discussion of the best-known Oliphant novels, while supplementing them with other works which have recently attracted interest (for example, *The Ladies Lindores*, 1883, in a Nineteenth-Century Scottish Women's Fiction series, 2008, and *The Wizard's Son*, 1884, in the *Selected Works*), or which seem to offer additional insights into Oliphant's values and opinions. All decades of Oliphant's output (except the 1840s, which produced only *Margaret Maitland,* are reflected in this study.

Critical Approaches

This volume draws on the many innovative critical approaches of recent years, both to Victorian fiction in general and specifically on Oliphant, who has been read as an anti-feminist, a proto-feminist, a lesser Austen, Eliot or Trollope, a social critic, a chronicler of the "everyday," a Scottish regionalist, a religious commentator, and above all, as a comic-ironic observer of social class interactions, moral dilemma and what Q.D. Leavis calls "painful situations." As Leavis herself indicates, Oliphant in fact "tried her hand, deliberately or instinctively, at every literary form known to her, even verse and drama" (Leavis, 1989: III, 175; 171). In 2015, a "Margaret Oliphant in Context" conference at the University of Leicester deployed terms such as "radical realism," "the disentangling of character," and "the self as archive," and explored her interest in the coinciding of gender and clerical concerns, the anticlimax of the happy ending, the divided mind, the financial novel, dress as an arbiter of taste, and the professional lives of publishers.[14] In the last few years, her novels have been shown to repay close attention to the language of the "classed" and "gendered" body, and the embodied subject, hence the increasing popularity of critical approaches derived from philosophers and theorists such as Pierre Bourdieu and Maurice Merleau-Ponty, or the field of clothing history and dress culture, as exemplified by Clair Hughes, Christine Bayles Kortsch, Patricia Zakreski, and Rosy Aindow. Masculinity studies, developed by theorists such as R.W. Connell, John Tosh, Herbert Sussman, Phillip Mallett, Rainer Emig and Antony Rowland have helped show just how far Oliphant departs from the Victorian masculine ideal in her characterizations of sons and suitors.

For all her ironic elusiveness, however, Oliphant's strongest values are clearly articulated, especially her belief that women are insufficiently appreciated, and men morally and professionally inadequate. The remaining chapters consider her work as a prolific reviewer for leading nineteenth-century periodicals, and her response to issues of gender in terms of roles within dysfunctional families. A chapter on "Clothes and the Body" drawing on theories of embodied subjectivity, interprets the many messages conveyed by physical appearance, distinctive hair, the touch of hands, beating hearts, flushed cheeks, lynx eyes, white and black dresses, jingling bracelets, and bushy beards. Discussion of Oliphant's writing about the supernatural, both in her short stories and at length in *The Wizard's Son* (1884), is contextualized by Judith Butler's interest in mourning and the "grievable" life, as well as by recent critical studies of Victorian women's ghost stories and their focus on haunted houses. Overall, Oliphant's world is full of shabby failures, hesitant lovers, and idealists, both men and women, whose manoeuvres to free themselves from states of impasse increasingly question the point of the marriage plot, yet search in vain for the alternatives Oliphant herself was actively living.

CHAPTER 1

"General utility woman" or Critic of the Age?

"I shall be glad to do a paper on Miss Martineau if you like for next month," Margaret Oliphant told John Blackwood in 1877, "and I think it might be made very amusing."[1] Around the same time, she consulted him about whether to buy the house she was renting, and wondered if she might have an advance of £1000 on a forthcoming novel.[2] In return, John Blackwood was if anything even more outspoken, alternately counselling his author and expressing his own views on the material she was addressing. "Do not review her for me unless you are prepared to be very distinct on her defects," he advised on the Martineau article, a review of the posthumously published *Autobiography*. "Nobody from her Mother downwards ever seemed to do right in the eyes of the spiteful old cat except her fulsome yankee toadies."[3] Provoked by the notoriously unpopular third volume, edited by Martineau's American admirer, Maria Weston Chapman, Blackwood's unguarded comments to Oliphant at the height of her reviewing career might imply that their relationship was frank and intimate, as between equals sharing dismissive opinions of other authors and editors. At times it certainly was, and Oliphant was sufficiently friendly with Blackwood to be invited to his house and to socialise with his family. On the other hand, her position with the Blackwood's firm remained ambiguous and insecure. Joanne Shattock describes author and editor as "never quite equals"

(2011: xx); while Oliphant, at the end of her life, concluded she had been their "general utility woman" (1897a: ii, 475). A phrase now widely quoted to summarize her role as reviewer for *Blackwood's Edinburgh Magazine*, it perhaps more accurately typifies Oliphant's half-hurt, half-ironic response to the retrospect of her own life and career: a metaphorical shoulder shrug which complicates her legacy as an arbiter of taste in literature and social mores, and cultural gatekeeper for half a century.

The object of this chapter is to investigate Oliphant's position as a critic of her society, especially in her response to the treatment of women, both in fiction and in the social context in which she passed her life. Her reviews also show that while her stance on women's issues is often opinionated, adhering to what she regarded as anti-theoretical common sense, she was capable of modifying her views in light of social change. Her notorious opposition to "sensation" writing was also less virulent than her reputation suggests. She not only openly admired Charles Reade's work, and conceded that Wilkie Collins in *The Woman in White* had created a superb villain in Count Fosco (Oliphant, 2011: 250), she also incorporated "sensation" elements into some of her own novels, especially *Salem Chapel* (1863), written at the height of the "sensation" decade. If we accept Kimberly J. Stern's argument that in the nineteenth century, "literary reviews often overlap with what we might designate as social and political commentary," Oliphant's straddling of both these fields makes the interplay of her literary and social criticism especially astute in its analysis of the ordinary, the sensational, and the believable in fiction (2016:17).

As Hilary Fraser and others have noted of the "multivalency" of the nineteenth-century periodical press, its journalism was "a fundamentally provocative and reactive medium, initiating dialogue on topics of the day, and demanding a response" (Fraser 2003: 1). The practice of anonymity allowed, even encouraged, contributors to be more opinionated than they might have been under a signature, and perhaps most importantly, their gendered identity was allowed to be ambiguous and invisible. On the other hand a journalist's individual opinions and distinctive "voice" might be distorted by the collective idiom of a house style. In Oliphant's case if it is hard to prove that anonymity made her bold, it at least suited her habit of "self-cancellation" (as discussed in the introductory chapter), affording some degree of protection, both for outspoken opinions, and for some subsequent backtracking. While an "Oliphant voice" becomes identifiable over time, it was sufficiently versatile to change genders (especially when talking about women's issues), to age as she aged, and to experiment with styles of humour and irony. Her mastery of succinct, memorable phrases explains why she is so frequently anthologized, especially for her animus against the worst excesses of the sensation novel. Specializing in English and European fiction, and novels rather than poetry (though she did occasionally write about both major and minor poets), Oliphant also tackled life writing, and changes in the laws affecting women, whether on marriage and divorce, or the suffrage.

It is appropriate to ask, as Solveig Robinson does, whether Oliphant's style changes significantly through her long career as a journalist. According to Robinson, the development of her "authoritative critical voice was a process that took decades" (Robinson, 2005: 199). At the same time, one could argue that she recycles certain themes and phrases, even obsessions, through her forty years of commentary, notwithstanding the invention of new voices and identities. Especially towards the end of her career she adopted fresh personae to express her views of both the literary and social scenes. These were as author of "The Old Saloon" series (shared with other authors, 1887–96) which ran in *Blackwood's* until she replaced it with "The Looker-on" (1896–7), "A Fireside Commentary" (1888) in the *St James's Gazette*, and "A Commentary from an Easy Chair" (1889–90) in *The Spectator*. She also made ten appearances in *Atalanta* (1893–4), a periodical for girls, under the shared signature of "The Brown Owl."[4] Like

Harriet Martineau, with her "From the Mountain" signature, purporting to be written by an old hermit in *Once a Week* during the 1860s, a desire to acknowledge her vantage point as an older person is complicated by her apparent preference for a detached, and occasionally masculine, identity at this stage of her career.

Blackwood's was a highly masculine journal, noted in the 1820s and '30s for its legendary pseudonymous male characters such as "the Ettrick Shepherd" (James Hogg) and "Christopher North" (John Wilson), and their "Noctes Ambrosianae" debates in Ambrose's Tavern in Edinburgh. Oliphant admiringly references this world in her opening paragraphs of "The Old Saloon" (January 1887), where she summons the memories of witty talk and the image of North, "with his head like Jove — one of the most splendid types of man that ever illustrated humanity," while admitting that alongside these godlike predecessors in journalism, she felt puny: "How does one dare to lift the small pipe of a lesser voice in presence of these shades?" (Oliphant, 1887: 126). Although its readership is also assumed to be predominantly male (as late as 1969, according to David Finkelstein, 82% of its readers were male) (Finkelstein, 2010: xviii), and its title page carried a picture of the Renaissance humanist George Buchanan (1506–82) from 1817 until the middle of the twentieth century, the paternalist "Maga" was also regarded by some of its contributors as a demanding female taskmistress. In their correspondence, which Oliphant cited in her history of the firm, *Annals of a Publishing House* (1897a), the original "cast" of "Noctes" and their friends habitually referred to the journal by female pronouns. The Reverend George Gleig, for example, characterised "Maga" as a woman to whom he felt unable to pledge regular sixteen-page articles: "She has my best wishes," he conceded, but "[…] it requires a great deal of writing to fill one of her sheets." Borrowing the imagery of a lady served in a medieval joust, Oliphant says of another contributor, William Maginn, that there was no one "who wore her colours with more apparent devotion" (Oliphant, 1897:

I, 486; 363). Although this chivalric atmosphere around "Maga" was a feature of the journal's heroic past, it inevitably positioned its women contributors, Oliphant included, outside the shared myth of masculine devotion to their mistress, or rather, never imagined them needing to be assigned a role in the fantasy. If we add to this picture the implications of Bourdieu's theory of the literary field (as outlined in the introductory chapter), and the division of authors into "heteronomous" best-sellers, or the "autonomous," immune to external influences, Oliphant's position as an author closer to the "heteronomous" model (subject to external influences) is further complicated as a reviewer straddling an insider/outsider relationship with the Blackwood firm.

Although Oliphant worked directly with the *Blackwood's* editors of the day, there is little sense of her being part of any social or professional group culture associated with the periodical: a point recently acknowledged by Kimberly J. Stern in her discussion of nineteenth-century women journalists' critical networks. Discussing Oliphant's relationship with *Blackwood's* "tavern sage" historical legacy, she cautions against assuming this was necessarily daunting for her, the very title "Old" Saloon, implying that its masculine atmosphere was a thing of the past. Instead, suggests Stern, Oliphant simultaneously invokes this masculine history and re-opens Ambrose's Tavern "under new management: it was, indeed, to be a more sober and inclusive version of the revelries for which the tavern sages had become famous" (Stern, 2016:11). She could not after all replicate the boisterous leg-pulling and "in" jokes of the original team, on her own, but she could experiment with the voice of the masculine reviewer, and develop a chameleon-like identity in tune with Maga's journey towards the *fin de siècle*.

As a reviewer, Oliphant is more like Harriet Martineau and Eliza Lynn Linton than she is George Eliot, in the sense that her career as a reviewer, like theirs, spanned her whole active professional life, rather than being an apprenticeship to recognition as a novelist. Beginning in 1854 at the age of twenty-six with a review of Mary Russell Mitford, Oliphant kept on reviewing not just for *Blackwood's* but for a range of mainstream journals until the year of her death, adding several new male-sounding personae to her identity as a reviewer: another example of Oliphant's ability to be simultaneously self-effacing and authoritative. These forty-three years witnessed major changes in reviewing styles (including the decline of anonymity in favour of reviewer signature), the entry of more full-time female reviewers into the profession, and the proliferation of the so-called "Little" magazines challenging the supremacy of the old heavyweight Reviews such as the *Edinburgh*, *Quarterly*, and *Westminster*, apart from "Maga" itself. These changes in many ways matched the shifting fashions of the novel, as social realism blended with, or gave ground to, sensationalism, and the three-decker format came to seem clumsy and wordy to the rising modernists, "New Woman" novelists, and "decadents" of the 1890s. Oliphant lived through it all, simultaneously writing and reviewing, in a lifelong dialogue between these two core activities of a professional writer.

Oliphant's correspondence with the Blackwood's firm shows that topics for her reviews were decided via an exchange of ideas. Usually they proposed the subject, but she was evidently free to make her own suggestions, which were often — but not always — taken up. When she offered to write on Carlyle, for example, drawing on her personal knowledge of the great man, *Blackwood's* were unenthusiastic, so she took it to *Macmillan's* instead.[5] At the very beginning of her reviewing career she had ambitiously proposed an overview of Thackeray, though aware that it would be as "a very small novelist reviewing a great one."[6] Although the firm rejected her offer in 1852, they relented two years later and the Thackeray article was published in their issue for January 1855, suggesting her ability, in Bourdieu's terminology, to straddle subgroups in the literary field. Meanwhile Blackwood tested her skills with the much "safer" offer of Miss Mitford, which she nevertheless seized as an immediate opportunity to comment both on the works themselves and Mitford's career as "one of the most womanly and unpretending" of "feminine writers" (Oliphant, 1854: 658). While fully aware of Mitford's unfashionable old-world style of narrative, Oliphant nevertheless respected her for avoiding all the sordid themes of modern times, which she herself came to find increasingly depressing as she moved forward in her reviewing career.

From the beginning of her relationship with *Blackwood's* it is easy to see that Oliphant makes the most of every opportunity to discuss both the work of other writers, and the way they represent women. As a new novelist herself she seems acutely aware of what other practitioners are doing, but also goes beyond mere analysis of their aesthetic qualities. For her, writing novels and reviewing them are complementary pursuits, mutually consolidating her preferences and forming her tastes. What interests her most is how contemporary fiction represents the ordinary daily experiences of parents and children, husbands and wives, and the ambitious young of both sexes making decisions about their future purpose in life. Laurie Langbauer has already drawn attention to Oliphant's interest both in "minor" novelists and their role as exponents of the everyday in fiction (1999: 70–71). In her very first review of 1854, Oliphant welcomes the apparent end of the historical fantasy and Gothic styles of the Scott and Radcliffe schools, in favour of the simple natural purity of Mitford's English villages. What most pleases her in Mitford is her "true and natural eye […] wise to see the unstrained and common emotions which lie warm in the bosom of ordinary life" (Oliphant, 1854: 658). In 1854, however, Mitford's work is essentially a throwback to the early years of the century, ignoring the radical irruption of *Jane Eyre* (1847) on to the literary scene. Throughout her reviewing career Oliphant struggled to reconcile her own preferences for the subtle everyday exploration of human psychology in mundane circumstances over the growing fashion for what she designated the "nasty" in modern novelists' preoccupations with crime and sexuality. Nevertheless — or because of this — Oliphant is now best known and frequently anthologized as a conservative critic determined to downplay the urgency of the social and gender issues to which sensation writing calls attention. At the same time, she was fascinated by the Brontës and Braddon, and as will be shown, engaged in her own literary dialogue with *Jane Eyre* (especially in her novel, *Janet*, 1891) over forty years after the novel was first published. This chapter will therefore begin with an overview of her changing responses to the roles and responsibilities of women, as expressed in her leading articles on the subject, which provides a context for her discussion of gender matters in her book reviews. It will be seen that for Oliphant the two were inseparable. How both women and men are represented in fiction was for her an indicator of how their roles were changing, not necessarily for the better, fiction at its best being for her essentially a reflection of contemporary society in its "truth to life."

"Mr Mill's crotchet": Oliphant on Women 1856–96
"Women's rights and women's duties have had enough discussion, perhaps even from the ridiculous point of view," Oliphant grumbled in 1867, the year in which John Stuart Mill proposed an amendment to the Second Reform Act which would admit women to the suffrage. "We have most of us made merry over Mr Mill's crotchet on the subject [...]" (Oliphant, 1867: 257; 275). She herself started "making merry" in 1856, with "The Laws Concerning Women," swiftly followed by "The Condition of Women" (1858). It was a topic to which she returned whenever there were new developments in the debate, right up to the year before her death, with "The Anti-Marriage League" (1896), her attack on Hardy's *Jude the Obscure* (1895). The fact that Oliphant kept returning to the subject, however, alongside her own changing position as a young wife and mother, and then a working widow, suggests that it engaged as well as irritated her, and that she wanted to review her thoughts on the needs

of women whose life experiences, like her own, had taken them beyond the presumed safety of the middle-class marital home. In this respect she resembled other professional female writers of the period, such as Eliza Lynn Linton and Charlotte Yonge: women who had not led quiet married lives (Yonge never married, and Linton separated from her husband), yet nevertheless upheld the conservative middle-class norm by not siding openly with the burgeoning movement for women's rights. Although Oliphant never strayed from the respectable boundaries of her widowhood, she nevertheless passed most of her adult life as a single mother of sons for whom she was essentially the sole breadwinner.

Oliphant's stance on women has been widely discussed in recent years, and perhaps most accessibly summarised by Elisabeth Jay in her *Literary Life*, which argues that the peculiarities of Oliphant's circumstances as a young widow and mother essentially "legitimised" her career as critic and novelist (1995. Chapter 2). While one might have expected her to be more sympathetic towards the practical needs of other women in similar circumstances, however, Oliphant disappoints in only gradually and grudgingly conceding that for a variety of reasons — or none at all — women might need to be better educated, to work, vote, or end an unhappy marriage. It was not just that marriage was, for her, the merging of two people into what she called a "double being," so far as their legal interests were concerned (Oliphant, 1869b: 589), though she also says this is a "mere trick of words" (Oliphant, 1856: 381). It was also that she felt the law was a clumsy and inadequate tool to mend the wrongs of an intimate and private relationship.

At the start of her writing career, Oliphant developed a line in loud, almost crude dismissals of there being anything wrong with the status quo. "Equality is the mightiest of humbugs," she scoffed in 1858 in relation to opening up the professions to women (Oliphant, 1858: 145); while in 1869 with a cry of "Where is this dismal country?" she poured scorn on John Stuart Mill's picture of female experience in *The Subjection of Women* (Oliphant 1869b: 576). One might legitimately ask why she sounds so hostile to the very notion of women's rights in some of her pronouncements, especially as her views mellowed over her lifetime, making her more sympathetic to the issues of property rights, single women's employment, and even the vote (although she remained equivocal as to wanting it herself). In 'The Grievances of Women' (1880), she admits to shrinking from the jeers of rude friends were she to attend any public pressure meetings on behalf of women: "We would rather, for our parts, put up even with a personal wrong in silence more or less indignant than hear ourselves laughed at in all the tones of the gamut and held up to coarse ridicule" (Oliphant, 1880: 698). Although ashamed of admitting it, by this stage Oliphant knows her own limitations as a campaigner. She is not in fact a campaigner at all, but a woman acutely aware of all the disadvantages of being a woman (both legal and physical), but accustomed to this position, and prepared to accept things as they are. Writing for the conservative *Blackwood's*, and depending on them for her livelihood, she perhaps had little choice. She was also aware of the advantages, especially the privilege of motherhood, and as her novels repeatedly demonstrate, declined to see women as necessarily unable to help themselves. Moreover, taking up her stance against Mill, she rejected "logic" and "theory" as the basis of argument, unashamedly admitting that as a woman logic was not her strongest hand: "We do not take our stand upon logic: let it be called instinct, intuition, or what you will" (Oliphant, 1866: 375).

Oliphant, in fact, twists this way and that in her determination to avoid any appearance of becoming overtly associated with campaigns for women's causes. When she was asked to sign the suffrage petition in 1866, she annoyed Barbara Bodichon by claiming there were only twenty names on it, but in this respect she was little different from George Eliot, a closer friend of Bodichon, but just as unenthused by petitions.[7] Instead, Oliphant

—like Eliot— preferred to show in her fictional exploration of individual women and their specific circumstances the challenges of fulfilling their personal aspirations while being constrained by ties to other people or lack of money. At least some of her work can be read as making the most eloquent statements attacking the status quo, though often in ironic asides which seem designed to protect her from seeming shrill. At other points, she rejects practical solutions because they fall short of the greater goals. One reason why she was unenthusiastic about legal reform, for example, was its obvious limitations: "It can give a woman a right to her own property," she concedes in her most "anti-feminist" phase, "So far well. It cannot give a woman a right to her own children, by far her dearest and most precious possession" (Oliphant, 1856: 383). At the time of writing, just a year before the passing of the Matrimonial Causes Act, custody of children over seven went to fathers and remained that way until 1873. In this respect Oliphant could be as forceful as Caroline Norton who spent years campaigning for the rights of separated and divorced mothers. The difference was that Oliphant's objections to the legal position of women come in throwaway remarks, ironic side-swipes at the complacent assumptions of male law-makers, rather than via closely argued pamphlets or concerted campaigns.

As time passed, Oliphant relaxed her views on some of the key issues affecting women's legal and social positions, but always with a residual conviction that having escaped the horrors of the violent revolutions which had raged through France and much of Europe, Britain was thankfully a staid and sensible country in which extremes of cruelty to women were too rare to require legal remedy. Nevertheless, she kept abreast of changes in the law, and read and reviewed the key publications on the subject, not only Mill's *Subjection*, but also Dinah Mulock Craik's *A Woman's Thoughts about Women* (1858), Josephine Butler's *Woman's Work and Woman's Culture* (1869), Eliza Lynn Linton's *Ourselves* (1869), and Barbara Bodichon's (anonymously published) *A Brief Summary in Plain Language of the Most Important Laws Concerning Women* (1854), which she proposed to John Blackwood as something she might discuss ("You would not object to my view of this question, I think," she reassured him (Shattock, 2011: 141)). On the 1857 Matrimonial Causes Act she allowed it was good that women trapped in brutal marriages should be permitted a means of escape, but many preconceptions and matters of principle, both religious and personal, on the oneness of husband and wife, prevented her from seeing such wrongs as sufficiently widespread to warrant legal intervention. Divorce was for her a shameful matter, as she indicates in 'The Condition of Women' (1858): "So far as women are concerned, it must always remain the dreadful alternative of an evil which has such monstrous and unnatural aggravations as to be beyond all limits of possible endurance" (Oliphant, 1858: 152). Legal separation was therefore for her preferable to the awful publicity and finality of divorce. In conceding this much she was beginning to shed some of her prickly complacency on the issue of women's rights. She had always known there were inequalities in the law, reflecting the biological inequalities of sex, but the question for her was how substantial these were, and to what extent Parliament needed to concern itself with correcting them.

If relatively little could be done for wives, she began to support the cause of single women, which was inseparable from the debates about education and employment. Though largely silent or suspicious on the subject of education (while keenly supervising her sons' progression through Eton and Oxford, and her nieces' artistic training), by 1869 she was declaring, of single women, that "They are as strong, as courageous, as clever as their masculine contemporaries" (Oliphant, 1869b: 591). By 1880, when, as Susan Hamilton notes, Oliphant had "done considerable rethinking on the subject," the problems of women in general seemed more attributable to "the great contempt in which they are held by men, not by a lack of education, political rights or abilities" (Hamilton, 2004: 215). This article ('The Grievances of Women', written for *Fraser's Magazine*) in fact becomes an impassioned plea for men to notice what women do, and to start valuing it. Citing the saying "A woman's work is never done," Oliphant describes a Victorian version of "multi-tasking," with no respite comparable with the husband's when he rests from work in the evenings: "But for this she gets absolutely no credit at all." Men are seen as working, and women as not, but rather living as their husband's dependant. As for pregnancy and childbirth — "the last extreme of human exertion"— this is one of the "unparalleled labours in her life to which the man can produce no balance on his side" (Oliphant, 1880: 704). From having been ashamed to be seen at public rallies, Oliphant now swallows her pride and insists that husbands acknowledge the full extent of their wives' contribution to the household. As for single women, she can see no reason why they should not train as doctors, nor why widows such as herself, as single householders, should not have the vote (1880: 707, 708).

What is also curious about Oliphant's about-turn in this article is her coining of what she herself admits is "coarse" language to enforce her argument. The truism that men have a superior role in society because they are physically stronger, is, she says, the "argument of the coalheaver" (Oliphant, 1880: 699), while "cowardly" women like herself, too embarrassed to stand up for women's rights, observe men's derision for the cause "and laugh on the wrong side of their mouths, to use a vulgar but graphic expression" (Oliphant, 1880: 699). Laughing on the wrong side of the mouth is a characteristically ironic expression for Oliphant, meaning to acknowledge some future (and deserved) reversal of fortune. In this case it hints that men may lose some employment opportunities to women entering hitherto male monopolies. Countering this kind of "vulgar" language with what she also admits is the "old-fashioned phraseology" of God-ordained roles (Oliphant, 1880: 701), Oliphant concludes that because most couples are happy enough, the sense of injustice handed down from mother to daughter becomes merely a "sentimental grievance"

(Oliphant, 1880: 705). Playing with the word "sentiment," right at the end of the article, she turns this back on the ungenerous husbands, concluding that until they abandon their "inexplicable sentiment" (Oliphant, 1880: 710) of undervaluing women's work, little progress can be made in advancing the equality of the sexes. As for the phrase, 'laughing on the wrong side of the mouth,' she recycled it in an 1894 article for *Atalanta*, transferring the image from "cowardly" women like herself to men, who "poor fellows, have their wrongs and their disabilities too" (Oliphant, 1894a: 734)

The twists and turns of her 1880 article (and indeed others) in many ways encapsulate the difficulty of appraising Oliphant's position on women's rights. They show she is familiar with the usual arguments and areas of grievance — the laws on marriage and divorce, employment opportunities, the vote, and the needs of single (and widowed) women — and that she feels strongly about at least some of them. In terms of style, however, she veers from outright condemnation of blatant inequality to a coy disengagement from the fray, on grounds of bad taste and a mismatch between her private sense of injustice and the confrontational "unfeminine" way in which it is publicly proclaimed. Ultimately, she deplores "theory" and prefers personal example: "I do not pretend to understand either Man or Woman, in capitals," she declares in 'Grievances', "I only know individuals, of no two of whom could I say that I think they are entirely equal" (Oliphant, 1880: 701). In the final decade of her life, she turned again, weary of the whole fuss about women, yet this period also witnesses her attack on Hardy's *Jude the Obscure*, which Hardy himself described as "the screaming of a poor lady in *Blackwood* that there was an unholy anti-marriage league afoot."[8]

An Old Person of Letters

In 1893, when she was writing desultory opinion pieces for the girls' magazine, *Atalanta*, founded by L. T. Meade, Oliphant admitted: "I am bound to confess that whenever I see the word Woman writ large, with a big capital letter, I consider discretion the better part of valour, and flee" (Oliphant, 1893:222). She felt so strongly about this that she repeated the statement in the same periodical the following year, further commenting that as "an old — let me say, Person of letters," she neither desired her work to be excused nor applauded, on the grounds that she was a woman (Oliphant, 1894a: 732). Perhaps this helps explain her outburst against Hardy's *Jude* (January 1896), about which she felt such qualms that she wondered if her "voice" was "authoritative enough to denounce it," another indication of her awkward position on the insider/outsider, heteronomous/autonomous borderline as a reviewer. She signed the article with her initials, as if to accept responsibility for any backlash. For all its virulence, her correspondence with her editor, Archibald McCall Smith, shows she was nervous about publishing the article, which she claimed was written "only under a sense of duty." This is a curious phrase, which implies a heavy sense of moral responsibility, presumably to protect both innocent readers, and the institution of marriage itself. Indeed, so far as she was concerned, there had never been anything in English print "so coarsely indecent as the whole history of Jude in his relations with his wife Arabella"— though her opposite, "the fantastic Susan," fares no better as Oliphant deplores her squeamish and inconsistent attitude to marriage (Oliphant, 1896a: 138). What also caught Oliphant's eye was Hardy's surprising treatment of his male characters, in the face of his remorseless women: "The men are passive, suffering, rather good than otherwise, victims of these and of fate. [...] This is one of the most curious developments of recent fiction" (Oliphant, 1896a: 140). If anything, she was acknowledging a development that had been surfacing for some time in her own novels, where many of her men are both passive and suffering.

There is perhaps a self-conscious perversity about Oliphant's opinions in these later articles, as if she is marking the right of an older speaker to have her say. By then she was writing under her own signature, though also under *Atalanta's* general signature of "The Brown Owl," which was used by several contributors, including Meade herself, and presumably considered a space for wise words to be conveyed to the journal's female readers. It allowed Oliphant to be as outspoken and even moodily out of sorts if she wished, as when she insists that women are "not specially ill-treated now" (Oliphant, 1894a: 734). By this stage she had run through a new set of pseudonymous identities for a range of periodicals which allowed her, identifying specifically as an older person, to range freely through current affairs and social criticism. While these are by no means confined to women's issues (she becomes more interested in the working conditions of men and women, as well as music, art, and the London "season"), she nevertheless, from her various firesides and easy-chairs, observes the changing fortunes of women in public life, often by asking awkward questions, and adopting unpopular standpoints. "A Commentary from My Chair," as she titles the first of a regular series of loosely-structured thoughts for *The Spectator*, begins benignly enough by contrasting her intended approach as a subtly female "grey-haired spectator of the game," with the poet Cowper's churlishness as he "looked forth upon the world," finding "nothing better to do than to rail at it" (Oliphant 1889a 805).[9] As Judith van Oosterom notes, "the role of the bystander clearly appealed to Oliphant," and she often uses such characters in her fiction to supplement her own observations as narrator (van Oosterom, 2010: 240). An example of such a character, contemporary with these late series of articles, is Janet Summerhayes, the governess heroine of *Janet* (1891), whose "strong sense of spectatorship" (Oliphant 1891a: I, 154) of relationships in the Harwood family of St. John's Wood is explicitly referenced, along with the notion of "seeing more of the game than the players did," echoing the "spectator of the game" terminology of "Commentary from My Chair" (Oliphant, 1891a: I, 245). While this might be assumed to be an objective position, it never is with Janet, who is drawn into the family's amorous rivalries, nor for long with Oliphant the journalist. Bystanding, for all its exclusion from the action, becomes in Oliphant's hands a position of low-risk superiority and power, while the "Commentary" is, by definition, a critical account of an observed event, usually by someone at a remove from it (such as a sports commentator). As she watches the rise of the trade union movement, for instance, Oliphant starts to question whether the work of female "rag-pickers," the lowest of the low in the textile industry, is honestly worth higher pay when they would be better advised to train as skilled needlewomen. No one forces them to do such shoddy work, she argues, adding: "Would it not be a good thing, before organising the rag-pickers, say, into a Union, to see if they could not be made to do work that was worth something more, a better process, surely, than endeavouring to force more pay for work that is worth very little?" (Oliphant, 1890: 375).

What begins as a detached observation in many of these articles quickly develops into a waspish argument disputing the accepted views of the 1890s and harking back to a more stoical and self-effacing culture of the present generation's grandmothers. Phrases such as "As a matter of fact," and "Why should they" mark the steps away from contemporary truisms back towards a time when women, motivated both by fear of scandal and good humoured resignation, simply accepted that their lot in life was harder than men's, but in other ways, as the bearers of children, also superior.

The proliferation of Oliphant's journalistic identities in the last decade of her life is usually explained by her perennial need for money, but it clearly served other purposes, including maintaining an input on social and political, as well as literary, subjects. Such was her enthusiasm for these new signatures that she was sometimes writing simultaneously under more than one at once, and when she stopped using one, she quickly acquired another, the last being the "Looker-on" column for *Blackwood's* (1894–6). Apart from the *Blackwood's* articles, many of these opinion pieces are brief

— often no more than two or three pages of newsprint, allowing a break with the formal style of the early decades of her career — and also more frequent (*The Spectator* was issued weekly, and the *St James's Gazette* daily). The "Easy-Chair" pieces appeared under the general heading of "Correspondence," followed by "Letters to the Editor," implying that Oliphant was more aligned to an external reader than a regular member of the team. She had in fact submitted a letter to the Editor, in 1874, headed "The Rights of Women," and signed merely "M," exasperated by the way women were being collectively insulted by journalists when assumptions were made about their political behaviour. Though it had never occurred to her "personally," as she put it, "to wish for a vote," she was nevertheless near to sympathizing with Mill's theories, "fantastic and contradictory to experience" as she had once thought them (Oliphant, 1874: 301–2). She was also fully aware of the "New Journalism," as she notes in one of the *Spectator* articles, the intensification of celebrity gossip and scandal-mongering, which while it had always been there to some extent, now acquired a new virulence and visibility. For her this was another opportunity to consider its impact on women, and to quarrel with the views of other newspapers, in this case the *Standard*, which declared that if a woman wrote an article for a magazine or newspaper, "she lays herself open to criticism." Oliphant countered firmly that such a woman "lays her subject and her style and her arguments open to criticism; but not, we think, in any way herself" (Oliphant, 1889b: 804–5).

Ironically, though, the more Oliphant addressed the social, rather than the purely literary, issues of the day, the more she used her pseudonymous personae to distance herself from the fray. The "Dowager" voice of the "Fireside Commentaries," for example, opines, in relation to old women, that the "nineteenth century has not much patience with us; nor, indeed, theoretically, I am afraid, has any century ever had" (Oliphant, 1888a: 5). What it does allow her to do is introduce a controversial topic — in this case women's political engagement — via a reminiscence from the days of a very different campaign, the anti-Corn Law agitation of the 1840s. Such was her eagerness as a fourteen-year-old "violent politician" in Liverpool, claims the "Dowager," that she and a friend devised their own "monster" petition in favour of repeal, and "wildly collected hundreds of signatures," in competition with a "legitimate" petition organized by a Mrs. Smith and a Miss Brown (Oliphant, 1888a: 5). It may, as she put it, have been her only "political exploit" (Oliphant, 1888a: 6), and she recounts it with characteristic self-mockery, but the passion was there, and when she attended a political meeting addressed by leading Corn-Law Repealers Richard Cobden and John Bright, she was thrilled by the fervour of both speakers and audience. At the same time, she defuses the political content of this episode by admitting that while she could not remember what anyone said, she retains a clear recollection of the speakers' clothes and hairstyles. Moreover the person she admired most was the "pretty young lady" secretary (Oliphant, 1888a: 6), on whom she developed an instant crush. Oliphant's abiding interest in clothes will be discussed in Chapter 3. In the meantime, she lovingly recalled in 1888 the girl's "large white collar" and "sweet complexion and pretty hair modestly parted on her fresh forehead" (Oliphant, 1888a: 6). The point perhaps is that female activists in the 1840s campaigned selflessly for the disadvantaged, while retaining their modesty and femininity, whereas in 1888 they had become loud and shameless.

Oliphant gained an obvious licence from these signatures to say what she wanted, both from the perspective of her own sex, and from a fabricated male perspective. As "a Dowager" in the "Fireside Commentaries" (though she soon dropped that signature, while retaining the article series title), she could reflect on her own girlhood, while as the male "Looker-on," she could view the next generation of young girls as the alien "Other." As many critics have noticed, there is a "world-weariness" about this character, and only six articles emerged under his signature

(Wilkes, 2012: 405). Opening in August 1894, at the end of the London social season, the first piece notes the "sense of dust, of shabbiness, of fatigue" (Oliphant, 1894: 285) in the air, matched by the increasing greyness of the country's Parliamentarians, while the sixth, in October 1896, identifies its author as "the last man in town," pleasantly surprised that Hyde Park, instead of "bearing the dismal traces of revelry departed," is actually blooming (Oliphant, 1896b: 481). Usually, however, he finds little to admire. There is nothing worth seeing at the theatre, he is bored with the "dull fellows" in his club, and by December 1895 "we have little or nothing to play with: there have been no pictures, there have been few books" (Oliphant, 1895c: 910). Inevitably he turns to the changing balance of power and behavioural norms of the sexes. Addressing the scandalous behaviour of the upper classes, and women's habit of inquiring into the sexual histories of young men before deciding whether they are safe to marry, the Looker-on of the first piece also admits to being "old-fashioned," and "perhaps prejudiced" (Oliphant, 1894: 288). In his view the season for women's agitation has passed. Whatever grievances they may have suffered before (and he admits these were real), they are now resolved and there is no longer any cause for women to "grow hot over wrongs that have long ceased to be" (Oliphant 1894: 290). Like Eliza Lynn Linton, with her "Girl of the Period" series (1868), Oliphant creates a new caricature of the modern woman, symbolised by a tall physique, the freedom of a latch-key, and a taste for music halls, as if these depressingly represent the height of their ambition (Oliphant, 1894: 290).[10] The "latch-key" indeed becomes a byword for emancipation in the writing of many *fin-de-siècle* journalists, and the liberty to enjoy risqué entertainment a symbolic right for young women ambitious for sexual equality with their brothers.[11] The Looker-on ratchets up the joke by proposing to patrol the streets with a police force of "herculean young women who are bigger than most of our soldiers and in perfect training for the purification of the Haymarket and other such regions" (Oliphant, 1894: 291). Although the series ranges freely round the arts, including the theatre and art exhibitions, and finally takes a stroll round Hyde Park in the style of a *flâneur*, the Looker-on never misses an opportunity, like his pseudonymous predecessors, to take further side-swipes, not so much at women themselves, as at what he witheringly designates the "Woman question," with its accompanying "Sex-literature" (Oliphant, 1894: 293; 295).

Ultimately the Looker-on is the archetypal grumbler, who feels permanently out of step and sympathy with his times. When he reaches the last paragraph of his final column in October 1896, he predicts that women are about to have their day: "It is quite true that we have made a sad mess of the world, and we sincerely hope they may do better" (Oliphant, 1896b: 507). The pronouns here may cause the reader aware of Oliphant's true identity some wry amusement over the distribution of responsibilities; but in passing the baton to women in the hope that they may make a better job of managing the world than have their husbands and sons, the Looker-on perhaps offers the last ironic word for a reviewer who tried to be both man and woman in her journalism, and despite her impatience with the "Woman Question," always maintained that women were the more capable sex.

"Nasty Novels": The Sensation Novel and Ordinary Life

Although Oliphant came to write more about the state of late nineteenth-century society in the final decade of her life, she never abandoned her interest in literature, or in discussing new novels as a "sign of the times." Even novels she disliked or felt uneasy about recurrently appeared in her reviews, perhaps for the very reason that they did disturb her. *Jane Eyre* (1847) was the earliest of these, to be followed by Mary Elizabeth Braddon's *Lady Audley's Secret* (1862). Though often vilified by Oliphant, the sensation novel remained, for her, a phenomenon that could not be ignored. For Charles Reade, however, now the least read of the principal "sensation" novelists (who include Wilkie Collins and Ellen (Mrs Henry) Wood), she had the utmost respect. This is an anomaly to be further explored in the final section of this chapter, along with her widely discussed apparent inconsistency in incorporating sensational elements into many of her own novels, where they seem to jar against the quiet monotony of her small town communities.

Oliphant attributed the change of tone in nineteenth-century fiction, from the realism of Austen and Mitford, to a salacious taste for what she loosely termed "vice," at least in part to the example of *Jane Eyre*, with its bigamy and seduction themes, and then to *Shirley*, with Caroline Helstone's overt longing for a husband, "a new sensation to the world in general" (Oliphant, 1867: 259). Her first major statement on *Jane Eyre* came in 1855, in a *Blackwood's* article at the end of which she is shocked to hear of Brontë's death, and hastily scrambles together a tribute. In private, though, she dismissed "the Jane Eyre school — those books which are so unwomanly that they only could have been written by women" — a typical Oliphant paradoxical phrase.[12] The idea that only women could write such "gross" books, or toy naughtily with what she calls "refined indelicacy" (Oliphant, 1855: 558) (prefiguring the phrase "innocent indecency," used in her "Novels" review of 1867: 274) exposes a more complex tension in Oliphant's writing about women than is always recognized in allegations that she inflates her ridicule in order to sound more like a male *Blackwood's* reviewer. The novels she targeted were not the genuinely fully adult, sexualised works of their European (mainly male) counterparts, which Oliphant gamely reviewed, but the self-consciously risky work of girlish Englishwomen with no direct experience of the smouldering relationships they tried to render.[13] On the other hand, after romping through *Jane Eyre* and making fun of its combative scenarios, she conceded that it "remains one of the most remarkable works of modern times" (Oliphant, 1855: 558). Though *Jane Eyre* was truly revolutionary, it was essentially its breaking with the idealistic tradition of romantic fiction that she regretted, where the men were chivalrous and "the ladies were beautiful" (Oliphant, 1855: 557); hence her distaste for English writers such as Rhoda Broughton, whose heroines are too freely-spoken and ready to be swept up in their lover's arms (Oliphant, 1867: 274). In effect it was the *faux*-knowingness of these increasingly physical scenes, never previously part of the English tradition of women's writing, that most upset Oliphant, along with their resultant vulgarity of language. Her own language breaks down in her "Novels" article of 1867 as she tries to capture the tone of "second-rate women's books" such as Broughton's (Oliphant, 1867: 266), and collapses into a vocabulary of "unloveliness," degenerating into "nastiness": Nell LeStrange of *Cometh Up as a Flower* (1867) engages in "light talk and nasty phrases" (Oliphant, 1867: 268), Ouida's are "very fine and very nasty books" (269), and overall she wishes someone would "put a stop to nasty novels" (275).

As with her comments on women's grievances, she felt these novels of the 1860s neither reflected the authentic experience of women in "real life," nor did women any favours in disparaging their dignity. A leading theme of Oliphant's fiction, which connects directly to her literary and social criticism, is the shame and humiliation women feel in allowing themselves to become emotionally involved with a man before he has proposed marriage. This experience occurs time and again in her novels, sometimes with two women simultaneously, as when both the gentle islander Oona Forrester and the good-natured heiress Katie Williamson, of *The Wizard's Son* (1884), are kept wondering for months whether the fickle Walter Methven, Lord Erradeen, has lost his heart to either of them; a further candidate, Julia Herbert, making up a third possibility as the novel works towards a melodramatic resolution of this impasse. Oliphant finds this an especially painful situation for modest women, such as Chatty Warrender, quietly loyal to Dick Cavendish, in *A Country Gentleman and His Family* (1886), and later for Gussy Harwood in *Janet* (1891), strung along by the philandering Charley Meredith. While this may be fairly standard fare for nineteenth-century fiction, peaking with Jane Eyre's apparently unrequited feelings for Rochester as he flirts with Blanche Ingram, Oliphant's anger at the indignity to which women are subjected by insensitive men is in its own more refined way as palpable as Charlotte Brontë's.

It may nevertheless be tempting to see Oliphant as preferring women to be patient victims, both in fiction and reality, rather than the ruthless adventurers of the typical 1860s "sensation" novel, but her response to this popular subgenre is neither consistent nor predictable. On the whole, for example, she preferred the male sensation writers, Wilkie Collins and Charles Reade, to the prominent women, Mary Elizabeth Braddon and Ellen Wood, though in a memorable phrase she credited Braddon with being "the inventor of the fair-headed demon of modern fiction," as well as with the "reign of bigamy as an interesting and fashionable crime" (Oliphant, 1867: 263). For both Collins and Reade she has considerable respect, for reasons which are worth investigating here. In Reade's case she distinguishes between the "coarse" and the "nasty," the latter signifying a clear breaching of the boundaries of good taste in relation to sexuality, whereas Reade's fiction is essentially "sound, wholesome and vigorous" (Oliphant, 1869a: 490). She particularly admired his strong and noble female characters, while identifying a triangular pattern not unlike some of her own: the positioning of "a very weak, sometimes contemptible, man" between "one brilliant, splendid woman" and "another simple, tender, feminine creature who is the rival" (Oliphant 1869a: 490). With Collins she praises the "naturalness" of events in *The Woman in White* (1860), especially the ordinariness and credibility of his sensationalism:

> We cannot object to the means by which he startles and thrills
> his readers; everything is legitimate, natural, and possible; all
> the exaggerations of excitement are carefully eschewed, and

there is almost as little that is objectionable in this highly-
wrought sensation novel, as if it had been a domestic history
of the most gentle and unexciting kind. (Oliphant, 1862:
566)

In other words, sensation writing becomes more acceptable to
Oliphant in proportion to its approximation to the mundane.
While regretting the more extreme incidents of Reade's *Hard Cash*
(1863), she nevertheless concedes that "everything that is absurd
and unlikely may, and does, happen in everyday life" (Oliphant,
1869a: 510).

It is here, perhaps, that we can expect to find some explanation
for Oliphant's apparent inconsistency in deploring the rise of
the sensation novel and the loss of a more old-fashioned kind
of genteel romance, while introducing sensational elements into
many of her novels. One of her recurrent tropes is the mysterious
history of both men and women whose hidden sexual past forces
itself on the shocked awareness of an otherwise quiet community
intent on its trivial rituals and small backbitings. The best-
known example occurs in the Rachel Hilyard/Susan Vincent
subplot of *Salem Chapel* (1863), which, once vilified by baffled
critics, is now defended as drawing attention to the permeable
boundaries between working- and middle-class experiences of
marital violence. As the Dissenting minister Arthur Vincent is
drawn into a destitute needlewoman's search for her abducted
daughter, along with Arthur's own sister, it is simply no longer
possible in Oliphant's world to cordon off unruly passion from
quiet respectability. In this respect, *Salem Chapel* pulls into its
"sensation underworld" a wider range of classes and characters
than *Lady Audley*, including the bigamous imposter Mr. Fordham/
Colonel Mildmay, who is also the half-brother of Lady Western,
the most socially elevated person in the community. While *Salem
Chapel* is perhaps the most extreme of Oliphant's novels in hinting
at possible abduction and murder, it also dispels the myth that

sordid goings-on are safely contained within the lower classes. A later story, *Queen Eleanor and Fair Rosamond* (1886), focuses on a middle-class wife's bafflement on discovering her husband has made a bigamous marriage, and the horror of having to tell her young adult children of their father's sexual misdemeanour.

The pervasiveness of unsuspected small town immorality was not, of course, Oliphant's discovery, but a staple feature of the sensation novel, which thrust bigamy, cruelty and coercion into the homes of the country gentry, if not directly into vicarages and the staid residences of houses like those of Carlingford's Grange Lane. In fact Carlingford is no more high-minded than any other fictional town where the surprising personal lives of its inhabitants and their friends and relations impinge on their neighbours. These are essentially sexual revelations of the very kind Oliphant deplored in "nasty" novels: for example, the havoc caused among the men of Carlingford in *The Perpetual Curate* (1864) by Rosa Elsworthy, a shopkeeper's seventeen-year-old niece, whose disappearance is (mistakenly) attributed to seduction by the clergyman, Frank Wentworth; or in *A Country Gentleman* (1886), a bigamy subplot involving Dick Cavendish whose supposed wife is living secretly in a neighbouring house of bad repute called "The Elms," the very mention of which sends shudders through the local community. Even worse, Theo Warrender, the moody undergraduate hero, becomes an abusive husband to Lady Markland and resentful stepfather to her clinging and precocious son Geoff. In *Hester* (1883) Edward Vernon both defrauds Vernon's bank, and absconds on a whim with Emma Ashton, who is desperate enough to marry anyone. Even Miss Marjoribanks is repeatedly fooled by the murky connections and the occasional false identity of the people she is trying to bring together socially, possibly with a view to marrying one of them herself.

Oliphant's fictional world is every bit as hazardous in its way as Collins's or Braddon's, but with a different emphasis. Her characters may be less charismatic than Collins's Count Fosco or Braddon's Lucy Audley, and by and large she avoids the more obviously sensational plot devices of the sinister madhouse or the graveyard revelation (*The Wizard's Son* is an obvious exception, with its menacing warlock-spectre), but throughout her career Oliphant deployed the sensational as both deeply embedded in the ordinary, and evidence of the "grievances" of women which her periodical articles only gradually conceded might actually be real. The hint of parody which emerges in the pious incredulity of village matrons, or the panic-stricken horror of their clergymen, is, however, enough to give her absorption of the sensational one further twist, which challenges the reader to know how seriously to take it. Her protagonists too, both men and women, must learn to become good interpreters of the socially and sexually confusing interactions that threaten the stability of Oliphant's fictional communities.

CHAPTER 2

Mothers, Daughters, Wives, Widows

"Yes, it is evident that I am much stronger than you are," Margaret Oliphant told her friend, John Tulloch, Principal of St Mary's College, St Andrews, in 1881. Though the two families were close for many years, Oliphant remained sceptical of the Principal's depressive tendencies, reminding him sharply, "think, please, if it had been me who had been ill, what would have become of me? — no income going on whether one could work or not — no wife to take care of me" (Oliphant, 1974:300). This passage, by turns proud, defensive, with more than an undercurrent of self-pity, in many ways encapsulates the essence of Oliphant's attitude to women and feminism. She saw women, above all, as practical, hard-working and self-sacrificing. They kept the household going when husbands and sons failed in their responsibilities. Her own experience, exceptional and tragic as it was, could not help but colour her views, and make her impatient, both with the feminist theorists of her day, and with everyone who undervalued women. Her fiction, however, represents a much fuller picture of women's experiences than her own situation, from the burgeoning desires of young girls, to the bustling activism of vigorous widows. Often dismissive of the traditional happy ending of the Victorian novel, she strained towards more radical denouements for her female protagonists, but at best often leaves them at a crossroads between marriage to a weaker man than themselves, or a life of lonely independence. Nevertheless, Oliphant's apparent timidity, like George Eliot's,[1] in failing to create alternative futures for her thoughtful and intelligent heroines, is offset by her awareness of their aspirations, and some instances of successful escape into careers such as book illustration and dress design. However small and infrequent these concessions, replicated as they were with her own nieces, they demonstrate Oliphant's ability to respond to social change. She was in fact disappointed when in 1893 her elder niece, Madge, abandoned her artistic training to marry a jute manufacturer in Dundee, exemplifying "over again," Oliphant grumbled, "the foolishness of giving expensive training to young women" (Oliphant 1974: 396).

One of Oliphant's most highly-strung early heroines is Hester Southcote of *The Days of My Life: An Autobiography* (1857), who recalls that at sixteen, "I was full of those endless metaphysical inquiries which youth — and especially youth that has nothing to do, abounds in — what was life for —what was it — what was the good of me, my particular self, and for what purpose did I come into the world?" (Oliphant, 1857: I, 100). These thoughts channel that cry of "What am I to do with my life?" which reverberates through so much nineteenth-century fiction, from *Jane Eyre* (1847) to *Middlemarch* (1871–2) and beyond, to the dramas of Ibsen, in *A Doll's House* (1879) and *Hedda Gabler* (1890). The only child of a reclusive father, and a mother who died in childbirth, Hester turns to her faithful attendant Alice for enlightenment, but Alice's account of a woman's life is far from reassuring. She was "happy beyond the common lot of women," Alice tells Hester, "but one by one everything I rejoiced in was taken away" (I, 104). Like Oliphant herself, Alice had children, but all died, and she is now resigned to making the best of what remains. In 1857, however, Oliphant was still a young mother in the early days of marriage, experiencing losses which were as yet nothing out of the ordinary. What is striking about this passage, therefore, is its bleak foreboding of the painful futility of women's lives. There is something especially claustrophobic about this novel, where there are few characters, and Hester is tricked into marrying her cousin, and returning to the isolated country house where she was raised by her introspective father.

Oliphant has been traditionally dismissed as a writer who was at best indifferent to the burgeoning feminism of her time, and at worst actively opposed to it. As her journalism (discussed in the previous chapter) shows, she felt no common cause with the younger generation of female activists, and deplored the "strange and humiliating notion" that women were a "sect," or special interest group, requiring particular consideration (Oliphant, 1870: 174). There were many reasons for her embarrassment, not least a sense on her part that it was degrading and immodest to insist on women's collective injustices, or to make herself in any way a public spokesperson for a cause. Certainly, Oliphant has been harder to recoup as a "neglected" female author, than, for example, Mary Elizabeth Braddon, because of her apparent reservations on the great causes of her day, especially the suffrage and sexual freedom. Barbara Leah Harman and Susan Meyer, in wondering why Sandra Gilbert and Susan Gubar omitted Oliphant from their *Norton Anthology of Literature by Women* (1985), suggest this was "because her novels do not question or challenge the prevailing patriarchy, nor does she treat her women characters as the oppressed "other." Equally, she has been faulted for her "political timidity" and "superficially emancipated heroines" (Harman and Meyer, 1996: 67–68). These are undoubtedly important charges, but perhaps the most significant is the issue of whether or not Oliphant "challenged the prevailing patriarchy." Magarete Rubik claims that she did, and that her "portrayal of women, in particular, is one of the most subversive aspects of her writing" (Rubik 1995: 51). This chapter, however, will argue that while she exposes many injustices, she fails to propose any really practical alternatives. Her women frequently outperform men in terms of resolving injustices, and demonstrate managerial talents often lacking in their male counterparts, but their opportunities to apply these to situations outside the home are limited. The notions of "performing" and "outperforming," nevertheless powerfully interact and overlap in Oliphant's fictional representation of women. Not only does she show her female characters self-consciously exaggerating a stereotyped role in order to reinforce its effectiveness: the role itself frequently requires strategic skills undeveloped in their fainter-hearted male counterparts.

These frustrations in defending Oliphant are familiar to those experienced in reading other Victorian women writers. Her women may perform as heroes, but they are not revolutionaries prepared to break taboos and bonds, like the heroines of George Gissing or Sarah Grand. This was partly because Oliphant was relatively uninterested in the great campaigns for women's education and employment; still less did she care about sexual freedom as an end in itself. For her, the domestic scene was women's natural habitat, which it was important to see as potentially a creative arena for more than basic household management, but not as a place for sexual pleasure outside marriage. Themes of patient endurance, of waiting for circumstances to change, rather than forcing them, are more to Oliphant's taste. There is a clear dividing line between *Hester*'s vulgar Emma Ashton, who is persuaded on a train to run away with Edward Vernon, and Chatty Warrender of *A Country Gentleman* who waits for most of the novel for Dick Cavendish to disentangle his complicated personal history. Oliphant creates Emma as a comic character, prepared to marry anyone who asks, whereas Chatty is refined, self-controlled, and dignified. While Emma accepts an impromptu offer from a man who meant to elope with someone else, Chatty behaves as a woman should, in Oliphant's eyes. She is fully vindicated when her lover's supposed wife admits they were never legally married.

If Oliphant has little sympathy with crude manifestations of sexual frustration, she remains concerned for the emotional fulfilment of older women, widows and patient spinsters, some enduring long engagements to college Fellows waiting for a "living" in order to set up house (as with *The Perpetual Curate's* Morgans). In *The Curate in Charge* (1876), both Mr. St. John's wives are past their first youth when they marry. The first, Hester Maydew (Oliphant has many Hesters in her novels), is already thirty when they meet, a vicar's daughter resigned to a life of parish duties, prompting an authorial observation that "it seems hard thus to wear away a life" (Oliphant 1987b:8). She then waits ten years before Mr. St. John finally secures a clerical post and feels ready to marry her. As the narrator puts it, "They were almost old people when they set off from the little church at Weston bride and bridegroom" (Oliphant, 1987b: 10). His second, his daughters' governess, Miss Brown (endowed with no other name), accepts a clumsy marriage proposal when the now widowed Mr. St. John has qualms about dismissing her on his teenage daughters' departure for school. Both wives are unsentimentally eliminated from the novel when they die after producing two children apiece, and interest shifts to the two daughters, Cicely and Mab. Like many of Oliphant's heroines they are girls full of potential, but trapped at home with an elderly father, and the twin toddler brothers he has irresponsibly fathered in his sixties. It is perhaps the sheer lack of other options that Oliphant most forcefully presents in so many of her novels, contextualized in situations where the women themselves are eager for a purpose in life, but persuaded to find it within the confines of their own home.

The upsurge of critical interest in Oliphant over the last twenty years has, however, produced many fresh approaches to tackling the internal tensions and contradictions of her fictional representation of women. D. J. Trela suggests that it "was more radical than her public political views" and that she was "constantly testing the limits" of societal and domestic conventions (Trela, 1995: 15–16), while Elizabeth Langland enlists Bourdieu's analysis of symbolic power in interpreting Lucilla Marjoribanks' consolidation of her managerial skills in a bourgeois community. Langland further notes how Oliphant's novels challenge "so many Victorian sacred cows—romance, angels, feminine duty, innocence, passivity, and the separation of home and state" (Langland, 1995: 153). Ironically, as Langland observes, Oliphant's own experience of being the overworked breadwinner for her children "became the basis for stigmatizing her achievement: she wrote too much and too quickly" (1995: 154). It follows that George Levine sees her as "conventional and unconventional at the same time," specializing in "disenchantment" with domestic life, especially the "psychological oppression of capable women trapped in conventional arrangements" (2016: 233–4). If Oliphant's "angels" are their household's salvation, one might argue, merging Langland's insights with Levine's, that many of them are disenchanted angels, determined to make the best of a situation by deploying their frustrated organizational talents. If these responses to circumstances amount to a version of Victorian feminism, it is very much Oliphant's own: anti-theoretical, realistic, and intensely practical. Above all, Oliphant privileges the taking of responsibility as something men avoid and women embrace, as they have to do when they have children. For Christine Bayles Kortsch the time has come for setting aside the question of whether or not Oliphant is a feminist, and focusing instead on the material culture in which she was "entangled," something I will also consider in the next chapter on dress and the body (2016:106). For now, the ways in which Oliphant represents the different stages of a woman's life in terms of her cultural "entanglement" will be the primary focus of this chapter. Given that such choices as were available to nineteenth-century middle-class women were virtually inseparable from consideration of their family context, it will also be helpful to understand more about how Oliphant conceived of the family as an arrangement which provided women with a purpose, but often at the cost of obstructing other, more individual, ambitions.

The Waiting Game: Young Women

Like many of her contemporaries, Oliphant often represents the family as fragmented and asymmetrical, dominated by widowed parents, with an emphasis on idle sons and vulnerable daughters whose purpose in society remains unclear. The juxtaposition of these two gendered classes repeatedly indicates an imbalance between young women eager to work, and their male counterparts, who (apart from conscientious doctors and clergymen) find it difficult to motivate themselves beyond a life of lounging and dissipation. Essentially, Oliphant approaches young women's lives in her novels through two main routes: social comedy, and a kind of long drawn-out waiting-game which often encompasses elements of sensationalism, notwithstanding her previously discussed notorious and public critical opposition to this developing subgenre of the mid nineteenth-century novel. The waiting-game is usually prolonged by the uncertainties of courtship and the awaited marriage proposal, one of Oliphant's favourite plot devices. This of course is common to many novelists, not least to Jane Austen, whose plots revolve around proposals which frequently arrive in the wrong sequence (as with *Mansfield Park's* (1814) Fanny Price and Henry Crawford, or Elizabeth Bennet's proposals from Mr Collins and a condescending Mr Darcy in *Pride and Prejudice* (1813). For Oliphant, however, the business of waiting for "a gentleman to speak," as Emma Ashton euphemistically puts it in *Hester* (1883), is not just heart-wrenching, but deeply humiliating. It becomes, in fact, emblematic of a woman's powerless position in the whole scheme of things. She needs to marry, but has to be chosen, and she must repress all unmaidenly promptings of desire before the man's proposal authorises them. For Emma Ashton, and indeed Phoebe Tozer, in *Salem Chapel* (1863), hovering hopefully around the new Dissenting minister, Arthur Vincent, the waiting game is crudely comic, and clearly in bad taste. For more sensitive Oliphant heroines, such as Chatty Warrender in *A Country Gentleman* (1886) and Oona Forrester in *The Wizard's Son* (1884), the on-off pressure of not knowing whether the hero reciprocates her feelings becomes both draining and degrading. While Walter Methven has become "the first object in her life,"

Oona Forrester assumes that she "counted for little or nothing in his" (Oliphant, 2015b: 159). Chatty Warrender, waiting for Dick Cavendish to clarify his position, undergoes a similar "pang of shame" as defined by the narrator's explanation: "A man is not ashamed of loving when he is not loved, however angry he may be with himself or the woman who has beguiled him; but the sharpest smart in a girl's heart is the shame of having given what was not asked for, what was not wanted" (Oliphant, 1886: II, 202).

This is the conservative position adopted by many nineteenth-century novelists who uphold the tradition that it was unseemly for a woman to register any sexual response to a man before it had been validated by a marriage proposal. Oliphant's young women, however, repeatedly respond emotionally and physically to the overtures of eligible men, most often through recurrent images of fluttering hearts and hands, followed by prolonged passages of introspection and resigned self-control, as exhibited both by Chatty Warrender over Dick Cavendish, and Gussy Harwood, with Charley Meredith, in *Janet* (1891). For other, more robust heroines, such as Lucilla Marjoribanks and Phoebe Junior, marriage is essentially a project undertaken in partnership with a weaker man. The woman still has to wait for the man to propose, but her confident sense of her own superiority makes the conventions of courtship less personally degrading. In Lucilla's case, the man's significance as a "project," whether with herself or in an arrangement with someone else, further complicates the issues of romance and rejection. The comic nuances of this novel are brought into full play as Oliphant's narration acknowledges Lucilla's tentative matching of herself with all the eligible bachelors in her circle, before sensibly dismissing them. Even when she thinks Mr. Cavendish[1] might be about to drop to his knees for a proposal, she pulls herself back to reality: "for though Miss Marjoribanks had a very good opinion of herself, it had not occurred to her that Mr. Cavendish was very deeply in love — with *her*, at all events" (Oliphant, 1988:182).

Not being in love when it would be convenient to be so, is another plot variation Oliphant exploits to the full in *The Curate in Charge* (1876), where the only real love-match is between Mr. St. John and his first wife Hester. While his second daughter Mab escapes into a career as a book illustrator, Cicely accepts loss of status as a village schoolmistress in order to support her baby brothers. Her position is almost that of a single mother, the text repeatedly stressing the absurdity and unnecessary existence of these two small boys, begotten so late in life by their father, and fatal to her own marriage prospects. In the circumstances marriage to her father's successor, Mr. Mildmay, an Oxford Fellow yearning for real "life," would be the ideal solution, but although he and Cicely feel a mutual interest, neither is exactly "in love." "What does he mean by life?" Cicely wonders in a self-conscious passage in tune with Oliphant's own meta-narrative about the triteness of marriage as a novel denouement (Oliphant, 1987b: 204). No downtrodden drudge, Cicely, her views echoed by the often intrusive narrator, makes several notable protests against the way her own life is governed by decisions made by men who have never experienced her own humiliating insecurity, but in the end, coyly admits to being in love with no one other than Mr. Mildmay (207). In subsequent novels, such as *Hester* (1883) and *Kirsteen* (1890), Oliphant found the courage to buck the trend and leave her eponymous heroines on their own— though Hester is too young to be left without at least a closing hint of romantic possibilities.

Marriage

Marriage remains Oliphant's solution for most of her young female characters, but one senses this is often done reluctantly (at least on the narrator's part), and in the knowledge that this is what novel-readers expect. As early as 1855, she professed to be bored with the traditional marriage plot, when she wrote "Modern Novelists – Great and Small," for *Blackwood's*: "People will be interested, we suspect, till the end of the world, in the old, old story, how Edwin and Angelina fell in love with each other; how they were separated, persecuted, and tempted; and how their virtue and constancy triumphed over all their misfortunes" (Oliphant, 1855: 555). Oliphant's novels usually challenge this popular stock of plot twists, discovering increasingly complex and prolonged reasons either for deferring the happy day, or for pursuing the couple into a strained and even violent aftermath of their romance, as in *A Country Gentleman* (1886) and *The Ladies Lindores* (1883). Her later novels attack marriages of convenience, and usually blame the husband for their breakdown, but the tribulations of *The Days of My Life* (1857) — which extend to all but the last few pages — are caused by a petulant heroine who feels aggrieved at being deceived into marriage, albeit with a man she deeply loves. Seemingly all the men she knows, including her own father, are in on the plot, which is benignly designed to restore Hester to the family estate and her children to their natural inheritance.

The comic novels, meanwhile, embed the happy couple in parallel plots of manoeuvres and machinations on the part of people determined to be married against the odds. For every romantic marriage, or those that are certain, but dependent on secure jobs and steady incomes, there are several that surprise people, and not just the random elopements, such as Edward Vernon's with Emma Ashton. *Miss Marjoribanks* (1866) is full of sudden, even underhand marriages, or unlikely alliances, that shake Lucilla's confidence, and illustrate the mysterious workings of sexuality, such as Archdeacon Beverley's marriage with the widowed Mrs. Mortimer, and Mr. Cavendish's on-off flirtations with Barbara Lake; or in *The Perpetual Curate* (1864) the shabby liaison between Rosa Elsworthy and Tom Wodehouse. Much of *Salem Chapel* revolves round suspected and shocking explosions of sexuality (as in Susan Vincent's apparent abduction by Mr. Fordham/ Colonel Mildmay), which contrast with the publicly conducted courtships of couples who take many months to resolve their differences and minor misunderstandings. *The Days of My Life* (1857) is fairly untypical of Oliphant in ending with a happy christening scene and assurance of many further progeny for the Southcotes after a bitter year of marital breakdown: "We have not only a second son now, but a third, and a fourth!" coos Hester, "and Cottiswoode is almost overflowing, and our patrimonial acres will have enough to do to provide for all the children with whom God has blessed us" (Oliphant, 1857: III, 293). This is relatively early Oliphant; her subsequent marital endings drag exhausted couples to an understanding somewhat less joyously and complacently, while her studies of marriage in the 1880s and 90s confront some of the worst abuses of married life, including sexual disgust, physical and emotional incompatibility, and the chronic depression that comes of being disappointed with children as well as husbands.

Judith van Oosterom has discussed these later novels in detail, noting the recurrence of estrangement from children in unhappy marriages. A classic example is Lady Caroline Lindores, forcibly married to Patrick Torrance, in *The Ladies Lindores* (1883), by a father determined on promoting his family's status and wealth through strategic alliances. Designating it "a pioneering work in its time in the manner in which it so explicitly touches on Caroline's repugnance of the physical side to her marriage," van Oosterom also notes that Caroline lacks the energy to change things (van Oosterom, 2004: 63). On the other hand, as Elisabeth Jay argues, Lady Caroline's situation triggers an indignant response in her younger sister Edith, and a wider debate among her friends and family (Jay 1995: 135). Edith's untried confidence in challenging her father, loudly expressed in cries of "I would not do it" (Oliphant, 1883a: 1, 124), is soon tested when he insists on her marrying the amusingly named Lord Millefleurs, heir to the house of Lavender: no brute like her brother-in-law Patrick Torrance, but a popinjay of a man, a "baby-faced and lisping adventurer" with "plump, delicate, pink-tinged hands" (Oliphant, 1883a: I, 296). Millefleurs is as sexually repugnant to Edith as Torrance was to her sister, and Oliphant sympathetically acknowledges it.

By 1883 Oliphant's wit, formerly levelled against the vulgar and ignorant, has refocused on the manoeuvrings of the upper classes in the London "season" as she addresses their attitude to matchmaking. In many ways it is no different from that of the middle and shop-keeping classes, as seen in *Salem Chapel* and *Miss Marjoribanks*, only by this point Oliphant's amusement is more noticeably barbed with anger. From the men's complacent perspective, they are offering potential wives "a post for life": "Thus the — we will not say candidates, rather nominees — possible occupants of the delightful and every way desirable post of Marchioness of Millefleurs," Oliphant narrates, "had every sort of inducement to 'go in' for it, and scarcely any drawback at all" (Oliphant, 1883a: II, 4). So far as Lord Lindores is concerned, the man's looks are unimportant: "he was not a hunchback, nor deaf, nor dumb, nor blind. Short of that, what on earth did it matter how a man looked?" (II, 8). This notion, of marriage as a job description and a project, which seemed so entertaining to Lucilla Marjoribanks and Phoebe Junior, had soured for Oliphant by the 1880s. Even within *Phoebe, Junior*, she tartly notes how the Dickensian Mr. Copperhead seems to have taken a feeble second wife, as "something belonging to him which he could always jeer at" (Oliphant, 1989: 10). *Kirsteen* (1890) goes further still in showing how Mr. Douglas, "after the few complaisances of a grim honeymoon, let his wife drop into the harmless position of a nonentity" (Oliphant, 1984a: 2).

Increasingly acknowledging the role played by the body in love and marriage (however much in her review articles she claimed to dislike its fictional representations), Oliphant could not, in her later novels, overlook physical incompatibility. If Patrick Torrance's bulbous bloodshot eyes and uncouth manners repel his wife, so do the "heavy fat cheeks" and "the same light, large, projecting eyes" of their children, which along with their coarse personalities, obstruct Carry's bonding with them (I, 181). Perhaps Oliphant's best-known study of sexual incompatibility, however, is her "Story of a Wedding Tour," first serialised in the *St James's Gazette* in 1894. Its orphaned heroine, Janey, who has been educated to be a governess, marries the first man who proposes to her, simply because he says he loves her, and she is moved and flattered by the idea. Oliphant's narrative, however, makes no secret of his ugliness, and a week of marriage is long enough for her to be "a good deal frightened, horrified, and even revolted, by her first discoveries of what it meant to be in love" (Oliphant 2013c: 255). It is not only her physical disgust which frightens Janey, however, but also the realization that her new husband has no interest in what she thinks or feels, or any regard for her as an individual. Having escaped his attentions when he fails to reboard their train after a station stop, she spends the night alone in a French hotel, already noticing her relieved expression reflected in the mirror: "It was full of life, and meaning, and energy, and strength. Who was it? Janey? Janey herself, the real woman, whom nobody had ever seen before" (2013c: 260).

What sounds like endorsement of Janey's feelings, however, becomes less clear as the narrative develops. Her husband's disappearance may be both empowering and liberating, but Janey is already pregnant. She warms to a mother and baby on the train taking her towards her new life in the South of France, but the image of Mr. Rosendale, preposterous in his rage, still haunts her in her happiness. Ten years later, the narrative cuts abruptly to his sudden reappearance in her quiet paradise, projected there by another train, and his rapid exit from it, already fatally ill: "A huge man, helpless, unconscious, with a purple countenance, staring eyes, breathing so that you could hear him a mile off" (2013c: 269). Although his death legitimises the end of their marriage, the legacy of guilt is permanent. Elisabeth Rose Gruner recounts her students' frustration at what they see as Oliphant's ambivalence about Janey's plight: "they, like me, preferred to see her as freed twice by the railway rather than trapped as she seems to be in the conclusion" (2005: 105). It may be that endorsing Janey's runaway single motherhood is one step too far for Oliphant. She had tried it before in *The Days of My Life* (1857) when Hester Southcote, piqued by her handsome, but deceiving husband, holes up with her maid in an obscure village hideaway, but then comes back and resumes her marriage. The likelihood is that, for Oliphant, however dreadful physical intimacy with a boorish husband may be (and she makes no bones about illustrating this), marriage is for life, and nemesis pursues those who try to break this bond. For genuine widows, however, there is always the reopening of possibility, and a chance to redress the mistakes of the past.

Mothers and Widows

Of the various ramifications of family relationships the ones that most interest Oliphant are those between parents and adult children: as Elisabeth Jay observes, there is surprisingly little in the novels about the pleasures of raising young children (1995: 133). Each of her major novels juxtaposes several contrasting mother figures, so that, for example, in *Salem Chapel* Arthur Vincent's mother, initially off-stage, is built up as a diminutive, but steely widow, devoted to her two adult children, alongside the mysterious Mrs. Hilyard, a separated wife desperate to protect her (also offstage) daughter Alice. In the comic-realist subplot of the novel, good-natured, vulgar Mrs. Tozer, the butterman's wife, like most of the other mothers in the Nonconformist community, hopes Arthur Vincent will choose her daughter as his bride. Among Oliphant's other popular novels, the mother-daughter relationships are often fraught and irritable, as in *Hester* (1883), where Mrs. Vernon's anxious fussing around Hester with her old-fashioned proud values infuriates her daughter, even as it betokens the mother's real concern for her child's wellbeing. Father-daughter relations tend to be less emotionally intense, especially where the fathers are old and unable to cope with practicalities (as in *The Curate in Charge*), or detached and independent (as with Dr. Marjoribanks), but there are exceptions. When Carry Lindores is forced by her insensitive father to marry the obnoxious Patrick Torrance, her mother can do nothing to halt the arrangements. Even a daughter on good terms with her father, Hester Southcote, finds that arrangements for her marriage cause a rift between them, as he is determined she should marry before he dies. It is with mother-son relationships, however, that Oliphant comes fully into her own, entering the field with a passion that betrays her own increasingly disappointed experience with her young adult sons, Cyril and Cecco. This experience is intensified in novels such as *The Wizard's Son* (1884) where there is no father-figure left in the family to break the pattern of mutual exasperation between mother and son, other than the terrifying warlock-lord, ancestral father of the race.

Mothers in Oliphant's novels are often widows, which makes these two roles difficult to separate in a comprehensive discussion of their purpose in her fiction. The 1871 Census for England and Wales, which surveys the population at the mid-point of Oliphant's most successful period of writing, conveys a sense of the instability of the Victorian family in terms of marriage duration. While most couples were seen to marry for the first time between the ages of twenty and thirty, the "probable duration" of married life was reckoned to be on average twenty-seven years; the proportion of widows to married couples being eleven, and widowers, nine, for every twenty-seven married couples.[2] In other words, a young adult son or daughter was likely to lose one parent just at the point when they were making their own decisions about marriage and becoming parents. The Census report also notes that remarriage is "of so much social importance" that it reduces the number of widows by about a quarter, and widowers by more than a third, causing them to be reclassified as married.[3] Oliphant's interest in the emotional lives of older people who have previously been married (as well as spinsters and bachelors past their first youth) therefore reflects a statistical reality which is largely neglected by novelists in the second half of the nineteenth century. According to Cynthia Curran (1993), however, there was a "dramatic fall in the remarriage rate from a high of 30% in the sixteenth to 11% in the nineteenth" centuries (1993: 227), most men preferring never married women as their brides. Frances Power Cobbe, addressing an "Excess of Widows over Widowers" in a *Westminster Review* article of 1889, claims that at this time widows outnumbered widowers by over 820,000 (1889: 501).

Inevitably, critics have speculated about Oliphant's own long widowhood and whether she was ever tempted to remarry. Elisabeth Jay recounts her relationship with the man who was "almost certainly, a suitor," the Reverend Robert Herbert Story (1835–1907), who became Principal of Glasgow University, and Moderator of the General Assembly (1995:17). Oliphant came to know him when she was researching her biography of the charismatic preacher and friend of the Carlyles, Edward Irving, and talks about him openly in her *Autobiography* as a "handsome young minister," living at that time with his widowed mother, "a handsome old lady full of strong character." What struck her most, however, was not just the man himself, but his family situation: instinctively, she saw them as "like a household in a novel" (Oliphant 1990: 94). There was also a sister, "very clever and bright" (1990: 105), while Story himself was "an excellent talker," who often made her laugh (1990: 105). They remained in touch, discussed and reviewed each other's work, and sometimes met, but Story's marriage in 1863 seems to have terminated Oliphant's brief experience of eligible widowhood, so far as further offers were concerned.

Nevertheless, widows in all their varieties, remain a disquieting presence at the centre of many of her novels: their sexual allure undimmed, along with their capacity for unsettling the vulnerable men of the parish. Even the timid and dowdy Mrs. Mortimer of *Miss Marjoribanks* makes a dramatic entrance "with a veil down, and a large shawl, and a tremulous air" (1988: 261), and ends up marrying Archdeacon Beverley, confirming Minnie Warrender's view (in *A Country Gentleman*) that "A widow is in the best position of any woman. She can do what she likes, and nobody has any right to object" (1886: 1, 142). A striking example is the glamorous Lady Western of *Salem Chapel* (1863), who might, with her sobriquet "the young Dowager," according to the butterman, Mr. Tozer, "lead a man out of his wits" (1986a: 43). Mrs. Tozer further adds that "by reason of having married an old man, she has a step-son twice as old as herself, and he's married; and so this gay pretty creature here, she's the Dowager Lady Western" (1986a: 45). Adelaide Tufton adds that Mrs. Hilyard "married a half-brother of Lady Western's — a desperate rascal he was. They had one baby and then she left him — one baby, a girl that has grown up an idiot" (1986a: 253). This misaligned family at the heart of the *Salem Chapel* sensation plot, splinters shrapnel in all directions, but most damagingly into the neat triadic Vincent family of widowed mother, son and daughter, who all become entangled with Lady Western's "desperate rascal" of a half-brother.

As if needing to step aside and debate widowhood and second marriages from all perspectives, Oliphant's story "Mrs. Clifford's Marriage" (1863), serialised soon after *Salem Chapel* in *Blackwood's*, largely consists of gossip about remarriage. At the heart of the story is Mary Clifford, widowed mother of five young children, with five thousand a year and "the handsomest house," and about to remarry. To one of her female neighbours, the decision to exchange "such exceptionally blessed circumstances," to stoop "her head under the yoke," is completely incomprehensible (Oliphant, March 1863: 284). Property inheritance is obviously another key issue here, with the assumption that Mrs. Clifford's assets will pass to her second husband, Tom Summerhayes, ominously introduced as "an idle fellow" (Oliphant, March 1863: 285). The warning signs are all too obvious, both to the female and male commentators allocated their own opening chapters. While the women wonder why she "can't be content" with her five children (Oliphant, March 1863: 285), the men wonder that

Summerhayes wants to burden himself with them. Both sets of gossips are concerned that Clifford left everything to his wife, making no provision for the children.

As the story develops, however, while Oliphant retains her scepticism about second marriages, she also baulks the reader's most obvious expectations about Mrs. Clifford's comeuppance for her foolishness. Tom Summerhayes' clumsy efforts to destroy her husband's will in a house fire rebound on him when the very lawyer he trusted discovers a legal loophole in the estate's entailment history, ensuring that the property legally passes, not to Mrs. Clifford, but to her eldest son Charley, cutting out Tom Summerhayes. Tom, in turn, proves to be an active manager of the estate, and not at all the idle wastrel of the standard Oliphant plot; in a further unexpected twist he concedes defeat in a gracious speech at Charley's coming-of-age celebrations, and retreats, with Mrs. Clifford, to the Summerhayes family manor house. What is most interesting perhaps, though, is Oliphant's final word on Mrs. Clifford, whose susceptibility to a controlling second husband has caused her children so much anxiety. Perhaps, says the narrator, she "had not been much more happy as Mrs. Clifford than she was as Mrs. Summerhayes," which may imply either that marriage is generally a fairly mediocre experience, or it is for a commonplace woman like Mary Clifford who lacks discernment and is quickly reassured (Oliphant, April 1863: 436). She was always, adds her sister-in-law Lydia, "a gentleman's beauty" (Oliphant, April 1863: 419); she is a type of "man's woman" unsympathetically identified by Oliphant as flawed and inferior, unlike the many astute and intelligent wives in her fiction all too aware of their husbands' embarrassing ineptitudes.

Thirty years later, in "A Widow's Tale" (1893), Oliphant revisited the theme of the young widow unprepared to see herself as sexually off-limits, in the story of Nelly Brunton, "the little widowed cousin from India" (Oliphant, 2013d: 205). From the start there is something amiss with all the female roles in the oddly lopsided Bampton household of naive, inexperienced women, where Julia "took the position of her father's wife rather than of his daughter," and is "a mother to May," her much younger sister (Oliphant, 2013d: 204). With "poor little" Nelly's entry into the family circle, as a widow of thirty, with two children (housed elsewhere), the family and their gentleman friend, Mr. Fitzroy, prepare to encounter all the sentimental clichés of widowhood, only to be confronted by a disconcertingly pretty face, with no widow's cap to cover her hair, and her evening dress of "very thin black stuff, almost transparent, faintly showing her shoulders and arms through" (Oliphant, 2013d: 210). The inevitable happens, and over songs at the piano, Fitzroy, who has already displaced another suitor for May, transfers his flirting, if not his marital intentions, to the more overtly sexually self-aware widow.

The narrator's voice in this story is self-consciously intrusive as she prepares the reader for Nelly's destruction of her young cousin's hopes and mysterious disappearance with Fitzroy: "I do not know how to justify Nelly's conduct in these circumstances," she apologizes, "and yet I do not think she was so much to blame as appears at first glance" (Oliphant, 2013d: 213). After all, Nelly's natural vitality tells her she is still young, and "her blood was still running fast in her veins" (213). Even Nelly's relative maturity and widowed status, however, fail to protect her from male ambivalence about commitment, which is such a recurrent theme in Oliphant's fiction, often conveyed through free indirect narration from the female victim's perspective. In this story the narrator fully enters into Nelly's self-defence, followed by her speculations as to whether Percy Fitzroy will visit her in her new home. The suspense of waiting for a "crisis" in their relationship climaxes in his thinly disguised offer to stay overnight by deliberately missing the last train home: a remarkably explicit proposition, which ends with his being firmly directed to the spare room. The shocking implication is that, as a widow, he assumes Nelly is sufficiently experienced to know the score. "What had he said?" she wonders afterwards. "Why had he said that and not something else?" (227), the "something else," presumably, being an honest proposal of marriage. Their different understanding of words is what forces Nelly's confrontation of their relationship in all its coarseness, and a realization of what her apparent acquiescence in his visits has authorized. A line has been crossed, and from this point on, Fitzroy's blatant irritation with her unexpected prudery, obliging him to consider "this brutal question of marriage" (238), exposes his own brutality and Nelly's residual propriety, as she repeats the phrase, "struggling with that burst and flood of misery which is one of the shames and terrors of a woman" (239).

For all her weak vacillation, Nelly is accorded a serious dark night of the soul as she weighs up the attractions of breaking with Fitzroy, and keeping a further tryst with him, supposedly to be married by licence. Citing George Eliot's Romola and her ability to fall out of love with her unworthy husband Tito, the narrator insists: "My own experience is all the other way. Life, I think, is not so easy as that comes to" (243). In other words, however badly Fitzroy behaves, the alternative— of being a good mother to her babies, who are "not companions for a woman in the full tide and height of her life" (242) — seems worse to Nelly, and the narrator at least credits her with feeling the genuine frustrated desire of a young widow kept under surveillance by her own household. Whether or not they ever do marry is left an open question, but all the evidence points the other way. All we know is that they lead a restless life abroad, and then Nelly returns, alone, dressed more like a widow than she had been on her first entry into the Bampton-Leigh household, "a shadowy figure standing over them, a woman in a travelling cloak, with a great veil like a cloud hanging over her face" (248).

It is easy to read both "Mrs. Clifford's Marriage" and "A Widow's Tale" as warnings against the temptations of desire in widowhood, and its conflict with the higher moral claims of children, but Oliphant characteristically complicates the message by conceding that a woman widowed in her thirties or forties may reasonably feel the need for an adult relationship with a man. The guiltier Nelly suffers more than Mary, however, and the ageing spinster Julia is rewarded with the love of Nelly's abandoned children. It is hard to avoid the implication that however tempting it is to succumb to male flirtation and love-making, a young widow is unlikely to find remarriage quite the idyllic second chance she dreamed of. Even Mary Clifford wonders for a moment what the arrangements will be in heaven when Mr. Clifford comes to claim her, and finds she has become Mrs. Summerhayes: testimony perhaps to Oliphant's underlying conviction that to marry a second husband is to betray the first.

Performing Widowhood

There is something theatrical about Oliphant's widows, with their cloudy veils and dramatic mourning dress. Not only do they confirm their identity, in Judith Butler's sense of constructing gender by performing it: their unpredictability is what repeatedly adds to their dangerous charisma in Oliphant's novels. By definition, they have a sexual history and a certain "knowingness" lacking in their inexperienced sisters, which in *Salem Chapel* (1863) is concentrated in the glamorous Lady Western, with whom Arthur Vincent enjoys a brief flirtation. In a novel remarkable for its lack of any real courtship plot for its moody and aloof hero, his widowed mother gradually assumes a much larger heroic role than any younger woman in his circle. Determined to defend both her troubled children, Mrs. Vincent (she has no first name) is never portrayed in a romantic light herself; instead, she becomes increasingly associated with the language of battle and martyrdom as she works to save both her children's reputations, and ultimately her son's post as minister with his socially inferior deacons and congregation. No "excitable, passionate creature," Oliphant insists in her narrative, "but a wholesome, daylight woman," whose suppressed emotions are signified by her often mentioned "clasped hands," Mrs. Vincent is the real hero of the story, as judged by her creator's moral and social standards for women (Oliphant, 1986a: 245). The phrase "a wholesome, daylight woman," is one of those surprising throwaway expressions that make reading Oliphant so pleasurable: a phrase that is all her own, capturing not just the widow's self-control and decency, but especially the author's relief in discovering a wholly trustworthy force for good in a novel full of people with murky histories. Mrs. Vincent apparently has nothing to hide as she goes forth bearing "Arthur's standard at this dangerous crisis of the battle" (230), and as the battle intensifies she delivers a "master-stroke" (365) in telling Tozer, the all-powerful deacon, that Arthur might simply "throw it all up" and resign (364). The style, in this stylistically rich novel, is often mock-heroic — "The widow's Parthian arrow had gone straight to the butterman's heart" (365) — but the impact of her simple phrase is no less powerful for that. It quickly becomes a narrative catchphrase representing the congregation's realization that their relationship with their pastor has reached a crisis.

Mrs. Vincent makes one further heroic foray into a chapel meeting, but this time heavily, perhaps ironically, disguised as what she already is, a widow: exaggerating her condition under "the thick veil of crape which she had worn in her first mourning. Nobody would recognise her under that screen" (379). As "The widow looked through her veil at the butterman and the poulterer with one keen pang of resentment, of which she repented instantly" (379), Oliphant reduces all the key players in this scene once more to their functional class designations. When the widow is joined by another social type, "the Back Grove Street needlewoman" (Mrs. Hilyard), who gazes at "the minister's mother" (383), their sympathetic connection is marked, as so often in this novel, by the touch of a hand: this time a "furtive hand" (Mrs. Hilyard's) that "took hold of the black gown" (383). As the next chapter will demonstrate, Oliphant deploys significant body language in her novels, along with frequent references to clothes, most often to delineate power structures. In this scene the body language works with the public masquerading of the clothed self (the widow in deep mourning, the shrunken needlewoman with her blue-stained fingers) to mark the silent alliance of members of a disregarded and powerless female underclass. Witnesses as they are to the bombastic and ungrammatical oratory of Arthur's detractors in this public meeting called to decide his future as their minister, the two women are almost erased by their dress, but they never lose their performative flair in deliberately over-acting their roles as defenders of a cause.

Mrs. Vincent's adventures in *Salem Chapel* provide a stark contrast with her daughter Susan's. Susan is either absent, as a missing person, for much of the story, or lying inert in bed, like a marble effigy, recovering from her supposed abduction. Almost the only meaningful thing she says for days after she is brought home is the melodramatic "I am not disgraced" (298). Although Susan's statuesque size and marble limbs eventually make her someone to be reckoned with— as she says at the end, "Somehow most people mind me now, because I am so big" (409) — she is also described as an "awful ghost" (263), a veritable woman in white to her mother's hyperactive widow in black. Arguably they are both female stereotypes which Oliphant exploits to the full, but while critics customarily regard this stereotyping as an awkward, even inexplicable lapse into the very sensationalism she deplored in her reviews of 1860s fiction, it is characteristically performed with wit and self-awareness throughout.[4] Although her social concerns are serious, her relish for parody, from the mock-heroic of Lady Western's sudden arrivals in her "heavenly chariot" (34), to Pigeon the poulterer's disingenuous declaration that "he would have held his peace cheerful if dooty had permitted him" (381), points to the possibility of a Bourdieusian reading in which an entire social structure is being ridiculed via the linguistic capital of the Salem community of self-righteous shopkeepers. Mrs. Vincent's advantage is that she has the time and the motivation to assert alternative values to those around her.

It is typical of Oliphant, however, that all Mrs. Vincent's efforts come to nothing when Arthur resigns anyway, notwithstanding placatory offers of a salary rise and a silver salver. Athough his mother loyally defends him to the last, Oliphant concludes that "It was with bitter restrained tears of disappointment and vexation that she heard from him" (455). The futility of heroism, a major Oliphant theme, while not completely corroborated by the intricate plot of this novel, nevertheless raises the question of whether Mrs. Vincent's utter dedication to her children is ultimately symbolic of a wider phenomenon: the futility not just of heroic gestures on behalf of others, but specifically of maternal self-sacrifice.

A Country Gentleman and His Family (1886)

Although a few mothers die young in Oliphant's plots, there are also many persistent survivors who, far from being pushed aside when their children grow up, and their husbands die, find themselves drawn directly into crises in their adult children's lives. Mrs. Vincent is by no means unusual in Oliphant's oeuvre in still feeling responsible for adult children, to the detriment of her own opportunities to enjoy her freedom. In an extreme example Mrs. Methven, for example, towards the end of *The Wizard's Son* (1884) rushes up to her son's country seat in Scotland to see whether he is still alive after an explosion and fire in a tower. More conventionally, Hester Vernon's mother (*Hester*, 1883) worries over her daughter's food, clothes, comings in and goings out, as if she were still a child. Phoebe Junior is unusual in being able to visit Carlingford on her own, to support her ailing grandmother, without her mother managing her daily activities. Oliphant's observations of these prolonged parent-child relationships (something she had experienced with her own two sons) recur in her fiction, viewed both from the child's and the parent's perspective, the angle varying from novel to novel.

The question of what to do with midlife freedom from marriage is something Oliphant explores two decades on from *Salem Chapel* in *A Country Gentleman and His Family* (1886), whose forty-five-year old widowed mother, Mrs. Warrender, is guiltily keen "to escape into some place where she could take large breaths and feel a wide sky over her" (Oliphant, 1886: 1, 52–3). Even within days of her husband's death, her eagerness for adventure shocks her more conventionally-minded adult children: "As she came into the room there came with her a brightness, a sense of living, which was inappropriate to the hour and the place" (1886: 1, 50). The narrative makes it clear that while she was a willing enough wife and mother, she is nothing like the dull and blameless husband she married, and finds her two elder children alien in temperament: both her tempestuous son Theo, and her self-righteously conformist daughter Minnie. In these sections of the novel, the narrator's voice takes over from the character's, providing a series of mini-essays on the tensions between dutiful widowhood and the discovery of a zest for life in someone who still has time to enjoy it. This is equally true of her younger counterpart in the novel, Lady Markland, who, before she has had any time to herself, succumbs to the suffocating attentions of Theo. It is important to the narrator that both women are allowed an identity of their own, apart from their children's demands on them. When Lady Markland's ten-year-old son Geoff assumes she will always be his "chief companion, always with him, his alone," the narrator's voice takes his mother's side: "How should she convey to him the first germ of the fact that mother and son are not one; that they separate and part in the course of nature; that a woman in the flower of her life does not necessarily centre every wish in the progress of a little boy?" (1886: II, 142). In a further twist, however, Oliphant captures Lady Markland's guilt at having to say this to Geoff: "To herself it was terrible, a thing foreign to all her tenets, to all her principles" (II, 142). Unlike the steadier Mrs. Warrender, who, though beleaguered by her children, is free of dictatorial suitors, Lady Markland's position is doomed from the start by her inability to free herself from the emotional demands of both child and husband. Oliphant's pre-Freudian triangular rivalry between parents and children is quite nakedly articulated in this previously overlooked novel, the merits of which have recently been rediscovered by George Levine and Barbara Z. Thaden. While Levine acknowledges that this is a "disenchanted" narrative, whose sexual and family tensions "hover on the edge of the kinds of dramas that Freud was imagining" (2016: 238–9), Thaden applies a psychoanalytic reading to Oliphant's reworking of the oedipal "Family Romance" which makes the woman protest, not as an aggrieved daughter, but as a mother. As she argues, for psychoanalysts, "the maternal function is always found wanting" (Thaden, 1997: 90). For Oliphant, on the other hand, as for Elizabeth Gaskell, with whom Thaden compares her, the mother of adult children remedies her position by forming "maternal circles" with other women, such as her daughter or daughter-in-law, and grandchildren. In *A Country Gentleman*, the circle embraces her son Theo's wife, Lady Markland, and her emotionally needy son, Geoff, who becomes, for Mrs. Warrender, an accepted grandchild when Theo rejects him.

Levine's reading of *A Country Gentleman* argues, however, that "This male *Bildungsroman* becomes […] a study of the women's repression"— both Mrs. Warrender's and Lady Markland's — as their disenchantment grows from their sense of disempowerment, while Theo's "grows from his fundamental assumptions about what he as a man is entitled to" (2016: 243). By planting two troubled women at the heart of Theo's *Bildungsroman*, Levine suggests, Oliphant is showing up the insensitivity of authors such as Dickens, who have seemingly no qualms about relegating women to the background of their heroes' quest for a meaningful life (2016: 244). Oliphant's women are no Miss Havishams, Estellas, or even Mrs. Joes, from *Great Expectations* (though Mrs. Warrender, like the first and last of these examples, lacks a first name, and Dick Cavendish's wife usually both): like Thaden, Levine observes "the bond that links mothers and wives together against the egoism and dominance of men" (Levine 2016: 246), even if there is relatively little either of them can do to avert the string of accidents and plot twists that control both their lives.

Two other women, Chatty Warrender, and Dick Cavendish's supposed wife, have an important role to play in this novel, however, which revives echoes of *Salem Chapel's* melodramatic subplot. Apart from the Markland subplot with its throwback to the eighteenth-century unreformed rakish husband, there is a house of ill-repute in the Warrenders' village, more characteristic of the Victorian "sensation" plot. With its bad drains, high walls, and mysterious inmates (who include Dick Cavendish's nameless wife), The Elms is a moral blot on the landscape: for little Geoff, an ogre's castle or a prison. Elisabeth Jay describes the fallen woman at the core of this story as a "good-hearted whore" (1995:112); the apparent impediment to Dick's marriage with Chatty, she first fakes her own death in order to release him, and is then discovered never to have married him at all.

In fact, Dick's two "wives," Chatty and the former circus performer he "married" in California, meet, both veiled, in the church immediately after the wedding, when the more deeply veiled figure confesses that she is "nobody's wife. I've been —a number of things. I like my freedom" (Oliphant, 1886: III, 118). This scene in the vestry becomes a kind of ritual "unmarrying," in which the surplus wife formally releases her "husband," having been already "dead to [him] these long years." As Levine observes, "The narrative seems to hold nothing against her or against Dick, who finds himself entangled against his better judgment in a mess from which the melodrama will finally extricate him" (Levine, 2016: 250). There are, after all, worse messes in the family, especially Theo's unhealthy obsession with controlling his new wife, Lady Markland, and his desire to be rid of his stepson, Geoff. As for Chatty, the daughter who started the novel with almost no personality, the Warrenders finally accept Dick Cavendish into their family, notwithstanding any squeamish reservations they might have had on her behalf. Mrs. Warrender's empathetic open-mindedness as a mother endorses the match, so that her younger daughter can marry the man with whom she has fallen in love. Mrs. Warrender's own plans to run away, however, come to nothing, much like Mrs. Vincent's plans for Arthur. As so often in an Oliphant novel, the exigencies of their children's lives prevent the mothers from pursuing their own independent desires.

Single Women

Early in *The Ladies Lindores* (1883), two servants, Janet and Agnes, compare the relative advantages of marriage and single life. Their mistress, Barbara Erskine, is also single, apparently by choice, but Agnes has never had any offers, despite being slim and pretty. "There's me and the mistress," muses Agnes, "we've stood aloof from a' that; bit I canna think it's been for oor happiness" (Oliphant, 1883a: 1, 166). This, like most of Oliphant's other novels, works on the assumption that most women will marry, and certainly most young women from their late teens onwards, will be considering their options. This is not only seen as natural and normal, but as more likely to be emotionally fulfilling than the old-maidism, which for middle-class women of adequate (if not plentiful) means, was the only realistic alternative. Although the possibility of late marriages interests Oliphant in several of her novels, including *The Perpetual Curate* (1864) and *The Curate in Charge* (1876), these are rarely seen as quite so satisfactory. Lucilla Marjoribanks is perhaps unusual in deliberately postponing any matrimonial intentions "until she was nine-and-twenty, and had begun to 'go off' a little" (Oliphant, 1988:73). Usually, Oliphant's women do not have the luxury of that option. The Rector's wife, Mrs. Morgan, for example, has certainly "gone off a little," in her ten years' wait, though Oliphant at least credits her with sharper wits than her bumbling husband. In her representation of single women past their prime, and childless older wives, Oliphant has it both ways. These women are easy targets for their detractors, but they are also strongly individuated, and frequently influence the fortunes, often benevolently, of the younger characters. Without obvious personal charms, and with time to interfere in other people's affairs, they often demonstrate a head for business lacking in their husbands or in younger, prettier married women. Lucilla Marjoribanks, deliberately fending off romance until she has completed her reorganisation of Carlingford's social and political landscapes, may be an extreme case of marriage deferral, but she is not alone in finding her single state more conducive to personal development — until, like Phoebe Junior, she realizes that partnership with a husband might take her even further.

Oliphant's ageing spinsters appear both singly and in clusters. In *The Perpetual Curate*, they are "worse than Fates" (Oliphant 1987a: 23) dominated by Miss Leonora Wentworth, who controls preferment for a church living, but they are supplemented in their covert observation of others, by the Miss Hemmings, and Mary Wodehouse (who accepts a late offer of marriage from Mr. Proctor). Both Mary Wodehouse and Dora Wentworth are shown on self-appointed secret missions under cover of darkness in the well-to-do neighbourhood of Grange Lane, noting the comings and goings of younger men and women. This is another example of Oliphant's comic-ironic adoption of the sensation mode, but while Dora can act only covertly in defence of her nephew, Leonora openly tries to manage his professional future, until confronted by Frank's rakish brother Jack. "I tell you, so far from rewarding him for being of the true sort," Jack tells his aunt, "you do nothing but snub him, that I can see" (Oliphant 1987: 501). This showdown between the reprobate nephew and the domineering maiden aunt is sprung on the reader as if once more to question conventional social attitudes. The reprobate is clearly correct in his judgement of the situation, and Aunt Leonora shamed into realizing she has been motivated "not by heroic and stoical justice and the love of souls, but a good deal by prejudice and a good deal by skilful artifice, and very little indeed by that highest motive which she called the glory of God" (506).

Oliphant challenges unjustified domestic tyranny wherever she sees it, and in many different forms, from tyrannical fathers to "strong-minded women." Like her Victorian contemporaries she is never entirely sure what to do with single women, and it may be unrealistic of modern readers to expect her, any more than George Eliot or Charlotte Brontë, to provide us with positive images of happy and healthy women content to pursue their own careers without the support of a husband. Two final case studies will at least show Oliphant's efforts to consider options for women other than marriage and motherhood, although characteristically they come tinged with ambiguity. The first of these is Catherine Vernon, twice acting head of Vernon's bank in *Hester* (1883), on each occasion occupying an interim role in place of a dishonest male defaulter. A natural leader, Catherine has lacked the anxieties of a married woman, living (Oliphant implies) an emotionally tepid life: "She had gone along peacefully, her own mistress, nobody making her afraid, no one to be anxious about, no one dear enough to rend her heart" (Oliphant, 2015a: 24). This sentence neatly summarizes Oliphant's reservations about singleness. While unmarried women escape the worst tragedies in life, they also miss the greatest joys. As it happens, Catherine treats her nephew Edward, who lodges with her, as a substitute son: grateful when he spends an evening at home with her, but aware of his gravitation towards a life of his own with Hester. In her portrayal of Catherine Vernon (now sixty-five), Oliphant pays tribute to her presence of mind and organisational skills, but shows her struggling to connect with the younger generation of Vernons. Explicitly compared with Queen Elizabeth I — "a dry tree — while other women had sons and daughters" (Oliphant, 2015a:24) — Catherine also seems like Queen Victoria, maintaining formal court ceremonial, while the younger, "fast set" in the family, "rampant, insolent, careless," go mad for Cousin Ellen's "dancing teas" (Oliphant, 2015a: 180). For all her superiority to every man in the novel, in terms of her managerial intelligence, Catherine is also taken in by everyone, and her reign seen as somehow anomalous and unnatural. While Catherine acknowledges Hester as her ideal successor — "you would be an excellent man of business" (Oliphant, 2015a: 370) — she also insists that this cannot be, and Hester must marry.

One late Oliphant character who never marries, however, is the eponymous Kirsteen (1890). It is fitting to close this chapter by asking why she was allowed to be both single and happy, fulfilled in her lifetime's career as a needlewoman, while a socially and intellectually superior woman like Catherine Vernon is not. The explanation lies partly in the opening image of her parents' marriage: her father "an arbitrary and high-tempered man, whose will was absolute in the family," his wife, "a nonentity," who after bearing fourteen children, falls into invalidism (Oliphant, 1984a: 2). This late novel, like many of its predecessors, explicitly debates the relative attractions of marriage and motherhood, but its setting "seventy years ago" (as its subtitle states), and initially "in the wilds of Argyllshire" (1), safely distances it from the reality of the urban English novel-reader's experiences in the *fin de siècle*. Kirsteen has to lower her social status to work for a mantua-maker in London, and override her romantic feelings for a lost lover, but her choices are firmly vindicated to the end. If her brother "Sir Alexander Douglas, K.C.B" (341), finds her actions difficult to approve, Oliphant nevertheless clearly affirms her happiness and status as "the best dressed woman in Edinburgh […] Miss Douglas of Moray Place" (342). Even if her family deplore "that she had no man" (341), Oliphant insists that "No one could be more cheerful, more full of interest in all that went on" (342).

Oliphant also notes significantly that Kirsteen is not alone in her later years, "her large house running over with hordes of nephews and nieces" (342). This is ultimately, perhaps, Oliphant's final position on women's lives, and one she took up herself as her sons died and she focused on the futures of her two nieces, Madge and Denny. She had examined the lives of women for half a century, without reaching any easy or complacent conclusions.

Marriage would always remain for her the most natural choice, the option best for most women; but her novels show how difficult this can be, surveying a panoramic landscape of roles for women of all ages, from the walk-on parts of the Carlingford wives and gossips, to the pioneering efforts of outspoken and independent-minded managers and organisers, such as Lucilla Marjoribanks and Catherine Vernon. If she overlooks the needs of the working-classes, what is most striking about Oliphant's representation of the middle and upper classes, is their articulacy and intelligence in continually questioning the fairness of other people's assumptions about their duties. The self-awareness of her strongest characters — Lucilla Marjoribanks, Phoebe Beecham, Mrs. Vincent, Mrs. Hilyard, Catherine Vernon — in affirming their role by exaggeratedly performing it — enhances their effectiveness in challenging those who disapprove. If the outcome of all this spirited performance is sometimes disappointing acquiescence in the status quo, each social unit has been shaken by events, and forced to listen to those it had brushed aside. Oliphant's transition from the Carlingford comedies to the more directly confrontational strategies of the later novels, marks her parallel transition from satirical anti-feminism to a serious and heartfelt study of women's options as they face the most crucial questions of their infinitely entangled lives.

CHAPTER 3

Mrs. Oliphant's Clothes and Bodies

"I acknowledge frankly that there is nothing in me— a fat, little, commonplace woman, rather tongue-tied— to impress any one"

(Oliphant, 1990:17)

Margaret Oliphant was someone who noticed bodies, starting with her own. She made significant artistic decisions about her characters' bodies, seeing them as tall and willowy (Carry Lindores), large and substantial (Lucilla Marjoribanks), or petite and pretty (Nettie Underwood, Ursula May). Her comic characters, especially, are physically present in ways rarely flattering to them, as with the simpering Phoebe Tozer of *Salem Chapel* (1863), "pink all over— dress, shoulders, elbows, cheeks, and all" (Oliphant, 1986a: 7), while the unusual eyes or hair of her more serious characters, such as Kirsteen Douglas, may be "quite out of accordance with the canons of the day" (Oliphant, 1984a: 3). Nor are male characters spared the authorial scrutiny of both clothes and bodies, especially beards (for example, shabby men like Tom Wodehouse and Fred Rider); even the most desirable catch on the marriage market, Lord Millefleurs in *The Ladies Lindores* (1883) is repeatedly mocked, both by characters, and narrator, for looking like a fat robin redbreast. With his upper-class lisp and puffy cheeks, Lord Millefleurs patently has no sexual allure for his would-be bride, Edith Lindores, but on the other hand he is also no kind of physical threat, unlike her brother-in-law, the brutish Patrick Torrance, notable for his protruding bloodshot eyes and hulking body.

Clothes, no less than bodies, are important to Oliphant. She had, after all, written a volume on *Dress* (1878) for Macmillan's "Art in the Home" series, and recommended her readers to "be individual" in their choice of attire, and to adapt it to their personal needs, without "abandoning fashion altogether" (Oliphant, 2005: 94). Where she mentions clothes in her novels, she makes them crucial to her portrayal of a character's values. Phoebe Beecham and Ursula May, for example, in *Phoebe, Junior* (1876), are known, respectively, at first, as "the young lady in black," and "the girl in white" (Oliphant, 1989: 23; 25), denoting the mature and daring sophistication of the one, and the naive youthfulness of the other, with perhaps a compliment to Wilkie Collins's *The Woman in White* (1860), though Ursula has more personality than Collins's Laura Fairlie and Anne Catherick. Meanwhile, Mrs. Vincent, in *Salem Chapel*, is characterised by her neat widow's cap and black silk dress, a sharp contrast with the "brilliant cherry-coloured bonnet" sported by Mrs. Tozer, a woman whose vulgarity is signalled throughout the novel, like her husband's, by her clothes, as well as her ungrammatical speech (Oliphant, 1986a: 239). Higher up the social scale, but no less vulgar in her way, is Ellen Merridew in *Hester* (1883), her wrists jingling with bracelets, and the "yards of silken train" in her dress "sweeping after her, and sweeping up too all of the mats at the doors as she went in" (Oliphant, 2015a: 56).

Remarkable clothes and bodies in Oliphant's novels (usually interrelated) may appear to be predominantly, if not exclusively associated with comic characters, in a quasi-Dickensian style: the "straight" protagonists, such as Arthur Vincent of *Salem Chapel*, Frank Wentworth of *The Perpetual Curate* (1864), and John Erskine and Edith Lindores of *The Ladies Lindores*, tending towards an abstract, conventional appearance, more in the manner of Jane Austen's serious characters. What exactly Oliphant does with clothes and bodies in her novels is, however, more complicated than appearances (literally) may suggest, as increasingly noted by critics. Galia Ofek's observations of hair in Oliphant's fiction, especially *Miss Marjoribanks* (1866) and *Hester*, draw attention to the Medusa theme, used differently by Oliphant and George Eliot, showing how Oliphant "tries to read the sign from a modern, feminine and unscholarly point of view" (Ofek, 2009: 174), re-appropriating the classical figure whose hair was made of snakes, and whose gaze turned men to stone. In *Miss Marjoribanks*, for example, Lucilla may still fix men with a hard stare, but essentially to manage a situation for the good of everyone: a corrective to the classical male interpretation of Medusa as "an emasculating woman" (Ofek, 2009: 174). *Salem Chapel*, meanwhile, has attracted debate about the sexualizing of Susan Vincent's white marble-like arms, and the blue dye-stained fingers of the mysterious needlewoman Mrs. Hilyard, the consequences of whose disastrous marriage now seem etched on her body, along with those of other impoverished women who survive on meagre earnings from harsh working conditions.[1] The bodies of Oliphant's men and women are both individually marked by their personal histories, and also representative of broader issues in the social and political debates of her time, such as changing gender roles, the pressures of poverty and disability, and the strains of mental breakdown. In feminist terms, Oliphant ensures that her characters are shown experiencing all the pleasures and discomforts of the body, which for women often include the oppressive closeness of men, and their physical restraint of women they try to control.

Theorizing the Body

Critical theory of the body in relation to its representation in literary texts has evolved significantly over recent decades. As the editors of the *Cambridge Companion to the Body in Literature* have noted in their overview from Foucault to Merleau-Ponty, Bourdieu, and post-Lacanian feminism, the theorised body has been shaped by its contemporary culture for centuries, especially in relation to notions of class, driven by socio-historical forces (Hillman and Maude, 2015: 1–9). The indissoluble relation between mind and body has stimulated some of the most wide-ranging explorations of how daily life is coloured by the experience of inhabiting a specific body, while at the opposite end of the spectrum the bodily pleasures of food, sex, and other kinds of sensuous enjoyment have prompted more popular approaches to understanding the connection between physical experience and material culture. While Fredric Jameson claims that new ways of thinking and talking about the body emerged in European literature in the 1840s, David Hillman and Ulrika Maude argue that the body, as a solid, visible, physical presence, simply does not exist in literature, as it would, for instance, in a film. Both fictional writers and critics have to find ways of creating and mediating the body through language. They have to make their readers aware, not just of a character's distinguishing features, but also of how their bodily experiences impact on their daily lives and social interactions: hence the vitality and variety of the body's significance in all cultures, from the medieval to the present day, and the demands it makes on our ability to theorise it. "Contemporary approaches to the body," Hillman and Maude demonstrate, through their essay collection, "tend to display an eclectic theoretical pluralism" (Hillman and Maude, 2015: 2).

Jameson's theory, in *The Antinomies of Realism* (2013), distinguishes between "affect," which eludes language, and "emotion," which is named (for example, as love, or hatred). For him, "affect" comes into being, or recognition, with the construction of the "secular or bourgeois body" (Jameson, 2013: 34); it is, indeed, bodily feeling that prompts the need for a new history of the body, as "an existential and class-social phenomenon, related to the emergence of new forms of daily life" (Jameson,

2013: 32). Of related interest here is the work of Maurice Merleau-Ponty (1908–61), whose rejection of Cartesian mind-body dualism in favour of the notion that "we are our bodies," develops the notion of the "body-subject." In *The Phenomenology of Perception* (1945), he argues that the body is one's "point of view upon the world," and also our means of communication with it (Merleau-Ponty, 2005: 81). The perceiving mind is thus an incarnated body, and the body itself a "grouping of lived-through meanings which moves towards its equilibrium" (Merleau-Ponty, 2005:177). As with Bourdieu's emphasis on habit in relation to the body, Merleau-Ponty suggests that habit helps to build this state of equilibrium. John Thompson, summarizing Bourdieu's notion of the "habitus" or set of dispositions which incline us to act in a certain way, explains: "It is because the body has become a repository of ingrained dispositions that certain actions, certain ways of behaving and responding, seem altogether natural" (in Bourdieu, 1991: 13). Bourdieu himself declared that "Habitus is a socialised subjectivity," meaning that our training or upbringing, especially in relation to social class, determines the way we view the world, which it may be difficult to transcend or escape (Bourdieu, 1992: 126). Another word Bourdieu coins is the notion of "hexis," which as Thompson elaborates, is "a certain durable organization of one's body and of its deployment in the world" (in Bourdieu, 1991: 13). "Habitus" and "hexis" are clearly closely connected, in the sense that they both refer to ingrained ways of viewing the world from a social perspective, often mediated through the body as a physical presence taking up space. Steph Lawler extends this definition to argue that habitus is evident in "ways of speaking (idioms as well as accent), in styles of dress, and so on" (2008: 129–130).

The usefulness of these theories to an enhanced understanding of Oliphant — an equally body- and class-conscious novelist, whose novels are all about the awkwardness of social interaction in hierarchical communities — should by now be becoming evident. Though in many ways a traditional Victorian middle-class woman, suitably circumspect in her approach to physical matters, including pregnancy and childbirth, Oliphant does write about sexual feeling, and is acutely conscious of the way people lose bodily control of themselves when afraid or excited. While much of this feeling is indicated in the expected ways through blushes and beating hearts, her characters are also troubled by red or pink complexions, lynx eyes, stolid physiques, bushy beards, or "weak-minded ringlets" (Oliphant, 1987a: 28). Like Charlotte Brontë's protagonists her more self-aware characters appraise each other critically or admiringly, and form what we might call a body-conscious community. As the autobiographical narrator Hester Southcote puts it in *The Days of My Life* (1857), when she first meets her relatives, Mrs. Ennerdale and her daughter Flora, "There are some people who make you conscious of your own appearance by the strange contrast which you feel it bears to theirs" (Oliphant, 1857: II, 206). Pale in the early stages of pregnancy, as well as in mourning for her father, Hester admires the innocent and fancy-free Flora "as only women can admire each other. I was not shy of looking at her as a man might have been" (Oliphant, 1857: II, 208). In later novels, such as *Miss Marjoribanks* and *Phoebe, Junior*, whole communities of women study each other's clothes and bodies, and compare them with their own, especially in the context of competition for the few available men.

Rather than itemize bodily attributes in detail, Oliphant generally works by focusing on one or two distinguishing features of her key characters, most commonly their hands, hair and eyes. Their bodies become disaggregated into agitated signalling systems as she looks for new ways of recording their physical responses to one another, especially their fear, excitement, and sexual attraction. Both Bourdieu's and Merleau-Ponty's theories of the embodied self, and the body as a place of "ingrained dispositions," are especially useful in drawing out her lifelong association of behavioural patterns with class and community values and predispositions. Many of her leading characters have a physical solidity which is a core aspect of their personality, largely derived from their family values, religion, or their trade or profession. While this is especially true of the lower-class, more vulgar characters, such as the Tozers, who are unflatteringly associated with the smell of hams and cheeses lingering in their parlour, like the Balzacian stale rooms cited by Jameson (2013: 33), bodily awareness occurs just as powerfully among her leading middle-class characters, both men and women, enhanced by the narrator's voice which communicates many of these observations.

Neat Bodies

A good place to start is with Nettie Underwood of *The Doctor's Family* (1862), Edward Rider's Australian sister-in-law by marriage, whose distinctive, self-sacrificing perspective on domestic responsibility is inextricably part of her physical presence, as viewed both by the novella's narrator, and by Rider, the eponymous "Doctor" of the title. Nettie essentially *is* her body, which is racially different from the "Saxon" type of blonde-haired beauty Rider had admired in his previous relationship with the symbolically named Bessie Christian. Nettie is, by contrast, piquant and foreign: a "little brown Titania" (Oliphant, 1986b: 68) with shapely hands, "brown and beautiful" (56), a tiny head "overladen with its beautiful hair" (68), and "brilliant, resolute, obstinate eyes" (74). The only member of her household with any energy, Nettie relocates her querulous sister Susan and Susan's three children from Australia to Carlingford, to be reunited with Fred Rider, Edward's idle brother, Susan's estranged husband, and the father of her children. One emphatic point is made about Nettie throughout: she takes responsibility as no one else does for housing this shambolic family and bringing order (so far as she can) to their chaotic living arrangements. The story is strangely prophetic of Oliphant's own future household of 1868–75, when she took in her widowed brother Frank and his family, but even by 1863 she had already settled into her strenuous life as a widowed working mother of three surviving children.

Nettie's brisk, neat body is frequently juxtaposed with Fred's, hulking and insensitive, which at the heart of the story invades her personal space, her own little sitting-room in their rented lodgings, and pollutes it with pipe smoke. This episode prefigures the scene where Fred, having toppled drunkenly into the canal, is brought home, a drowned corpse, covered with Nettie's shawl, and laid to rest in "the little silent womanly room" (115), as Oliphant calls it. As she removes the shawl, Fred's "dead eyes" stare back at her (116), and her own response to this sudden family tragedy is registered by Oliphant in a succession of bodily references. Having gazed at the covered body with "a sob of excitement and agitation swelling into her throat" (115), she sends a message to Edward Rider, "with lips that trembled in spite of herself" (116–17). Later she is shown sitting outside her own parlour door, "without her shawl, and with her tiny chilled feet on the cold tiles" (120). This way of writing about the whole body as acutely sensitive, from quivering lips to trembling hands, encapsulates a technique of Oliphant's, established early in her career, which connects individual "ingrained dispositions," as theorised by Bourdieu, with broader generic associations of class and gender. Whether a woman is small and tidy (though in Nettie's case saved from being entirely childlike by her luxuriant and unmanageable hair), or large and stately, like Lucilla Marjoribanks, matters to Oliphant, as she records their involuntary physical response to the stresses of living in families and communities.

The Touch of Hands
Nettie's body-language also expresses the physical and mental frustrations of being the unappreciated manager of the household, too proud to ask for help, or even to acknowledge openly that she has needs of her own, in her growing feelings for Edward

Rider. Barbara Korte's study of body language as "an important signifying system" in literature, suggests that it "constitutes one subsystem of the text's entire sign repertoire" (1997:4). Among other things, non-verbal behaviour reflects the power structures in communities and relationships, as we see repeatedly in Oliphant's writing. One of her favourite ways of indicating varieties of feeling difficult to verbalise is through what Korte calls "haptic behaviour," or forms of touching, of which the most intensive is the wringing of a person's own hands, "tight in each other," as she shows when Nettie is ambushed by Rider in a flurry of packing for the family's abrupt return to Australia (Oliphant, 1986b: 173). The play of their two pairs of hands is intricately described: he seizing her "busy hands" (172), "hoarse and violent, grasping the hands tighter" (172), she "drawing her hands from his grasp" (172), and he recapturing them, once more "clasp[ing] the firm hands which held each other fast" (173). Oliphant is here exploiting to the full the options she has, as a Victorian woman writer, albeit at the start of the "sensation" decade, for representing a crisis in feeling between two people struggling to act on their attraction to one another in the face of family duty.

Hands are especially important to Oliphant as involuntary signalling systems when individuals come under increased pressure from a society intent on surveillance of relationships, as often happens in her fictional world of Carlingford or George Eliot's Middlemarch. As Daniel Karlin has noted, in relation to the "whip hand" in Eliot's novel, *Middlemarch* repeatedly notices hand gestures, and "hand work" — ways in which hands are employed in work and recreation (such as piano-playing) — as well as the bodily management of others by application of the restraining or controlling hand. He adds that when characters lay their hands on those of someone else, such moments almost always "represent ambivalent impulses, in which affection or even apology co-exists with the desire to dominate" (Karlin, 2002: 31–2).

The desire to dominate is certainly evident in Edward Rider's

97

physical interactions with Nettie. In a novella where everyone tries to control everyone else, whether physically, or by passive-aggressive behaviour, while also being controlled, Rider acts as if the only way to save her is by overriding (with a pun on his name) her family's determination to keep hold of her forever. Saved by Susan's announcement that she is going to marry the bearded "Bushman," Richard Chatham, a suspected rival for Nettie's hand, Rider, in a comic *volte-face*, "stretched out both his hands and grasped the gigantic fist of the Bushman with an effusion which took that worthy altogether by surprise" (176). Even after this apparent resolution of their problems, Nettie has one further hand to unlatch from her own, or find a way of accommodating: that of her young nephew, little Freddy, who rejects his new stepfather and demands to stay with Nettie: "He made a clutch at Nettie with one hand, and with all the force of the other thrust away the astonished doctor" (187). In a play of male hands for ownership of Nettie, she in turn clinging to a desperate sense of her own domestic usefulness, Oliphant shows how the family literally restrains her from fulfilling, or even acknowledging her own emotional needs. At the same time, while turning Rider into her forceful saviour, she leaves the reader uneasy about Nettie's fate, as she starts her new life as Rider's wife with Freddy as their needy nephew and stepson.

Oliphant remains fascinated by the play of touch, especially hands on arms, as she develops more complex relationships between men and women in her longer novels. Hands in themselves, even when lying idle, are used to denote the strengths and weaknesses of character. In *The Perpetual Curate*, for example, Gerald Wentworth's wife Louisa is fragile and helpless in the face of his determination to risk his family's welfare by leaving the Church of England to become a Catholic. Fearing that as a Catholic priest he would have to abandon his wife and children, Louisa begs him not to forsake her:

He took her little hand and held it between his own, which
were trembling with all this strain — her little tender helpless
woman's hand, formed only for soft occupations and softer
caresses; it was not a hand which could help a man in such
an emergency; it was without any grasp in it to take hold
upon him, or force of love to part — a clinging, impotent
hand, such as holds down, but cannot raise up (Oliphant,
1987a: 153).

There is nothing particularly subtle about this play of gendered
hands, but it conveniently represents a theme often deployed by
Oliphant in her lifelong study of close-knit communities, to denote
energy-sapping marital relationships. Her language here seems to
sentimentalize the "little tender helpless woman's hand," while, in
accumulating slightly too many adjectives, in a style reminiscent
of Browning's dramatic monologues, indicating the damage it
wreaks on the man hopelessly tied to her. Browning's Andrea del
Sarto (1855), for example, tells the unfaithful Lucrezia, "Your
soft hand is a woman of itself;/And mine the man's bared breast
she curls inside" — a phrase both bizarre and oddly repellent,
especially in the circumstances of her adultery with her "cousin"
(Browning, 1989: 115). It suggests, as does Oliphant's more
prosaic passage, not just the physical delicacy of the woman, but
also her selfish power to manipulate by dragging the man down.
By contrast, Frank Wentworth, in *The Perpetual Curate* (1864),
unfairly accused of having seduced the shopkeeper's niece, Rosa
Elsworthy, tries to reconcile with Lucy during her father's illness,
by taking her hand "and holding it fast — a hand so different from
that weak woman's hand that clung to Gerald without any force to
hold him, in Wentworth Rectory" (1987a: 95).

While these examples mainly stress the mutually controlling
hands of husbands and wives, in *Salem Chapel* the hand upon the
arm is wielded by characters of all class and gender combinations
in a variety of passionate attempts to restrain or simply connect,

while the memories of previous connections serve to intensify the physical sensation of touch. Mid-way through the novel, for example, Arthur Vincent is detained by Mrs. Hilyard, even as the sound of carriage-wheels evokes the memory of Lady Western, and the "sweet hand she had laid upon his arm," a sharp contrast with the bony fingers he sees "with the blood pressed down to the very tips, holding with desperation that arm which had the power of life and death" (Oliphant 1986a: 314–5). Nor is Arthur's mother safe from the "furtive hand" of Mrs. Hilyard, who clutches the widow's gown as they attend the crucial chapel meeting which will decide Arthur's fate as minister to a dissatisfied "flock" (383). Both women are shown wringing their own hands with suppressed impatience, as Nettie does: the physical clinging to another alternating with the driving inward of feeling, only partially resolved when Susan returns, "clasping close, as if never again to lose them, her mother's tender hands" (408). Where women clutch each other for support, men pull at women's clothes, especially in *Miss Marjoribanks*, where Archdeacon Beverley grabs Mrs. Mortimer's sleeve —"not her hand — as if to convince himself that it was something real he saw" (Oliphant, 1988: 212), and in *Phoebe, Junior* where Clarence Copperhead "held Phoebe by the sleeve, that she might not escape him" (Oliphant, 1989:328). In *The Wizard's Son* (1884), another lover, Walter Methven, finds himself comparing the hands of two women he admires: the wealthy Glasgow heiress Katie Williamson, with her "very firm and true" hand (Oliphant, 2015b: 222), and the woman he eventually marries, Oona Forrester, whose supporting hand, "as soft as snow," was held out to him at a time when he was tormented by a sense of spiritual and supernatural haunting (Oliphant, 2015: 222).

Finally, in *Miss Marjoribanks*, where there are few physical gestures of affection between the title character, and the father who never seems to appreciate her desire to "be a comfort" to him, a valedictory touch softens Lucilla's last memory of him.

On the final evening of his life, when he says good-night, "his hand drooped upon Lucilla's shoulder, and he patted it softly, as he might have patted the head of a child" (Oliphant, 1988: 400). So unusual is his attempt to be a comfort to her, that Lucilla remembers it recurrently through the next chapters, building a link with the lawyer's disclosure that when he realized how little he had to leave his daughter, Dr. Marjoribanks said to himself "Poor Lucilla." "'And he patted me on the shoulder that last night,' she said, with tender tears" (413). In relationships where direct confessions of love, even between parent and child, are hard to utter, the slightest touch, for Oliphant, is eloquent of many years of repressed feeling.

Such is Oliphant's reliance on the touch of hands as an indicator of fluctuating emotional temperatures and finely differentiated relationships, that it persists as a key trope through her career. While it is often deployed in assertive confrontations where a misunderstood lover tries to bring a woman to an understanding of the truth, touch is also used sensitively among women to reassure or support. A scene of this kind occurs towards the end of *Hester* (1883), where the eponymous heroine and her forbidding relative and benefactor Catherine Vernon come together in their mutual disappointment at Edward Vernon's betrayal, both of their trust, and of the bank, which Catherine must now, for a second time, rescue from collapse. Both proud women, it takes a significant gesture from Hester to break the ice between them as "She made a step or two forward, and then dropped upon her knees, and touched Catherine's arm softly with a deprecating, half-caressing touch" (Oliphant, 2015a: 337). Startled by the intensification of Hester's grasp, and the drooping of her forehead on her arm, Catherine (like Dr. Marjoribanks, soon to die) is at first tempted to "snatch her arm away," but reciprocates by laying her "other hand upon the drooping head" (Oliphant 2015: 338). When Hester leaves her for a while, "She patted the girl's arm softly with her hand. Their amity was too new to bear caresses" (361).

The "patting" gesture is similar to Dr. Marjoribanks's final touch: emotionally awkward, it is nevertheless a reaching out, a token of parental affection which means more in an undemonstrative relationship than a more passionate gesture. The touch of hands in Oliphant's novels thus becomes a means, not just of reinforcing connections and registering the balance of power between people, but also a nuanced system for recording the gamut of feelings all her characters experience in a culture where more overt displays of physical emotion, especially between men and women, must be carefully managed.

Large, Tall, or Stout?

As is increasingly recognised in discussion of Oliphant's fiction, the presence of the embodied subject is more than just a casual character sketch, but a factor crucial to the unfolding of plot and the reinforcement of socio-cultural themes: no more so than in the characterisation of Lucilla Marjoribanks, whose solid physicality looms large over the chronicle of misunderstandings and social manoeuvrings that constitute one of her best-known novels. From the start, Oliphant is careful to describe Lucilla's physique as "large" rather than "tall" —"which conveys an altogether different idea" — that she is physically mature, and with the potential to become "grandiose" (Oliphant, 1988: 26). At fifteen she is "full and well-developed," with "a mass of hair," well-shaped hands and feet (27). Already womanly for her age, Lucilla is also keenly aware that by twenty-nine, she will be "going off a little" (69). There is nothing static about her body, however monumental.[2] Big women, in Oliphant's novels (Susan Vincent of *Salem Chapel* is another example) are respected by their more insignificant-looking friends and relatives, and have the potential to disrupt, merely by thrusting their corporeality into the domestic scene, but their influence may be a passing phenomenon. This is also true of her rival, Barbara Lake, a self-promoting drawing-room contralto, who is described as "not stout as yet, though it is the nature of a contralto to be stout; but she was tall, with all due opportunity for that development which might come later" (58). In other words, both Lucilla and Barbara are the possessors of unstable bodies, liable to coarsen and lose their ephemeral appeal. In a nice plot twist, it is Mr. Cavendish, possible suitor to both Lucilla and Barbara, who "goes off" and becomes "stout." "Stout," rather than "large," bears the signs of being a carefully-selected word in this context, suggesting a stolidity, stockiness or corpulence that comes from over-indulgence. In an interview with Lucilla, his body is, like hers, portrayed as changing: "he was getting large in dimensions and a little red in the face" (382). Repeatedly described as "getting stout," Mr. Cavendish seems to be visibly and actively swelling in a way that betrays his coarse sensuality (Lucilla is reminded of George IV (394)). When Barbara also turns out to have "gone off, like himself" (443), and also to have become "large" — he first identifies her in the distance as "the figure of a large woman in a large shawl, not very gracefully put on" (442) — the relationship between the two is fittingly revived. Oliphant's use of "large" as a term of approbation has transitioned with it to denote a coarseness both Lucilla and Susan Vincent have managed to avoid, apparently through their innate discretion and good taste. When Tom Marjoribanks reappears, eager to marry Lucilla, and her cook Nancy describes him as "'big and stout, and one o'them awful beards'" (478), his size (and beard) establish him as no longer a "boy," but a mature man, of a fitting physique and prowess to mate with Lucilla: his 'stoutness' more acceptable, perhaps, as the result of ten years' hard work in India, rather than overeating and drinking at home.

The narrator's voice meanwhile registers unease about Barbara's "straight black eyebrows, very dark and very straight" (58), her most dominant feature (like those of the Pre-Raphaelite "stunner" Jane Burden, who had married William Morris in 1859). While they listen to her music Barbara's audiences cannot ignore her body, which like Lucilla's intrudes into their space. Still more unsettling is the intense gaze Barbara returns to her audience ("that defiant look which was chiefly awkwardness and temper, but which looked like pride when she was standing up at her full height" (107)), but when the audience heartily applaud the performance, Barbara "flushed into splendid crimson, and shone out from under her straight eyebrows, intoxicated into absolute beauty" (108). Barbara's inability to control her physical responses warns of her emotional and moral volatility as she dallies with Mr. Cavendish, one of several possible candidates for Lucilla's hand.

It may be no coincidence that both Lucilla and Barbara are bold and confident, determined to manage their own destinies and rise above the level of the ordinary, but falling either side of the crucial demarcation line of "vulgarity." While Lucilla comes dangerously close to crossing this line, with her "tawny curls" (69) and habit of wearing a white dress with green ribbons when "a critical observer might have said that her figure was a little too developed and substantial for these vestal robes" (70), her behaviour, unlike Barbara's, is governed by impeccable self-control. Of all Oliphant's protagonists Lucilla is the one whose physical appearance we are least allowed to overlook, and which drives the ways in which her body, in Merleau-Ponty's terms, becomes her point of view upon the world. Yet although her size gives her power beyond her years, and much is made of her ability to suppress her feelings, her body still gives her away on occasions of extreme pressure or disappointment: as when she is preparing for a grand dinner at her father's, at a point when various relationships in her circle are coming to a head. Even Dr. Marjoribanks notices that his daughter is "flushed" and asks: "'is anything going to happen?'" (304). Although she assures him she is "quite well," the narrative continues: "But there could be no doubt that Lucilla had more colour than usual. Her pulse was quite steady, and her heart going on at its ordinary rate; but her admirable circulation was nevertheless so far affected, that the ordinary rose-tints of her complexion were all deepened" (304).

By contrast, Mrs. Woodburn, Mr. Cavendish's sister, who fears some public exposure or humiliation of her brother, is less able to manage her "heightened colour" (305): "Neither her pulse nor her heart would have borne the scrutiny to which Miss Marjoribanks's calm organs might have been subjected with perfect security" (305). While this physiological language is aligned with the mock-heroic style used to describe Lucilla's social campaigns, it also heightens our sense of the body's integral engagement with the emotions, and the unavoidability of its self-betrayal, even in this most familiar of middle-class rituals, the formal dinner party.

Disabled Bodies

While Oliphant writes mainly about young and healthy bodies, she also includes in her novels a number of disabled characters, especially women, who mainly act as spectators and moral commentators on the activities of the young. These figures include Adelaide Tufton of *Salem Chapel*, Alison Milnathort in *The Wizard's Son*, and Mrs. Harwood in *Janet* (1891). Recent advances in feminist disability studies have theorised the disabled, or "non-normative" body as marking the physical borderline between what a culture deems acceptable and abnormal. By definition, the disabled body does not comply with the standardized physical norm as endorsed by the dominant culture, and therefore may be seen as representing a form of degeneracy or inferiority. When the disabled subject is also female, she is doubly at odds with societal norms, especially in the nineteenth century when femininity in itself is medically theorised as disabling. According to Rosemarie Garland-Thomson, a feminist disability approach "fosters complex understandings of the cultural history of the body" (2011:16). It includes issues such as "the status of the lived body, the politics of appearance, the medicalization of the body, [and] the privilege of normalcy" (Garland-Thomson, 2011:16). In seeing disability as a "culturally fabricated narrative of the body, similar to what we understand as the fictions of race and gender" (17), Garland-

Thomson applies the terminology of writing narratives, and interpreting cultural assumptions in a way that is especially useful for studies of novelists such as Oliphant, who also address social issues via the inclusion of clearly-differentiated bodily types. Social scientists and feminist disability theorists further examine the ways in which neoliberal cultures enforce universalising norms and privilege the able-bodied, white, male, heterosexual figure as their ideal. Put simply, feminist disability theory challenges these suppositions by "unseating the dominant assumption that disability is something that is wrong with someone" (Garland-Thomson, 2011:18). In an earlier review article for *Signs* Garland-Thomson cites the many disability narratives written by women who challenge "normalist" perspectives, both contemporary and historical, but designates their available options as all "prejudiced, oppressive, and disempowering": for example the biomedical, sentimental, catastrophic, or abject (2005: 1567–8). Martha Stoddard Holmes, indeed, in *Fictions of Affliction* (2004), argues that Victorian representations of disability define it in terms of emotional excess and melodrama.

Stoddard Holmes's study includes an "Appendix of Physically Disabled Characters in Nineteenth-Century British Literature" (197–200), which lists many familiar names from Dickens, Charlotte Yonge, Dinah Mulock Craik, and Wilkie Collins, among others, but nothing from Oliphant's novels. While it would be difficult to claim for Oliphant's disabled women any startling deviations from the patterns established by her contemporaries — essentially people on the margins of their societies, often debarred from marriage and motherhood, but endowed with an astute compensatory wisdom — her disabled female characters are presented as eagerly engaged with the world from which their physical condition excludes them. Adelaide Tufton, the Dissenting minister's daughter in *Salem Chapel* for example, is often brought into play as a commentator on the community's behaviour. An otherwise minor character in the drama, she is explicitly defined as a "very pale, emaciated, eager-looking woman, not much above thirty," who, though sequestered from the outside world, is nevertheless keenly observant of her friends' interactions (Oliphant, 1986a: 25). Despite her limp appearance, however, Adelaide is seen by those who know her, as appearing "to indemnify herself for her privations" (26). This is a curious phrase, which suggests that Adelaide somehow insures herself, in a business-like way, against loss. She has also, in a phrase that seems to anticipate the language of feminist disability theory, "managed to neutralise her own disabilities, and to be acknowledged as an equal in the general conflict, which she could enter only with her sharp tongue and quick eye" (26). Brushing away all references to her misfortune, she employs a brisk vocabulary of "Stuff" and "Bother" (28), and knows as much about her neighbours as if she were actively mixing with them. In the terminology of the "Looker-on," which Oliphant adopted as her pseudonym for her own final set of observational articles for *Blackwood's Magazine* (1894–6), Adelaide Tufton is an observer of other people's follies from a safe remove: something she accomplishes without leaving the overheated home she shares with her elderly parents. "'I put things together, you see,'" "the daring invalid" tells the Dissenting minister, Arthur Vincent. "'[…] I shake them well down, and then the broken pieces come together'" (29).

In this novel where characters are differentiated by reference to distinctive bodily features, even Mrs. Vincent's "lynx eyes" are quelled by Adelaide's sharp gaze, and her talk of the congregation "killing" Arthur with their constant harassment. Adelaide's compensation for her disability appears to come in the form of a licence to speak her mind. Meanwhile, the Tufton family's static configuration — the elderly parents and the invalid daughter all confined to their chairs — is invoked several times in the novel at points where a crisis looms elsewhere in the parish. The very air of their parlour is "motionless" (440), Adelaide "immovable" (440), and the house itself "unchangeable" (440): the place where

Adelaide "had surely never once altered her position, but had knitted away the days with a mystic thread like one of the Fates" (440). Oliphant is determinedly unsentimental about Adelaide, even demonising her through her cold, pale blue eyes and "loveless eagerness of curiosity" (442), which ultimately sends Arthur Vincent home feeling thankful to be alive and free to make his own destiny. While he pities her frustrations, her "life in death" (443) as he sees it, his own energies are renewed for the final battle with his congregation, and ultimate resignation of his post.

While Adelaide is still relatively young, Alison Milnathort, of *The Wizard's Son* has only the appearance of youth, and that in a disconcerting way. When Walter Methven (newly designated Lord Erradeen) first meets her in her Edinburgh home, shared with her lawyer brother, he sees only "a piece of whiteness, which was a female countenance" (Oliphant, 2015b:65). While this gradually resolves into a human form, there is nothing reassuring about her "preternaturally young, almost childish" face, and overall appearance of "a girl dressed for some simple party" (72). In fact she is at least as old as his mother, and self-confessedly "just a cripple creature" (65), badly injured in an accident thirty years earlier. The accident turns out to be highly pertinent to Walter's situation, haunted as he is by a ghostly male presence when he goes to claim his inherited property in Scotland. Miss Milnathort encountered the same mysterious figure in her youth when she was engaged to an earlier Lord Erradeen, but ordered by the ghost to give him up. Fleeing from "Him" (the mysterious presence, whose mission is to control the life choices of his descendants), she fell from the walls of an old ruin and was severely crushed. This apparition is further discussed in my chapter on the supernatural, but in the meantime Miss Milnathort advises Walter that it may be possible to defeat him if he is confronted by two people of one mind: Walter and the woman who truly loves him (Oona Forrester). Her role in the novel is therefore fairy-godmother-like: a white haired Dickensian child-woman, often tearful, whose words close the novel, as she is reunited with Walter to bless the young couple who faced out the threat she was unable to defeat.

Alison Milnathort is a more generous observer of life than the final invalid to be discussed here: Mrs. Harwood, of *Janet*, chair-bound wife of a husband who was presumed dead but by her own management confined to a closed wing of the house as a "madman." While he is beyond recovery, Mrs. Harwood, though prematurely aged, "with white hair, a white cap, and a white shawl over her shoulders" (Oliphant, 1891a: I, 33) is the dominant figure of the household, apparently crippled with rheumatism, but according to her daughter Gussy, both too "stout" and too "lazy" to get out of her wheeled chair (I, 40). As with Adelaide Tufton and Alison Milnathort it is the unchanging nature of her presence which at first lulls Janet into a false sense of security. Even by the final volume Mrs. Harwood is still where she was, forever knitting (the favourite occupation of Oliphant's invalids), until the cataclysmic moment when she realizes her husband's hiding place has been revealed: "and with a sudden wrench, as if she were tearing herself like a limb from its socket, the disabled woman rose" (III, 76).

In a middle-class house of secrets, Mrs. Harwood's paralysis is surely symbolic of the way her life has been held in lock-down until this moment of what Martha Stoddard Holmes defines as the "melodramatic" outcome of a woman's desire exploding in conflict with intractable conditions. In one further revelation, the reappearance of Dr. Harding, Janet's devoted lover, prompts a temporary collapse in the invalid, further exchanges of touch in Oliphant's characteristic style, and the entry of "a man in a wheeled chair with white hair and beard" — a man scarcely distinguishable in his whiteness and disability from his half-conscious wife (III, 261). If whiteness and colourlessness distinguish Oliphant's disabled characters, their bland appearance is in disproportion to their ability to disrupt the respectability of family histories and expose their suppression of fraud and moral bankruptcy. Mrs.

Harwood's situation is further complicated by a wish to protect her husband from being sent to an asylum. The fact that her home becomes the asylum (as in *Jane Eyre*) shows Oliphant towards the end of her career adopting what was by then a well-worn convention from the "sensation" fiction she had openly attacked in the 1860s.

Oliphant's frequent recourse in her fiction to bodily characteristics, gestures, discomforts and disabilities, reinforces her awareness of the restrictions in women's lives and their often subordinate position in terms of physical space and power. Throughout her writing we find images of men firmly seizing women's arms and hands. Men's bodies are shown invading women's rooms, and polluting their space with pipe smoke; they lounge on sofas while women scurry about; and their beards and hulking physical presence seem to demand attention and obedience. While women's hands are also shown clutching the arms and clothing of others, these gestures often symbolize urgency or neediness more than physical restraint. In her depiction of dress codes, Oliphant similarly both reflects social attitudes, and subverts them: here more directly through the independent outlook of some of her boldest female characters in their interactions with would-be suitors and rivals.

Dress

At the end of *Janet*, the heroine's middle-aged doctor-wooer, now much improved by some smart clothes, promises his fiancée a day's clothes shopping, for "dinner-dresses, morning-dresses, ball-dresses." "To buy," adds the narrator, "is a pleasure to every woman — to get a number of new dresses, is a delight to any girl" (III, 269). As the examples in the previous section indicate, Oliphant's awareness of bodily types and characteristics is often associated with clothing that further inflates or suppresses the identity. As Rosy Aindow suggests, citing Elizabeth Wilson, "clothing has a unique relationship with the human body, linking 'the biological body to the social being, and public to private" (2016:1). For example, plump and sociable Phoebe Tozer dresses in a shade of pink that augments her size, while the elderly female invalids, like Brontë's Lucy Snowe in *Villette* (1853), with her white hair under a white cap, "like snow beneath snow" (Brontë, 1979:105), are reduced to "pieces of whiteness" (as with Miss Milnathort) or piles of white fleecy knitting. Though a plain dresser herself, Oliphant's volume *Dress* (1878) cited at the start of this chapter, remains, according to Elisabeth Jay "of more than period interest because she sees dress as more than either merely functional or wholly superficial adornment." Jay also observes that Carlyle's *Sartor Resartus* (1833–4) will have "alerted her to the subject's metaphorical application," though she angled it more towards the discussion of art (Jay, 1995: 304). Taking the reader through a history of dress, with an emphasis on its more ridiculous aspects (she is especially scornful of Elizabethan trunk hose), Oliphant's prevailing message is that women's dress should be comfortable, tasteful and practical. She professes to favouring "subdued tones of dark blues, dark greens, and soft neutral tints" (Oliphant, 2005: 77), but also approves of "individualism" in dress, especially in choice of colour and shape (Oliphant, 2005: 81). Patricia Zakreski makes a convincing case for seeing *Dress* as "[m]ore polemic than advice manual," which argues that dress "must be taken seriously, and its power as a social force recognized and understood" (Zakreski, 2016:56). Oliphant was in fact praised by "Deliverance Dingle" of *The Lady's World* for her interest in representing fashion in fiction (Dingle, 1887: 266).

A politicised aspect of taking dress seriously was for Oliphant the plight of seamstresses and the contradictions between creative needlework and the remorseless conditions of the London "sweatshops," which she frequently discusses in her late journalism, especially her "Commentaries" for *The Spectator* and the *St James's Gazette*.[3] *Salem Chapel's* Mrs. Hilyard, "working busily at men's clothing of the coarsest kind, blue stuff which had transferred its colour to her thin fingers" (Oliphant 1986a:

20) — which also sometimes bleed — eloquently testifies to the physical toll on seamstresses toiling at home to make a meagre living. Christine Bayles Kortsch proposes that we "thicken" our reading of Oliphant's career by examining the material culture in which it was entangled — that of "women's dress culture" (Kortsch, 2016: 106) citing *Kirsteen* (1890) as her "romanticized portrait of dressmaking" (19). In this novel, the eponymous dressmaker heroine ultimately becomes the equivalent of a leading fashion designer with a particular flair for adapting existing styles and inventing new combinations of colours and materials, "as a painter likes to arrange and study the more subtle harmonies of light and shade" (Oliphant, 1984a: 165). Nevertheless, as Kortsch suggests, the novel's backdating seventy years dissociates it from all the more painful controversies around seamstresses later in the nineteenth century, including sexual promiscuity, "fallenness," and exploitation. The novel's initial precise dating, to 1814–15, the period of Napoleon's exile to the Isle of Elba (1814) (1984a:6), makes Kirsteen herself contemporary with Jane Austen's *Emma*, and Walter Scott is frequently referenced as the family's choice of reading. The novel as a whole effectively both pre-and post-dates Gaskell's *Mary Barton* (1848) and *Ruth* (1853), implicitly inviting comparisons between past and present conditions for dressmakers, and Kirsteen's successful career with Gaskell's more pessimistic outcomes. Kortsch does, however, notice Kirsteen's erotic embroidery of her lover's initials into a handkerchief, using threads of her own red hair: a more benign version of the intimate relationship between sewing and the female body that stains Mrs. Hilyard's hands, and perhaps, in its secret messaging, becomes a metaphor for women's writing, If Oliphant's texts are full of secrets, so were the identities of many female authors, from Austen to George Eliot, at the start of their careers; and when Kirsteen embroiders the initials 'R.D.' into the handkerchiefs, her modesty is similarly protected by the fact that they are also her brother's initials, and no one need know of her unsanctioned romance.

Recent studies of dress in nineteenth-century fiction have emphasised its importance in helping readers to understand the nuances of social relationships, class identities, and perceptions of an individual character's taste and morality. Despite its apparent stratification in terms of class norms and standards (for example, the white dress as a marker of the middle-class young woman's unmarried status), dress also emits ambiguous and contradictory signals in many Victorian novels. As Clair Hughes argues, of Henry James, "The language of dress always means more, has deeper social and textual meanings, often excessively confusing ones" (2001: 13). Hughes also suggests that James's deployment of clothes references "not only develops across his work but also operates in distinct ways in each novel or tale" (2001: 4). Much the same could be said of Oliphant, in whose works clothing sometimes passes with scarcely a mention, while in others, especially the early Carlingford novels, *Miss Marjoribanks, Phoebe, Junior, Hester,* and *Kirsteen*, it drives social interactions, denotes obsessions and preoccupations, and often undermines the credibility or dignity of core characters.

Close reading of Oliphant's novels uncovers a lively commentary on dress which in itself forms a significant cultural narrative of women's attempts to assert both their individuality and ambition in a predominantly small-minded society. Questions of taste, in Bourdieu's sense of being the preserve of those possessing cultural capital (particularly education) concern Oliphant throughout her writing career. Like Bourdieu she is interested in the processes by which those with cultural capital achieve social dominance, whatever their other credentials, and ironically the least secure are those who boast about having "taste." In *Hester* (1883), for example, Mrs. John defends her husband's "beautiful taste" in the face of Hester's view that his former home, the White House, "is a vulgar staring place" (2015a: 88), while the spiteful Misses Vernon-Ridgway, who live as Catherine's pensioners, titter over her lack of taste: "Her worst enemy never accused her of *that*" (66). Taste (or lack of it) is also a running joke in the history of the Tozer family from *Salem Chapel* (1863) to *Phoebe, Junior* (1876), as we follow the rise of the butterman's plump pink daughter Phoebe through marriage to an ambitious Dissenting clergyman, Henry Beecham. When we meet them in *Phoebe, Junior*, Mr. Beecham is ministering to an affluent London congregation resplendent in "velvet, silk, lace, trinkets, and furs" (Oliphant, 1989:4), but their "refinement" is largely of the "surface kind, that which you buy from upholsterers and tailors and dressmakers" (5). Oliphant's undisguised disdain for the Tozers and Beechams and the standing they have achieved through shallow gentility contrasts with her more serious treatment of the innately refined Anglican clerical family, the Mays. While the Mays are much poorer than the Beechams, they have titled connections, and Ursula's father is "a man of some culture" (67). This cultural conflict involving the brash business people, the Copperheads, as well as the Mays and Tozers, in some ways prefigures the awkward collisions of Wilcoxes and Schlegels in E.M. Forster's *Howards End* (1910), and it culminates, like Forster's novel, in the revelation of an exploitative history between the two principal families, when Mr. May is discovered to have forged Mr. Tozer's signature on a promissory note. Meanwhile Phoebe Beecham, who is not allowed to cook or take the "Cambridge examinations" because of her father's determination to safeguard her gentility, electrifies the guests at Mr. Copperhead's ball by appearing in a black gown.

Patricia Zakreski has explained the powerful impact of Phoebe Beecham's choice of black for a society ball where the norm is to dress in white or pastel shades signifying the innocence of young womanhood (Zakreski 2016: 69). Whereas black was at that period normally a colour associated with mourning, or the discreet invisibility of age, widowhood, or servitude, it was by no means always easy to decode, especially when not modestly shrouding a widow. As Anne Hollander puts it, "A lady in black is not only dramatic and dignified, but also dangerous" (Hollander,

1993: 376). On Phoebe it causes a sensation, and is read as a sign of her daring and confidence; yet, normally dressed in a dowdy brown, to the despair of her grandmother, Phoebe is not overtly sexual. As Zakreski indicates (2016: 66), she chooses black because, unlike green, it will tone down her pink complexion, and white "shows no invention" (Oliphant, 1989: 19). In this intergenerational dialogue Mrs. Beecham grudgingly allows her daughter to revolutionize her appearance, though Phoebe is careful to distinguish her mother's black velvet with Honiton lace from her own black tulle, "flounced to distraction, and largely relieved with blue" (Oliphant, 1989: 20). The pleasure of enhancing a dress with additional flourishes is something Oliphant often mentions in her novels, so while Phoebe's designation by the awe-struck ball-goers as "the young lady in black" (23) marks her out as bold and mysterious, the poor clergyman's daughter Ursula May is dismissed by a male bystander as "a chit in a white frock" (25). The black and white ball gowns quickly establish Ursula and Phoebe, respectively mainstream Anglican and Dissenter, as the polar opposites around which their society refocuses its values. Ironically, though both dresses attract notice, and become the talk of the ball, neither girl is a good match for an aspiring suitor because of their social insignificance.

White dresses are especially important in Oliphant's novels. By an agreed common code, they mark out young women as both artless and available, yet for Oliphant the simple white dress, arguably an avoidance of fashion choice, is also more than a naive blank canvas. Lucilla Marjoribanks, for example, insists that the only thing to wear for dinner (and only if there are ladies present) is "A white frock, high in the neck" (Oliphant, 1988: 74). Even so, white dresses come in many varieties, and much is made of Barbara Lake's "limp" muslin, "six times washed" (1988: 106). It is not just that she is poor: her "limp" dress hints at bohemianism, and when her father buys her a new one, its replacement is just as disconcerting: "She had her new dress on, and though it was only white muslin like other people's, it gave her the air of a priestess inspired by some approaching crisis, and sweeping forward upon the victim who was ready to be sacrificed" (128–9). In terms of Bourdieu's theory of cultural capital, Barbara Lake's uneasy relationship with the white dress, which is such an instinctive matter for Lucilla, denotes her class insecurity and lack of social confidence. Although the Lakes consider themselves, as a family of artists, superior to the bourgeois doctors and businessmen of Carlingford, they nevertheless fall foul of the social codes promulgated by those they look down upon.

Kirsteen, as befitting a novel about dressmaking, includes a lengthy discussion of the simple fashions of 1814, as the family seamstress, Miss Macnab, prepares to turn a roll of muslin into evening dresses for the Castle ball. Notwithstanding the modest connotations of such dresses, Kirsteen's sister Mary recalls the occasion when her mother's "spangled muslin" was torn by an officer's spurs (Oliphant 1984a: 45), and Miss Macnab fits every line of the new dresses so that the narrow skirt clings to the body of each sister. Oliphant's narration stresses the skills required by a dressmaker in Miss Macnab's position: without knowing the future demands of her profession, with its emphasis on "draping and arranging" (53), she nevertheless is "an artist in her way" (54), and she moulds the white gown "with something like a sculptor's art" (54). At the ball itself, Kirsteen and her sister Mary appear modestly ornamented and lightly protected with a "little tucker or lace against the warm whiteness of the bosom" (62), but their clothes are not striking enough, unlike Phoebe's, to compensate for their outsider status.

In *Hester*, Hester Vernon's dresses for her cousin Ellen's *Thés Dansantes* are taken just as seriously and attract more notice, though she too is initially an outsider, and an impoverished one. Nevertheless Mrs. Vernon excitedly arranges for her daughter to have two new tarlatan dresses with silk slips, and "crisp puffings" (Oliphant, 2015a: 181), complemented with her mother's pearls, white shoes, white gloves, and white flowers in her hair. Despite initial objections to all this fuss, Hester gains confidence from how she looks, and "stood up in her virgin robes with a sense of delightful security" (181). Her cousin, and putative suitor, Edward Vernon, is captivated and hails her as "Cinderella" (182), which Hester takes as an insult. Oliphant never particularises dress in this much detail without an ulterior purpose, and here she shows how Hester's quiet pleasure in her own appearance is tainted by Edward's compliment, ostensibly because it seems patronising, but perhaps too because the whiff of sexuality compromises her more innocent enjoyment of her looks. "'I am no cinder-wench, Mr. Edward Vernon,'" she said, "'I have given you no reason to call me so. It is a pitiful thing for a man to notice a girl's dress. If I am dressed poorly, I am not ashamed of it'" (182). Edward hastily apologizes, comparing her instead with the moon emerging from the clouds.

Kimberley Reynolds and Nicola Humble capture these awkward, contradictory sensations when they claim that "clothing in the nineteenth-century novel almost invariably makes visible the body in a way detrimental to the heroine. It produces her for the gaze of the spectator, and its qualities are generative of pleasure only for that spectator, and not for the woman herself" (Reynolds and Humble, 1993: 59). While Oliphant's novels register the spectatorship of both male and female admirers of women's dress, there is something specifically disquieting about male admiration such as Edward's, even though, of all the men in her limited social circle, he is the one Hester is most interested in attracting. Unlike Jane Austen's Henry Tilney in *Northanger Abbey* (1818), who is well-informed, but sexually unthreatening in his familiarity with women's dress materials, as much of his knowledge comes from his sister, Edward's tone is misjudged: "'Nothing could be sweeter than that little house-frock you used to wear out on the Common […] But to-night you are like a young princess'" (Oliphant, 2015a: 183).[4] The "little house frock" sounds condescending in this context, both in terms of Hester's youth and status, and his manner assumes a right to congratulate her on her improved, more grown-up appearance. Oliphant thus uses dress to destabilize relationships between her characters, and to capture the slippage from friendship into something more overtly sexual. Furthermore, the attention Hester attracts with her pretty dresses and her mother's pearls rakes up the family history, as the pearls should have been handed over to her father's creditors after he absconded from the bank, a family story kept from her for much of the novel. Her mother's hapless position in this shameful episode of their past, when her husband abandoned both her and the bank, is reinforced by reference to her "short sleeves" and "pretty feet in sandalled slippers" (Oliphant, 2015a: 14). Mrs. John, "this poor, fine lady, sitting in her short sleeves on the edge of the volcano" (13), was dressed to host parties, not to rescue the bank. As the narrator puts it, the businesslike behaviour of modern women "is in great part to be put down to high dresses and long sleeves. In these habiliments a lady looks not so very different from other people," whereas the kind of low-necked white muslin dress Mrs. John was wearing seems to segregate its wearer "from everyday life" (14).

Hester reads at times like a response to Jane Austen's statement in *Northanger Abbey* that Catherine Morland cannot be justified in thinking too much about what gown and headdress to wear for her next ball: "Dress is at all times a frivolous distinction, and excessive solicitude about it often destroys its own aim" (Austen 1972: 92). While Hester's dialogue with Edward about her new dress seems to suggest otherwise, Oliphant also notes that the greatest admiration for dress and jewellery tends to come from other women. Her frivolous cousin Ellen encapsulates this appeal for the young and impressionable Hester early on in the novel when she appears in a flurry of rustling silks and jingling bracelets which to Hester seem "like silver bells, a pretty individualism and sign of her presence" (Oliphant, 2015a: 59). Returning from her honeymoon later in the novel, Ellen sports sealskins (also favoured by Lucilla Marjoribanks as high-end accessories), much to the admiration of Mrs. John. "It was at the time," notes the narrator, "when sealskins were rare, when they were just 'coming in'" (Oliphant 2015a: 170). Equally, as Ellen notes, the crinoline "is certainly going out" (146). At fourteen, Hester is easily impressed, while to the ironic narrator and most of the Vernon family Ellen's cheerful chatter about fashion, complete with pretentious name-dropping, and perfumy kisses is something to exchange snide smiles about. By contrast, if Ellen represents the modern brash married woman who will never have to work, Catherine Vernon, who rescues the bank twice in the course of the novel, is rarely described in terms of her clothes, other than the "costly silken skirts" she gathers about her as she withdraws to read the newspaper at a family party (146). With Catherine her body, especially her "heart" (both in the physical and metaphorical sense) is what counts. Childless and temperamentally ironic and self-contained, Catherine dies at home in her early sixties, when her heart gives out. Ultimately, what anyone wears, whatever pearls or sealskins they flaunt, seems immaterial, in light of the failed relationships and betrayals suffered in this novel alike by young and old.

Men's Clothes

Little has been said in this chapter about men's clothes in Oliphant's novels: partly because the next focuses more fully on her portrayal of men, but also because her male dressers are for the most part less extravagant and noticeable than her women. Clothes historians have tended to play down the significance of male dress: Anne Hollander, for example, refers to the "slow advance" of male fashions, and men's tendency in the nineteenth century to be "more subdued and abstract" in the way they looked (Hollander, 1993: 360). Oliphant, however, references male dress, as she does female, when it significantly displays character. A strong belief that emerges from her short treatise on *Dress*, is that clothes should express individuality without becoming eccentric, and this applies as much to men as it does to women. Like her women, her fictional men are often characterised by a single item of clothing which distinguishes them, so, in *Phoebe, Junior,* Phoebe Beecham's striking black dress is matched by Clarence Copperhead's "large shirt front" and "very long great-coat" (Oliphant, 1989: 198), and Ursula May's innocent white ball dress with Mr. Northcote's "black frock-coat" and "semi-clerical, and yet not clerical" appearance, as befitting a gentlemanly Non-conformist clergyman (100). Elaborating further on Mr. Northcote's attire as representative of his social and religious position, the narrator explains:

> His dress was one of the signs of his character and meaning. Strong in a sense of his own clerical position, he believed in uniform as devoutly as any Ritualist, but he would not plagiarise the Anglican livery and walk about in a modified soutane and round hat like "our brethren in the Established Church," as Mr. Beecham kindly called them. (Oliphant 1989: 113).

Mr. Northcote is like Arthur Vincent of *Salem Chapel* in being anxious to separate himself from the lower-class Dissenting circles that dominate "the connection" (as its members designate themselves), but without being mistakable for an Anglican. In Oliphant's novels the most tasteful and trustworthy men avoid both facial hair and clothes that draw attention to themselves, but the effect of this is to make them as heroes abstract and generalised. Thus Arthur Vincent is as difficult to visualize as Frank Wentworth of *The Perpetual Curate*, or Reginald May of *Phoebe, Junior,* described as "A slight young man, not very tall, with dark hair, like Ursula's, and a somewhat anxious expression, in correct English clerical dress" (Oliphant, 1989: 63). At the lower end of the social scale, Mr. Tozer the butterman of *Salem Chapel* welcomes Arthur to six o'clock tea in his house, "fully habited in the overwhelming black suit and white tie" which he wears every Sunday at chapel (Oliphant, 1986a: 7), as do all the other men at the party. As suggested at the start of this chapter, it is essentially the male comic characters in Oliphant's novels who stand out as noteworthy in terms of their appearance, and here it is the one word "overwhelming" which tells us everything we need to know about Tozer's oppressive personality.

Oliphant's particularising of clothes and the body in her fiction is not only key to achieving the class nuances integral to her writing: it is also essential to her tracing of the fluctuations of social and sexual relationships, and the instability of the human body as a register of troubled responses to competition, intrusion, and anxiety. When clothes and bodies fail or reward their owners, in terms of self-possession or correct judgement, relationships shift and change. It sometimes seems that for every triumphant dress or warm, supportive hand, Oliphant provides an undercutting aftermath or social *faux pas*. There is, however, a uniquely touching moment in *The Curate in Charge* (1876), harmonising the symbolism of bodies and clothes when the frail clergyman of the title, Cecil St. John is found dead on the morning he is due to leave his curacy. Having failed, both in his career and management of his home and finances, Mr. St. John has achieved the one thing that eludes his upcoming rival, the aesthete Roger Mildmay, and that is a loving relationship with a woman, his first wife Hester Maydew. When his body is found, sitting up, he is seen to have a woman's cloak and hat on his knees: Hester's old garments, preserved in his room for many years. The oddity of his behaviour on the very brink of death disconcerts those who think he should have been focusing on "the golden city with the gates of pearl," rather than on these homely relics of his first love: "there was a dreadful materialism in the cloak and hat. But most people felt a thrill of real emotion" (Oliphant 1987b: 180). In anticipating his reunion with Hester, Mr. St. John tacitly acknowledges the powerful meaning of clothes as emblems of his marriage and its lost companionship. He has fetched her cloak and hat and is waiting to meet her.

Quiet failure in more than one aspect of life remains a major theme for Oliphant in her study of middle-class men, as will be shown in the next chapter. If Hester Maydew had met her "ideal man," the narrator muses, that man would not have been content to wait ten years for her father to die so that she and he could be married (1987b: 9). Mr. St. John, however, waited then, and now he waits again: the embodiment of meek passivity, unable to move without her companionship. While Oliphant's men often struggle on their own, their entanglement with women usually involves them in new complications. Even when they inherit property and women fall in love with them their course through life is rarely straightforward. Why she persistently sees men as weak and self-sabotaging (probably more than any other Victorian novelist) will be further investigated in the next chapter.

CHAPTER 4

"Only a Man": Oliphant's Masculinities

At a family party in Margaret Oliphant's novel *Hester* (1883), a new young man makes a startling entrance: Roland Ashton, tall, imposing, with "a fine mass of dark hair, wavy, and rather longer than is now permitted by fashion, fine features and dark eyes, with a paleness which was considered very interesting in those days [...]. They all appraised him mentally as he came in—" (Oliphant, 2015a: 140–1). The appraisers, ranging from the sixty-five-year-old unmarried matriarch of the family, Catherine Vernon, to the rival young men, respond "with various degrees of quickened curiosity and grudging" (141). All are aware that this apparent paragon of masculinity will disrupt assumptions and alliances within an already disunited community, but his two main rivals, Harry and Edward Vernon, while assuming he must be a "coxcomb," are especially worried: "They divined that he was the sort of fellow whom women admired, and scorned him for it — as women perhaps now and then indulge in a little sneer at a gentleman's beauty" (147).

The many nuances of this scenario, as Oliphant captures the intermeshing of individual jealousies with assumptions about other people's attitudes, demonstrates not just her acute awareness of the social malaise of tightly-knit family groups, but also her sensitivity to the ripples of heightened sexual feeling in an everyday domestic setting. In offering a feminist perspective on

Oliphant, this volume must also consider the positioning and motivations of men in communities that intersect with those of her ambitious female characters. Oliphant's men are essentially the sons, brothers and husbands of middle-class women, and like the women, facing choices and dilemmas about their future lives. Their collective insecurity suggests that Oliphant's conception of masculinity was, like today's theoretical models, very far from being a monolithic social construct synonymous with virility, and frequently undermined by cultural change.

In the 1990s, claim Rainer Emig and Antony Rowland, "men replaced women as the problem sex in public debates" (2010: 6). For Oliphant much the same might have been said of her experiences a century earlier. In the 1990s men were perceived to be losing ground at school and work, even personal confidence and general wellbeing, while women were forging ahead, often in areas from which they had previously been excluded. In the 1890s, for Oliphant, men were a problem chiefly because of their inertia. Not that her female characters are by any means exempt from making mistakes or behaving foolishly, as Chapter 2 has illustrated, but Oliphant's writing nevertheless conveys a sense that men's problems are more intractable, and their attempts to resolve them more bedevilled by innate personal failings of long standing. When the Wentworth family of *The Perpetual Curate* (1864) refer to the mysterious "Wentworth complaint," which runs in the male line, and "never attacks women" (Oliphant, 1987a: 480), this seems like a metaphor for male susceptibility to moral and physical decline, to which its stronger-minded sisters are immune.

Overall, her female protagonists feel more equal to handling practicalities, as a brief example from Chapter XXX of *Salem Chapel* (1863) indicates. In this chapter Mrs. Vincent is sitting by her son's side, urging him to have patience with his "flock" as they challenge him to improve his performance as Dissenting minister. She feels she could deal with the situation herself, but worries about her son's ability to intervene effectively in a crisis:

he who was a young man, and took his own way, and did not know, as Tozer said, how to keep things straight? When Mrs. Vincent thought of her son in personal conflict with Mrs. Pigeon, she lost faith in Arthur. She herself might have conquered that difficult adversary, but what weapons had he to bring forth against the deacon's wife, he who was only a minister and a man? (Oliphant, 1986a: 344)

This passage is typical, in several ways, of Oliphant's style of writing about young men. For a start, it positions the son in opposition to his mother as she shakes her head over his impetuous way of managing his affairs. Father-son relationships in Oliphant's fiction are far less interesting to her than the lifelong emotional tension, mixed with pride and forgiveness (on both sides), between sons and their mothers. Additionally, the ironic narrative voice, with its free indirect style following the mother's thoughts in the crisis rather than the son's, privileges the mother's perspective, without altogether upholding her viewpoint as the only legitimate response. Mrs. Vincent's habit of treating her adult son like a small boy, and interfering in his professional life, like the other mothers, aunts and wives of Oliphant's clerics, is not necessarily in Arthur's interests, or fully approved by the narrator. The final phrase of this excerpt — "only a minister and a man"— is repeated, with variations, at crisis points in this and her other novels, with clear, if benign, irony, subverting the expected "only a woman."

Oliphant, as is well known, mercilessly undercuts her male protagonists — indeed her varied supporting cast of men as well — whenever she has the opportunity. Like Trollope's, whose Barsetshire series provided at least a partial template for the themes of her Carlingford novels, her heroes are normally middle-class in the most successful phase of her writing (often clergymen, sometimes doctors), later more likely to be country gentlemen, owners of landed estates, or stockbrokers, but they also include Parliamentary candidates, students, businessmen, shopkeepers, artists, bankers, lawyers, men of independent means, and a large number of hangers-on, with no particular profession. Unlike Charlotte Yonge, she has little interest in the military, or like Elizabeth Gaskell, in men who go to sea. Although she tentatively explores a few "new" male professions (such as engineering), she largely avoids detailed discussion of scientific or technological careers. Unlike Gaskell or Eliot, she has few working-class heroes, more often creating a comic chorus of self-righteous commentators out of her Carlingford small traders, such as Tozer the butterman and his fellow Dissenters. Like Eliot, however, she names some of her novels after male protagonists or their professions, such as *John Drayton* (1851), subtitled *A History of the Early Life and Development of a Liverpool Engineer*. Although she was only twenty-three when she published this "plain story of true and common life" (with no author's name on the title page), she adopts the authorial voice of "Mr. Mitchell," an elderly grey-haired schoolmaster, though again, self-consciously male-sounding narrators are unusual in her fiction (Oliphant, 1851: I, l). Other novels named after male protagonists include *Harry Muir* (1853), *The Perpetual Curate*, *The Curate in Charge* (1876), *The Wizard's Son* (1884), *A Country Gentleman and His Family* (1886), *The Son of His Father* (1887), *The Railway Man and His Children* (1891), and *Old Mr. Tredgold* (1896); there were also short stories, such as "The Scientific Gentleman" (1872), and "Mr. Sandford" (1888), considered one of her best, but as she privately observed, written "in a sort of cheerful despair" about her own and her sons' prospects (Oliphant, 1990: 158). Interspersed with these titles were the names of her five full-length biographies: all male, starting with *The Life of Edward Irving* (1862), and ending with *Thomas Chalmers, Preacher, Philosopher, and Statesman* (1893). As Elisabeth Jay has noted, Oliphant seemed to be drawn to men who had been brought down in their professional lives for maintaining passionately-held convictions, usually about religion (Jay, 1995: 142). The crossover between her biographical and her fictional narratives is self-evident in these stories of rise and fall, influenced by reckless or self-sabotaging behaviour, which Oliphant indicates is more characteristic of men than it is of women.

Underlying all these narratives, however, is her own personal experience, first with her brothers, Frank (c. 1816–75) and Willie (c.1819–85), then with her husband, another Frank (1818–59), and finally with her sons, Cyril (1856–90) and Cecco (1859–94). The recurring patterns of male failure in Oliphant's life, as shown in the Introduction, were so marked that it is difficult to avoid a largely biographical explanation for their recurrence in her fiction, and the consequent appeal of flawed biographical subjects (though she began writing about these long before her sons' decline into career failure and ill health). Perhaps, overall, she found it hard to associate masculinity with success. Even when some modicum of professional security is achieved in her fiction and biographies, it is soon lost, partly via circumstance, but also by her protagonists' inability to maintain an equilibrium in their personal or professional lives. In the most tormented passages of her *Autobiography* (1899), when she tries to identify what went wrong with the Oliphant men, she falls back on weary generalities. Her older brother Frank, who was "a kind of god" to her in childhood, died "old and suffering and deteriorated, he and I so far apart," while "poor Willie," the younger, "was our sore and constant trouble" (Jay, 1990: 19). As for her son Cyril, born strong and healthy, with promising prospects, the "clouds" gathered at Oxford, and bachelor dissipation became a settled way of life, while chronic ill-health kept Cecco from ever establishing a career, along with what he (perhaps half jocularly) described as a "cordial detestation" for having anything to do: "In complete idleness alone is true happiness to be found" (Oliphant 1974: 402). Temperamental inertia, combined with heavy drinking, was the curse of the Oliphant men, acting on weak, tubercular constitutions to end their lives prematurely. The opening pages of her short story, "Mr. Sandford" show how easy it was for idling

through the day to become habitual for young men living at home
with their parents. The artist's younger son Harry is described
as "one of those agreeable do-nothings who are more prevalent
nowadays than ever before, a very clever fellow, who had just
not succeeded as he ought at University or elsewhere, but had
plenty of brains for anything, and only wanted the opportunity to
distinguish himself" (Oliphant, 2013b: 154).

Another example, treated at greater length, is Walter Methven
of *The Wizard's Son*, characterised by his "somewhat volatile and
indolent disposition, and no ambition at all as to his future, nor
anxiety as to what was going to happen to him in life" (Oliphant,
2015b:7). In her journalism of the late 1880s and 90s, Oliphant
imagines the possibility of forcing spoilt idle men into hard
physical work. In one of her "Commentaries in an Easy Chair"
for *The Spectator*, for example, where she attacks the London
and Southampton Dock Strikes of 1889–90 for their "insolent
insubordination," she wonders "why the young men who are
not made to succeed in examinations [...] whose only prospect
is the Colonies and backwoods [...] do not organise a brigade
of poor gentlemen to replace these arrogant and skilless dockers"
(Oliphant, 18 October 1890: 521). Writing about the unskilled
masses prompted thoughts of the equally unskilled classes above
them who were somewhat closer to home, though in passages
such as this Oliphant often sounds both irritated with the young
men who are so hopeless, but also tired of the endless complaints
about them in the press.

If Oliphant sees this state of male middle-class idleness
as something of a national blight in the final decades of the
nineteenth century, her novels provide only vague explanations,
chiefly insufficient pressure to leave comfortable homes and easy-
going social circles. In reality, career options were becoming more
difficult for undistinguished middle-ranking young men fresh out
of university, with no taste for the traditional occupations of the
church, the law or medicine, and even qualified lawyers frequently

appear in Victorian fiction as "briefless" barristers, Mr. Sandford's elder son Jack among them. Leonore Davidoff and Catherine Hall chart the movement towards "masculine identification with occupation" in the first half of the nineteenth century, which was further reinforced by the broadening use of occupational categories in the decennial Census for England and Wales (1997: 230). New categories were added every ten years, so that between 1851 and 1871 —the twenty years covering Oliphant's early career — occupations such as "Bank service" and posts on the railways were appearing. The number of Church of England clergymen held steady at between 18,000 and 20,000, but were overtaken by railway employees and government civil service posts (over 49,000 and 28, 000 by 1871).[1] The category of "Unoccupied" (unemployed) was introduced in 1881.[2]

A further factor which may have influenced Oliphant's pessimistic portrayal of male employment was the introduction of competitive examinations: for example, the Indian (1854) and home Civil Services (1870) had made it harder for men of Oliphant's class to transition effortlessly into a career in public service, and when Cecco did pass an examination to work for the British Museum, he was turned down on health grounds (Oliphant, 1974: 348). In *Kirsteen* (1890), set back seventy years, the narrator's voice grumbles that it was "more easy in those days to set young men out in the world than it is now. Your friends thought of them, your political leaders were accessible" (Oliphant, 1984a: 33). In this novel the aggressive Drumcarro, father to seven sons, "contrived to get appointments for them" in the King's or East India Company's service (Oliphant, 1984a: 33), and a belief that positions for young men should be obtained via personal connections lingers in her writing. In "Mr. Sandford," for example, the artist is urged to "speak to Lord Okeham about Harry" (Oliphant, 2013b: 155), but while he feels awkward doing so, Oliphant was more pushy on her sons' behalf, even wondering if John Blackwood would introduce her to Lord Salisbury (whose sons had been in the same Eton house as hers), "with the view of asking him for a Foreign Office nomination for one of my boys" (Oliphant, 1974: 279). When Cyril obtained a post in Ceylon working for the Governor, Sir Arthur Gordon, and it had to be terminated because the climate was ruining his health, she found him small literary tasks to do, including a volume on Alfred de Musset for the Blackwood's Foreign Classics for English Readers series. Cecco, more fragile, but more willing to make an effort, worked for a while as Queen's Librarian at Windsor Castle, and helped his mother with *The Victorian Age of English Literature* (1892). Oliphant regarded him as "his mother's boy all his dear life" (Jay, 1990: 79), born as he was after his father's death. After his own, she described him as "my child still, though a man, my dearest friend and closest companion" (Oliphant, 1974: 411).

Oliphant was both proud of what was good about their relationship, but also dismayed that all her efforts to give her sons a happy childhood and first-class education should have amounted to so little. In summarizing her sons' failure to achieve even a steady humdrum career, she admitted: "They were well-equipped and beyond the average in ability, both, but did nothing to verify this to the world" (Jay, 1990:80). In her novels she indicates that this lack of ambition was less common in girls who were eager to do something meaningful with their lives. We see this in Hester Vernon, who at fourteen wants to teach what she calls a "*cours*" (Oliphant, 2015a: 57), while in *The Ladies Lindores* (1883) one of the young heroines, Nora Barrington, observes to the apparently inactive hero, John Erskine on the appeal of life "in town," "'Men seem to like that do-nothing life. It is only we girls that are rising up against it. We want something to do'" (Oliphant, 1883a: I, 228). Oliphant clearly thought better of leaving John Erskine in idleness, as in her short sequel to *Lindores*, *Lady Car* (1889), she turns him into "one of the most important men in the district, member for his county, trusted and looked up to" (Oliphant, 2013a: 202). While the opposite trajectory is traced by the gentlemanly Edward Beaufort who becomes Lady Car's second husband, and never progresses beyond his initial dilettante elegance, youthful lack of purpose was, in the Lindores novels at least, by no means irredeemable if suitably motivated by frugality, ambition, and a happy marriage.

Juliette Atkinson, in her study of Victorian biography, devotes a chapter to "Tragic Failures" and "Happy Mediocrity," proposing that the so-called "failed life" may be "a life of quiet influence" or "a sign of integrity and heroism" (2010:116). Indeed she includes in this category one of Oliphant's own biographical subjects, the charismatic preacher Edward Irving (1792–1834), whose professional and personal lives quickly unravelled after a stellar beginning, when his congregation began speaking in tongues, and he was expelled from his Church. While Atkinson's categories of "failure" offer a more positive approach to the examination of some nineteenth-century male lives, other, less inspiring, examples were common among the children of Oliphant's fellow authors. For every Arthur Hallam (1811–1833), the young man full of hope and promise, whose sudden death inspired much of Tennyson's poetry, culminating in *In Memoriam* (1850), there were apparently dozens of youths with no intention of ever doing anything. Among these were Mrs. Humphry Ward's son Arnold (1876–1950), and most of Dickens's, whom he packed off to sea or far-flung continents in the hope of shocking them into a sense of purpose, but probably hastening the deaths of at least three, Walter (1841–63), Francis (1844–86) and Sydney Smith (1847–72). Elizabeth and Robert Browning's son Robert Wiedeman ("Pen") (1849–1912), achieved a longer life, and some modest success as a painter and sculptor, but his father frequently despaired of him: "You see that all my plans are destroyed by this double evil," he complained to his brother-in-law, George Barrett, when Pen was in his early twenties, "— the utmost self-indulgence joined to the greatest contempt of work and its fruits" (Finlayson, 2004: 609). Fictional representations of a similar disinclination or ability to work abounded in the novels of Oliphant's contemporaries: for example Dickens's Richard Carstone of *Bleak House* (1852–3), and James Harthouse and Tom Gradgrind of *Hard Times* (1854), Elizabeth Gaskell's Osborne Hamley of *Wives and Daughters* (1864–66), and George Eliot's Fred Vincy of *Middlemarch* (1871–2). The heir to the throne, Prince Albert Edward of Wales ("Bertie"), seemed to embody, at the very pinnacle of Victorian society, a lack of academic ambition, combined with a susceptibility to other pleasures. Yet the middle decades of the nineteenth-century were widely seen as a time of entrepreneurship and fresh energies in the fields of business and philanthropy, not least by men and women driven by a social conscience. If a social conscience existed in Oliphant's sons, or the idlest of her male protagonists, it made a poor showing, but there may have been broader cultural reasons for their professional failure. Donna Loftus suggests that by the later decades of the nineteenth century, "mid-Victorian entrepreneurial culture" (Loftus 2012: 197) was giving place to "gentlemanly capitalism" (202–203), which required a different skillset and circumstances from those acquired at university by Cyril and Cecco. With no family business to inherit, or finely-honed professional skills, Oliphant's sons floundered in a world where it was necessary to pass examinations and work hard in order to "get on." Middle- to upper-class male withdrawal from the competitive marketplace, which Oliphant saw as a feature of her times, impacted on her representation of masculinity in ways that explore the problem, but as with her portrayal of women's domestic frustrations, struggle to propose realistic alternatives.

Critical Approaches to Masculinities

While Oliphant's portrayal of men seems consistent and easily explained in light of her own experiences, new critical approaches to the study of "masculinities" may help develop a fuller understanding of the range of issues she examines over six decades of writing. Since the early 1990s, starting with Judith

Butler's *Gender Trouble* (1990), there has been an intensification of interest in discovering more finely nuanced theories of what we understand by "patriarchy," "manliness," and what Joseph Bristow has called "the intricate ways in which types of maleness emerge in diverse circumstances" (in Emig and Rowland, 2010: ix). Because masculinity has for so long been taken for granted as the "norm" and therefore culturally invisible, it has been problematised only relatively recently in ways that are particularly relevant to Oliphant's difficulties with men. Herbert Sussman, focusing specifically on Victorian masculinities, argues the value of foregrounding "the social construction of what at any historical moment is marked as 'masculine'". In other words, it is important from the start to acknowledge the "plurality of formations of the masculine among the Victorians" (Sussman, 1995: 8). Sussman himself declines to privilege the popular area of "homoerotics," which was emerging in the 1990s as the key theme of *fin- de-siècle* masculinities, but covers a range of other topics in his study, including "the many psychological and social forces that troubled Victorian manhood, among them industrialization, the development of bourgeois hegemony, class conflict, the feminization of culture" (1995: 10).

From this list we can quickly eliminate some areas that Oliphant avoids. Foremost among these is homoerotics (Oliphant is no forerunner of Oscar Wilde, though her novels include some Wildean aesthetes and dilettantes); nor is she an expert on industrialization and the business entrepreneur.[3] Instead her fields are primarily Sussman's final three: "bourgeois hegemony, class conflict, the feminization of culture," which accord with my previous contextual framework derived from Bourdieu. Sussman further links these themes with the necessity for self-control and the management of dangerous energies in men, drawing on other theorists, including Peter Stearns' *Be a Man!: Males in Modern Society* (1990), whose distinction between working- and middle-class men in the nineteenth century "provides a valuable corrective to the continuing tendency of Victorianists to conflate certain specifically bourgeois forms of manliness with Victorian manliness in general" (Sussman 1995: 12). While Sussman's study focuses on writers and artists, however, Oliphant's most successful novels of the 1860s and '70s concentrate on clergymen and doctors: men who are more directly enmeshed in small-minded communities, and whose professions give them fewer opportunities to distinguish themselves, irrespective of the crowd's disapproval. When her later novels drift more towards the world of the landed gentry (as in *The Ladies Lindores, Lady Car,* and *The Wizard's Son*), her male protagonists become more like generic types, less individualized than the caricatured figures surrounding them. Oliphant thus creates a male type who is pleasant, presentable, well-intentioned, but almost without character, representing masculinity at its blandest. Such an example might be John Erskine of *The Ladies Lindores* (1883), who is introduced as not perhaps looking "like a hero of romance, but he looked like a clean and virtuous young Englishman" (Oliphant, 1883a: l, 159). Ironically, he is later taken into custody, suspected of being instrumental in Patrick Torrance's murder (a riding accident): Oliphant's comment perhaps on an average appearance and personality being no protection against the general suspicion of young men being subject to fits of dangerous energies such as Sussman discusses in his theories of Victorian masculinity.

Sussman also argues that "manhood" is a state of manliness that is not innate, but has to be achieved through "arduous public or private ritual"; nor is it achievable by all, or once achieved, necessarily easy to maintain (1995: 13). He designates its "plot" or "narrative" as a story of "manhood achieved and manhood lost" (13), through plots derived from the possible routes of entrepreneurship, or the literary, artistic, or "prophetic" forms of creativity. These terms are especially helpful to building an understanding of Oliphant's male plots which generally juxtapose scenes of public performance (especially in the pulpit) with private attempts to win approval from the woman they want to marry.

"Manhood," moreover, as a state of achieved and maintained manliness, in Sussman's terms, is always seen in Oliphant's novels as especially difficult to uphold in the face of all the challenges levelled at her beleaguered ministers and doctors. In some ways, as with George Eliot's Adam Bede, strong, uncomplicated masculinity is easier to find in the working class, as with Oliphant's own John Drayton, "the good pondrous [sic] fellow" whose "figure and strength were Herculean," without the coarse brutality of Patrick Torrance in *The Ladies Lindores* (Oliphant, 1851: I, 17), as discussed in Chapter 1. Phillip Mallett adds a further reminder that "Masculinity is ineluctably a relational construct, shaped by and within the totality of gender relations, and as these change, so too does the notion of what constitutes the manly" (Mallett, 2015: vi). Oliphant's men are always seen as enmeshed in a complex social structure more akin to Barchester or Middlemarch than Jane Austen's Highbury, where not only issues of gender but also different generations and cultural expectations restrict what a man can do to achieve his ambitions while maintaining his values and integrity. These communities, moreover, especially in the Carlingford novels, are often dominated by at least one strong woman, such as Frank Wentworth's aunts, in *The Perpetual Curate*, Lucilla in *Miss Marjoribanks* (1866), or Catherine Vernon, in *Hester*; all single women with a tight grip on their dependants' futures.

The questions we might ask of Oliphant's masculinities are many. While the issues of languor and failure have to be at the forefront of this discussion (the opposite of the uncontrollable violent energies that trouble Gaskell, Dickens, Browning, or Carlyle), we might also want to consider to what extent men have any power in her communities, and whether their private and public lives are as mutually entangled and destructive as they traditionally are for the female protagonists of Victorian novels. How, too, do Oliphant's men relate to women, and what do they want in order to achieve the personal fulfilment both sexes are actively seeking in her novels? Roger Mildmay of *The Curate in Charge* is a classic example of an Oliphant man who knows his life is unfulfilling as an Oxford college aesthete, but is unsure what to do about it. "What was life?" he asks himself at the height of his crisis, knowing that he has no inclinations towards either dissipation or marriage. "How then was he to know life, and have it?" (Oliphant, 1987b: 73). This is a question both men and women ask themselves in many of Oliphant's novels, as indeed they do in the works of many other Victorian novelists, but her heroes' inward traumas lack the strenuous spiritual and intellectual soul-searching which we find in men such as Kingsley's Lancelot Smith of *Yeast* (1851) or George Eliot's Daniel Deronda (1876). While the answer is elusive for both sexes, it seems particularly difficult for Oliphant's men to achieve, even in mid-career, any permanent sense that what they are doing is either socially useful or emotionally, still less spiritually, fulfilling.

Fathers, Sons, Brothers, and Husbands

Oliphant explores all the key male family roles and relationships in her novels and short stories, often combining or merging them with studies of their professional lives, from which their personal difficulties and dilemmas emerge in more or less equal measure. Outside her biographies, Oliphant is not particularly interested in tracing the experience of new fatherhood in her younger male protagonists, her Carlingford novels usually ending at the point of marriage. This is a marked departure from her biography of Edward Irving, for example, where the birth, illness and death of Irving's baby son at fifteen months are narrated with empathetic reverence. "So far as I can perceive," Oliphant concludes, "no other event of his life penetrated so profoundly the depths of his spirit" (Oliphant, 1862: 114–15). This profound feeling for the wonders of fatherhood and the tragedy of a baby's loss (the first of three) is not something she transfers to her novels, where her father figures are generally older men, such as Dr. Marjoribanks, Lord Lindores,

Mr. May, Mr. St. John, or Mr. Wodehouse. They are largely gruff and emotionally detached parents, irritated by children who want something other than the norm. Several of them die in the course of the novel, precipitating their children into crisis; few are portrayed as wise and reliable providers. While this is a common feature of nineteenth-century novels, in order to throw the children upon their own resources, Oliphant rings additional variations on the theme, by making her father-figures not just poor managers of the family finances, but occasionally reckless enough to create additional families. The most prolific of these is Squire Wentworth, of *The Perpetual Curate*. As Oliphant tartly puts it, when explaining Frank's antecedents, "the respectable Squire his father had indulged in three wives and three families, and such a regiment of sons that all his influence had been fully taxed to provide for them" (Oliphant, 1987a: 21). In *Kirsteen*, Drumcarro fathers fourteen children, and cares only about the boys, while, as we saw in Chapter 2, the elderly Curate in Charge, Cecil St. John, is left, "a poor man of sixty-five, casting piteous looks at the two babies whom he had no right, he knew, to have helped into the world" (Oliphant, 1987b: 33–4). In such cases as these the fathers' irresponsible sexuality is pitted against the older children's prim horror and disapproval: both the St. John daughters and Frank Wentworth finding it much more complicated to marry than it was for their fathers, both because of endless misunderstandings, and a sense of living in a more socially tangled world.

Oliphant's fathers do worse things, however, than continue procreating into old age. Mr. St. John fails to provide for any of his four children, and sleepwalks into eviction from his curacy when his successor is appointed. Mr. Lycett-Landon, of *Queen Eleanor and Fair Rosamond* (1886) abandons his wife and children in Liverpool and establishes a new bigamous household in London, Ursula May's clergyman father, in *Phoebe, Junior* (1876), forges a signature to manage his debts (as does Tom Wodehouse, Lucy's brother, in *The Perpetual Curate*), Hester Vernon's father ruins the bank and absconds, and even the more worldly-wise Dr. Marjoribanks, Lucilla's father, makes bad investments and leaves her nothing except the house and "some little corners and scraps of money in the Funds" (Oliphant, 1988: 414). Where fathers are more financially competent, they try to manipulate their daughters' emotional lives by pressurising them into mercenary marriages, though not always successfully. Although Lord Lindores forces his sensitive elder daughter Caroline into a miserable marriage with Patrick Torrance, his younger daughter resists all attempts to make her marry the unmanly Lord Millefleurs, just as Kirsteen refuses to be bundled into marriage with "old Glendochart" at her father's behest. Oliphant throws in the detail that Mr. Douglas previously owned slaves in the West Indies, and is still taunted by his Scottish neighbours for being "an auld slave-driver" (Oliphant, 1984a: 32), a habit of mind borne out in his family relationships. Even a more benign father, Mr. Southcote, from *The Days of My Life* (1857), orders his only daughter Hester to marry her suitor Harry Edgar in a space of three weeks. While this is a well-intentioned plot to secure her inheritance of the family estate through marriage to a cousin living under a false name, Hester is so offended by the deception that she flees her marital home and gives birth to their first child in a cottage, attended only by her faithful servant. Perhaps the most grotesque father of all Oliphant's creations, however, is the white-bearded King-Lear-like Mr. Harwood of *Janet* (1891), the family's closet madman, who finally emerges from a mysterious annexe to their suburban house, to rave about the debts he thinks he owes.

There are, of course, kindly fathers in Oliphant's fiction: indeed many of the fathers who unintentionally ruin their daughters' lives do so because of incompetence, rather than ill-will or cruelty. In that respect they are slightly better than the violent husbands several of her characters encounter through bitter, ill-matched marriages. While abusive men appear relatively early in Oliphant's career, most notably in Colonel Mildmay/Mr.

Fordham, Mrs. Hilyard's estranged husband, in *Salem Chapel*, the worst of these is probably Patrick Torrance of *The Ladies Lindores*, whose philistinism is coupled with a mixture of sneering pride in his sensitive wife, and contempt for that very sensitivity and coldness that made her a valued prize. Physically brutish and ugly, his sexuality is clearly something his wife dreads, and which she is relieved to be spared by his accidental death. As she tells her mother, "'To think I shall never be subject to all *that* any more— that he can never come in here again—that I am free—that I can be alone—'" (Oliphant, 1883: II, 265). Almost as brutish, though less personally repellent, is young Lord Markland of *A Country Gentleman*, who, having "run through" the fortune his wife brought him, spends much of his time away from home. Like Carry Lindores, Lady Markland maintains a discreet silence during his lifetime on the subject of their private relations (Oliphant, 1886: I, 61). Her second marriage, to Theo Warrender, proves to be just as miserable, owing to his controlling nature. Oliphant, as narrator, interjects a comment on Theo's intolerance of any opposition from a wife: "Perhaps this was because of that inherent contempt for women which is a settled principle in the minds of so many men […] To continue perfect in his eyes, after their marriage, she would have needed to agree always with him, to think his thoughts" (Oliphant, 1886: III, 151). In this late and disillusioned study of marriage, even Mrs. Warrender's uneventful years as a wife are remembered as a time of deep disappointment with a lack of compatibility at all levels, including the discovery that her children are essentially her husband's by nature, and not hers, an experience she shares with Carry Lindores.

Where husbands are not physically brutal or controlling they can be rogues and swindlers. John Vernon in *Hester*, though absent in person from all but the opening pages of the novel, is essentially the cause of the Vernon bank collapse and its subsequent ramifications. Oliphant this time makes his widow uninterested in remarrying, and also stubbornly loyal to the man who squandered all their money and abandoned both his wife and daughter. Hester herself nearly marries her cousin, Edward Vernon, who absconds in a similar way, implying that "bad blood" corrupts the male line of the Vernons, while the women twice intervene to save the family business. Most commonly, however, Oliphant's husbands are dull and bumbling, rather than sensational brutes. Some of her more finely nuanced studies are of well-meaning men such as the Rector of Carlingford, Mr. Morgan, a former Fellow of All Souls, who waited ten years for a "living" (a clerical post), which would enable him to marry. Gently satirised, the Morgans are past their prime, and victims of their own (especially his) prudence. Such outbursts of regret as Mrs. Morgan expresses occasionally are kindly attributed by him to "nerves": "Mr. Morgan looked very blank at her as she sat there crying, sobbing with a force of sentiment which was probably untranslatable to the surprised, middle-aged man" (Oliphant, 1987a: 118). Within even the best of marriages in Oliphant's fiction, men display a degree of emotional obtuseness, which makes their companionship in these earlier novels particularly frustrating.

Most disappointing of all, however, of Oliphant's survey of male familial roles, are the sons: the most longed-for, and with the most potential to compensate for their mothers' unhappy marriages or early widowhood, but almost invariably directionless and irritable. Such is this pervasive pattern for Oliphant that she identifies it in British history as well as in fiction: for example, in the case of King George II's wife, Queen Caroline, and her difficult relationship with her eldest son, Prince Frederick. While assuring readers that the Queen treated him with the "same, almost unearthly tolerance which she showed to his father," Oliphant admits that Frederick became his mother's political enemy, "the unmannerly and unmanly lout" (Oliphant, 1868: 216–17). The theme of mothers alienated by their sons because of their resemblance to brutish or otherwise incompatible husbands, is especially a feature of her later novels. It starts early with Carry Lindores, who feels no natural kinship with her son Tom, in every way his father's child, while Mrs. Warrender, in *A Country Gentleman*, regrets the reappearance of her husband's dull conventionality in her young adult children. Other sons, such as Walter Methven of *The Wizard's Son*, exasperate their mothers with their sheer apathy. The narrator's special pleading in the opening pages of this novel suggests that Oliphant was drawing on autobiographical experience, as she describes Mrs. Methven's defensive awareness of the neighbours' comments about "her foolish indulgence, or her sinful backing-up of his natural indolence […] Under the guidance of a foolish mother, a young man always went wrong" (Oliphant, 2015b: 10). "Perhaps I did not take the right way with him," Oliphant admitted of her son Cyril shortly after his death in 1890 (Oliphant, 1990: 45). What exasperated her most was his wasted potential: something Mrs. Methven also deplores when she compares Walter with her neighbours' sons who are all doing well: "not one of them was worthy, she thought, to be seen by the side of her boy; but they had all got before him in the race of life" (Oliphant, 2015b:13).

The sons in her novels are equally exasperated by their mothers, apparently locked in a cycle of carelessly affectionate dependence and eagerness to escape. This occurs even with mother-substitutes such as Catherine Vernon in *Hester*, and her companion and heir-presumptive Edward Vernon who lives with her, although he has parents elsewhere. Despite his dutiful appearance, Edward is as frustrated with his home life as his counterpart Hester, living with her widowed mother: "'Home is a kind of irons,'" Edward complains, "'handcuffs, ankle chains. One is always like an unhappy cockatoo on a perch. Any little attempt at flight is always pulled back'" (Oliphant, 2015a: 150). Both Edward Vernon and Walter Methven resent the lonely dependence of their mother-figures, the watching of their sons' comings and goings, and speculating about their future, while in *Janet*, Dolff's physical colourlessness, and lack of anything but a generic personality as a "vulgar, music-hall frequenting, loud and foolish young man," marks Oliphant's despair over the apparent ubiquity of the mediocre son of the age (Oliphant, 1891a: 11, 66).

As brothers, too, such men offer little support to their sisters. One of Oliphant's earliest novels, *Harry Muir: A Story of Scottish Life*, establishes the pattern of a brother sinking into what are euphemistically described as "poor and petty sins" (chiefly alcoholism), while his sisters maintain themselves by hard work (Oliphant 1853: I, 75). When Harry inherits a family estate, he briefly takes up farming, but is led astray by a dissolute relative, and dies after falling from his horse. His faithful eldest sister, Martha, who has raised him like her own son, and now inherits the estate, restores it to a sound financial footing, proving, as so often in Oliphant's fiction, that women can be better managers than men because they have a strong work ethic, and as home-loving women, are immune to dissolute habits and worse company. In her later novels, Lucy and Mary Wodehouse, of *The Perpetual Curate*, are ashamed of their shambolic brother Tom, Lord Rintoul, in *The Ladies Lindores*, tries to force both sisters into marriages of convenience, and Theo Warrender, of *A Country Gentleman*, bullies his sisters, disregards their needs, and when annoyed by their lack of support, "turned upon his sisters and slew them" (Oliphant, 1886: I, 94). Although the term here sounds extreme (a metaphor for berating them for not trying harder to keep their mother at home), the narrator remarks that "Brothers and sisters are permitted to be brutal to each other without much harm done" (95). While sisters in Oliphant's novels often feel strong affection for brothers, they are frequently ashamed of their decline into selfish apathy. She knew perhaps, they were no more to be trusted than errant husbands and idle sons, and would ultimately also need looking after.

Carlingford Men

Not all of Oliphant's men are hopeless cases, however. Her most thoughtful and heroic protagonists are to be found in her

Carlingford novels of the 1860s, especially *Salem Chapel* and *The Perpetual Curate*, which feature young clergymen (Arthur Vincent and Frank Wentworth) setting out in life with hopeful ideals. Frank Wentworth was one of her own favourites (Oliphant, 1974: 191), described as "a man of the present age—reasonable to a fault, and apt to consider other people as much as possible from their own point of view" (Oliphant, 1987a: 256). All the more disconcerting then, that towards the end of the novel, he feels "that it was chiefly the impatient and undutiful who secured their happiness" (481), a realization that motivates him to make a stronger claim for Lucy Wodehouse's hand. Oliphant draws deepening parallels between Frank and Arthur Vincent, showing that the Dissenting minister of the earlier novel, and the eponymous Perpetual Curate of the later, are similar in outlook, notwithstanding their opposed religious positions. As an employee of the established church, and descended from a landed gentry family (his father is a Squire), Frank appears to have all the advantages in terms of social position, but Oliphant quickly explains that his circumstances are actually "as delicate and critical as can be imagined" (Oliphant, 1987a: 2), not least because he has established "a kind of impromptu chapel" (4) in the impoverished canal district of Carlingford without the Rector's authority. As Oliphant explained to her publisher, Frank "is working *in the* parish with which he has nothing to do, and which it is in reality high treason for any one, even the bishop to interfere with" (Oliphant, 1974:192). Arthur, meanwhile, arriving at Carlingford, fresh out of training college, and "as fully endowed with natural good looks as the young priest" (Oliphant, 1986a: 18), "white-browed, white-handed, in snowy linen and glossy clerical apparel" (3), is also drawn towards the poor and suffering while also colliding with authority, in the form of his deacon, Mr. Tozer. Though both unwittingly become enmeshed in compromising situations, Arthur is the more directly exposed to "the dark sea of life" (102), seething with tragic histories and violent passions: a world from which Frank is largely protected, despite a wrongful accusation of having seduced a shopkeeper's daughter, Rosa Elsworthy. Both men are irritated by the way their work is hampered by small-minded people, and both find themselves arraigned before their congregations, mistakenly accused of immoral actions and disgracing their "flocks." The difficulty for readers is to understand why, in two successive novels featuring virtuous and intelligent young clerics, Oliphant is determined to subject them to a series of mishaps and crises mostly arising from misunderstandings or the actions of other people, rather than from their own behaviour.

The clue may lie in a comment from *The Perpetual Curate's* narrator at the height of the Rosa Elsworthy scandal: "Mr. Wentworth was quite well aware that the character of a clergyman was almost as susceptible as that of a woman, and that the vague stigma might haunt and overshadow him all his life" (Oliphant, 1987a: 257). In both novels, young clergymen are scrutinised as intensively as any young woman. Any reluctance to accept social invitations is held against them, and their movements after dark down the dimly-lit streets of Carlingford are frequently observed alike by well-wishers and enemies. Older clergy offer advice, as do elderly relatives. Moreover, the thin line between male respectability and its opposite, shame and disrepute, is as easily crossed for a man regarded as a moral leader as it is for a woman. If anything, there are more pitfalls for a man: not just illicit sexuality, but heavy drinking, smoking, gambling, and the temptations of petty crime. A professional man is also permanently on view, tied to a relentless programme of parish duties, sermons, services, and social gatherings. While no one in *The Perpetual Curate* seems intent on vilifying Rosa — repeatedly described as "a little girl" (129), though she is actually seventeen — most assume the worst of Frank, rather than attribute blame where it is actually due, to Tom Wodehouse, brother of Frank's adored Lucy, whom he wants to marry. Frank later admits that he made too little effort to vindicate himself: a victim, like Arthur Vincent, of his own snobbery and pride in his class status which, in his view, should have been sufficient for his parishioners to trust him.

Arthur's entanglement in the Carlingford underworld arises from his associations with Mrs. Hilyard and her separated husband, encountered through his efforts to rescue his sister Susan. In both plots therefore, there is, at least potentially, a "fallen woman" story which reveals not so much the loose morals of the women as the multiple identities and vices of the men. It is not entirely clear why Oliphant needed to add Jack Wentworth, a scapegrace brother (Oscar Wilde-like, in name and behaviour) to the *Perpetual Curate's* imbroglios, except perhaps as an example of how masculine idleness in the more comfortably-off classes can degenerate into selfish decadence, as harmful in its way as Tom Wodehouse's more overtly offensive swearing and shabbiness. While Frank is desperate to recover his reputation, Jack lies on the sofa, watching the moths fluttering to their deaths in the lamp, and worrying that his "heart will be torn asunder for the rest of the evening by the sight of suicide" (Oliphant, 1987a: 284). More surprising, therefore, is Jack's defence of Frank towards the end of the novel, when he tells their Aunt Leonora how his brother "has been carrying other people about on his shoulders, and doing his duty" without the support of his family (501). In this respect Frank is like Nettie Underwood, of *The Doctor's Family*, or even Oliphant herself, while Tom Wodehouse, with his large shambling body and clouds of pipe smoke, reprises Fred Rider, the doctor's "self-ruined" older brother (Oliphant, 1986b: 44). Jack, meanwhile, before disappearing into the darkness, propounds his own philosophy for success: "'The man who gets his own way is the man who takes it'" (p. 502). Stunned by what appears to be a wake-up call to greater selfishness, Frank repeats these magical words to Lucy Wodehouse, regains control of his life, marries Lucy, and becomes the Rector of Carlingford, amid many self-conscious references in the closing pages to the endings of "trashy" novels and fairytales (Oliphant, 1987a, pp.535–6).

Salem Chapel's Arthur Vincent too embraces a new way of life "with the sensation of an enchanted prince in a fairy tale" — not via promotion within the Dissenting ministry, but by going into "literature" as a periodical writer, like Oliphant herself, and living with his sister and Alice Mildmay, the woman he seems destined to marry. "Life became glorious again under their touch," the narrator reports, "He could not tell what wonderful thing he might not yet do in this wonderful elevation and new inspiring of his heart" (Oliphant, 1986a: 460–1). Oliphant rarely writes again with such effusion and optimism about the future of her male protagonists. The awkward, ironic, humorous, apologetic tone of these two closing summaries, with their endorsement of each man's selfish decision to put his own needs first, complicates the final message. It seems to be an emboldening of men (and by implication, women, as the parallels with women's lives are so apparent) who are too passive for their own good: a philosophy which can quickly turn ugly, and which brings its own hazards to her later fiction.

Country Gentlemen

"'On the whole,'" says George Vavasour in Anthony Trollope's *Can You Forgive Her* (1864–5), "'I don't know that there is any kind of life better than that of an English country gentleman in his own place'" (Trollope, 1986: 84). In adopting this idea in several of her novels (and extending its reach to Scotland), Oliphant was contributing to a social theme already popular with some of her contemporaries, particularly Anthony Trollope, Elizabeth Gaskell, and George Eliot. In her interwoven narratives of the Gibsons, Hamleys and Cumnors in *Wives and Daughters* (1864–66), Gaskell, for example, explored the permeability of class boundaries which allowed the doctor, Squire and landed gentry to interact within a small country community, and form alliances which lift three of the women (the Cumnors' governess, Hyacinth Kirkpatrick, and her daughter Cynthia, and Dr. Gibson's daughter Molly) into securer social positions. While the first two women marry professional men (Cynthia after escaping a sleazy connection with Mr. Preston, the Cumnors' land agent), Molly marries the Squire's second son, the scientist and explorer Roger Hamley. Eliot's novels similarly allow the proximity of landed gentry such as the Cheverels in *Mr. Gilfil's Love Story* (1857), the Donnithornes in *Adam Bede* (1859) and the Chettams in *Middlemarch* (1871–2), to impinge on the lives of their middle- and rural working-class neighbours. In the novels to be discussed here, however, Oliphant seems primarily interested in the ways in which new inheritors of landed estates (often from middle-class origins) respond to their good fortune: not so much in terms of the support they can give their tenants, or the improvements they can carry out on their land, as in their own psychological turmoil in managing their elevated social position, and forming supportive alliances through marriage. Significantly, she provides little detail of the day-to-day running of the estates: Walter Methven, of *The Wizard's Son*, for example, makes only one significant decision, when he halts the eviction of crofters on his land. Instead, she takes a more generic interest in how an idle young man like Walter handles his new status, servants and neighbours, and copes with the haunting of a mysterious man associated with the estate's history. In other respects his resemblance to the other callow youths of Oliphant's fiction is soon evident. Like Frank Wentworth of *The Perpetual Curate*, he feels he has no choice in anything: "It seemed that he was never to have any control over himself," he notes when he hears of the immediate ordeal he is expected to face at Kinloch-Houran, where the mysterious man will make an appearance: "He had barely escaped from the tutelage of home when he fell into this other which was much more rigid. 'Poor mother!' he said to himself, with an affectionate recollection of her many cares, her anxious watchfulness; and laughed to himself at the thought that she was being avenged" (Oliphant, 2015b: 69). Walter's association between the demands of his mother and the commands of the

147

family nemesis is presented with Oliphant's characteristic irony. Perhaps her men never feel free because there is always a woman expecting something better of them, and the women are nearly always in control of their homes and finances. Even on a humbler scale, in *A Country Gentleman*, when Theodore Warrender inherits the modest family estate, the first obstacle to his new-found freedom is the presence of his relatively young mother, whose refusal to fade into a shadowy grief-stricken widow marks her out as superior to her conventional children. While they expect her to withdraw into the background, she is a constant presence in the novel, a wise counsellor to her children, and the protector of little Geoff, the emotionally needy son of Theo's second wife, Lady Markland.

The Marklands, the Warrenders' immediate neighbours, represent a very different kind of landowner, closer to the eighteenth-century aristocratic model where in fiction, at least, the husband is "wild" and rakish in his behaviour. By the sixth chapter Lord Markland has died after being thrown from his horse (like Patrick Torrance in *The Ladies Lindores*), and his wife left to manage their decaying estate. The novel thus quickly establishes a contrast between two types of "country gentleman": as Oliphant herself notes, in introducing her readers to the Warrenders' circumstances, "The county gentry of England is a very comprehensive class." Ranging from "the truest nobility, the finest gentlemen" to the "most limited, dull, and commonplace that human experience knows," this class, in Oliphant's hands, provides substantial scope for human dramas within their secluded woods and properties, without the need for a finely-differentiated contextual community on the scale of *Middlemarch* (Oliphant, 1886: I, 16).

Oliphant is perhaps most interested in the transition phase, from obscurity and middle-class values, to responsibility for a country estate, because it enables her to probe the differences between the establishment and her own class, where more effort might be required to maintain social position and stability.

For Theo Warrender, the crisis comes after he has observed the requisite period of mourning for his father and must decide whether to resume his education at Oxford or begin actively managing his estate. As with George Eliot's Fred Vincy and Tom Tulliver, it is clear that his education has poorly prepared him for a life of practical responsibilities: an agricultural college, as he mentions sulkily, having more to offer than its Oxford equivalent. On the other hand, he is no farmer, but a country gentleman. Again, it is the women of the novel who seem most energised by this idea, and his opportunities for making a difference, or, at the very least, upholding the dignity of the family. Theo's sister, the insufferable Minnie, who will later marry a clergyman and defer entirely to his opinions, sounds like Trollope's George Vavasour in declaring that "'a country gentleman is just the very finest thing a man can be [...] Why, Theo, there is not such a position in the world! We are the bulwark of the country. We are the support of the constitution'" (Oliphant, 1886: II, 6). Less pompously, their mother envies Theo the opening of such prospects, having never had any exciting opportunities in her own life, but all he does is squander them, becoming Geoff's tutor in order to spend more time with Lady Markland. In this case the alliance of country gentleman and aristocratic widow does nothing to enhance the position or happiness of either: the birth of twin girls seeming more of an absurd encumbrance, than a joyful sealing of their relationship. "'Poor Theo!'" says his mother "'He is pleased, of course, but I think half ashamed too. It seems a little ridiculous to have twins, and the first'" (Oliphant, 1886: III, 159). The twin girls seem to mirror the twin boys with whom the elderly Mr. St. John of *The Curate in Charge* is blessed in his second marriage: a double helping of responsibility for which neither man is remotely suited, and who must therefore become someone else's burden. By contrast the roguish Dick Cavendish, who eventually marries Theo's younger sister Chatty, has the energy to make a fresh start after a foolish "marriage" in America. He is one of the few men in Oliphant's novels whose potentially dangerous energy levels, as identified by Sussman as a nineteenth-century male characteristic, help him overcome his risk to the family and community, to become a genuinely reformed character and devoted husband.

Oliphant's growing interest in the landed gentry, however, takes her higher than the level of "country gentleman," especially in the two Lindores novels. Her credentials for writing about this class seem flimsily derived from living in Windsor, near the Queen, and being, as she told John Blackwood, "gloriously Tory now and then" (Jay 1995: 251). In some of her later periodical articles, such as her "Easy-Chair" series of the 1890s in *The Spectator*, Oliphant writes of the London "season," as if she belongs to the class that abandons the heat and dust of the capital in the summer months to cool off in the countryside (9 August 1890: 177–8). Yet the titled and landed characters she includes in her novels are often caricatured. At one extreme she laughs at plump little Lord Millefleurs of *The Ladies Lindores*, with his lisp and other speech mannerisms, while at the other, the horrifying bully, Patrick Torrance, is described by Lady Lindores as "'a rich fox-hunter, with the mind of a ploughman'" (Oliphant, 1883a: I, 98). The novel's short sequel, *Lady Car* traces the development of the couple's son Tom into a replica of his father, especially in his attitude to women, from his mother and sister to the lower-class woman he jokingly marries under a false name when he is under age. The key difference between them, however, is that while his father chose a middle-class woman with style, grace and intelligence, to enhance his home, Tom falls into a casual alliance with a woman first introduced to the reader (and Tom's mother) emerging from an argument with him, "in very fine, but flimsy attire, her face flushed with crying and quarrelling" (Oliphant, 2013a: 207).

Lady Car focuses specifically on the definition of a "gentleman," contrasting Patrick and Tom Torrance with Lady Car's second husband, the highly civilized, but ineffectual Edward Beaufort.

While a simple comparison between the two types might have been expected to produce a clear endorsement of "Beau," as the children call their stepfather, Oliphant quietly dismantles the better man's advantages to the point where Lady Car simply dies of disappointment, with him and every other aspect of her life. "'What's a gentleman?'" Tom asks rhetorically as he assesses his own prospects and values compared with his stepfather's, "'A man that has a place of his own and lots of money, and no need to do anything unless he likes — if that's not a gentleman, I don't know what is'" (207). Beau's definition, by contrast, is dismissed as "'all kinds of nonsense; that it's not what you have but what you do, and all that'" (207). The text, however, unequivocally states from the start that "Mr. Beaufort was a gentleman" (151), here defined as "a man of great cultivation of mind" and "an excellent scholar" (151). A former tutor and companion to Lord Millefleurs, Edward has perhaps benefited from his exposure to the finer things in life, but he never writes the great work his wife expects of him, and too easily slips into dilettante ease, playfully preparing Tom for his inheritance by encouraging him to design a flag, like the Royal standard, to be hoisted over their Surrey villa when his mother is in residence. Oliphant seems to blame Edward as much for his air of superiority to his uncouth stepson, as she does Pat Torrance for his bullying vulgarity, and he is unable to divert Tom from turning into a cheap imitation of his father. Nor is Lady Car's brother, Robin Lindores, who becomes Lord Rintoul when his father unexpectedly inherits an Earldom, any better. Introduced as a shallow and undistinguished young man who "knew himself to be wiser than his mother, and to know more of life than even the governor himself," Rintoul adopts the slang of his day, and insists his sisters marry for wealth and status (Oliphant, 1883a: I, 262).

If Edward Beaufort fails as a man while upholding the characteristics of a gentleman, Oliphant looks elsewhere for her masculine ideal. In *The Ladies Lindores*, this is John Erskine, another middle-class man who inherits an estate, albeit a much smaller one than the Lindores' property. The details of his successful progression from insignificant all-round "good fellow" and "honest gentleman," to leading man of the county, are left vague, perhaps because Oliphant was not entirely sure how these miraculous careers came about. The difference between their fates Oliphant implies, has, however, less to do with money than with character. Moreover, this influence passes to the next generation, with John's son, "little Jock," already, at fourteen, holding a place at Eton above his older cousin Tom.[4] The absence of charismatic male role models is undoubtedly an issue in Oliphant's fiction. With no one in the previous generation to look up to (their fathers are either already dead, or a poor example), Oliphant's few exemplary leading men are usually motivated in their careers by a combination of financial necessity, desire to marry a virtuous wife, and by their own emerging integrity and ambition: less for their own distinction and success, than for the good they can do their community and family.

If the single most important necessity for these men is a sense of purpose, accompanied by a belief in their own abilities to make a difference to their family and community, by 1888, Oliphant was feeling that, in comparison with women, men were becoming progressively weaker. "As we women grow more energetic," she claimed in the *St. James's Gazette*, "the men grow less so" (1888b:6) Where this crucial sense of purpose is missing, it needs to be bolstered by a wife who is intellectually capable of directing her husband's career: Lucilla Marjoribanks, for example, Phoebe Beecham, or Walter Methven's wife Oona. Far from being dragged down by their families, as Oliphant was herself, she indicates that the majority of her men self-sabotage the most when they are alone and dependent on their own initiatives, or (paradoxically) when they are dominated by their mothers, and feel not just demeaned, but emasculated by them. When after his father's death, in *The Son of His Father*, John Sandford's mother tells him "'unfortunately you cannot be free of me and my authority'" (Oliphant, 1887: I, 291), this seems only a slight exaggeration of many other sons' situations in her fiction, where the absence of supportive male companionship is both cause and effect of this maternal ascendancy. Novel after novel depicts a subculture of dishevelled, bearded men smoking on sofas by day, and drinking or pursuing unsuitable women by night. There is no Wildean glamour about these provincial bachelor lifestyles: only a decline into resentful defensiveness in the face of disapproving relatives. The lack of any responsibility for wives or children, in all but a few cases (Fred Rider, for instance) further discourages effort, and perhaps explains why Oliphant's female characters tend to be more energetic, motivated as they are, either by concerns for others, or their own survival in a culture that suddenly deprives them of fathers or husbands, and with them a sustainable income. While Sussman's theory of dangerous masculine energies may fit a few of Oliphant's villains (such as Pat Torrance, or Colonel Mildmay), and some of her early heroes, such as Arthur Vincent, Oliphant's men are more often blighted by inertia, ineptitude, and passive vices. Moreover, they are for her a sign of their times, her acknowledgment of the *fin-de-siècle* cultural changes that made her later middle-class men, of whom Harry Vernon and Algernon Merridew of *Hester* (1883), or Dolff Harwood of *Janet* (1891) are representative examples, banal stereotypes. With a taste for golf and football, music-halls, popular songs, slang, and a pretty girl, they are a far cry from her earnest young curates, Arthur Vincent and Frank Wentworth, whose stubborn idealism and family pride may have derailed their progress, but which ultimately reward them with a lifelong purpose and a loyal family.

CHAPTER 5

"What did it mean? Oh, what did it mean?" The Sensational and the Supernatural

"What do we know about the mysteries of life and death?" Oliphant asks in her biography of her distant relative Laurence Oliphant (Oliphant, 1891b: II, 320). By this point in her life such questions represented more than a passing curiosity. Five of her six children had predeceased her, along with her parents, husband, both brothers, and a nephew. Even by Victorian standards this was an abnormally tragic tally, and her remaining son, Cecco, was to follow in 1894. Envying Oliphant his ability to feel his deceased wife's presence as "part of his being," she regretted that "[s]uch strong consolations do not come to us, for whom, perhaps, the long endurance, the aching void, the blank of separation, may be needful" (Oliphant, 1891b: II, 320).

Unlike some of her more sceptical contemporaries, such as George Eliot, however, Oliphant had not lost her religious faith, and indeed retained a sense of the afterlife as a tangible place where the dead were individually tested and rewarded. Although the number of her supernatural tales is relatively small, and her fictional writing did not take this turn until the mid-1870s, her contribution to an increasingly popular subgenre is significant. Moreover, what looks like a departure from her usual realist style of writing, is not such a sharp break with the past as it might seem.

155

Most of her classic ghost stories, such as 'The Lady's Walk' (1882–83) and 'Old Lady Mary' (1884), are set in comfortable middle-class homes experiencing family and financial pressures. Idle youths flourish there, just as they do in her mainstream fiction, as do agitated parents, and troubled women and children. It is not until we reach her 'Little Pilgrim' tales (1882) and others set in the afterlife that they seem to cross new boundaries in terms of style as well as subject matter, and adopt an appropriately strange amalgam of dystopian vision and *The Pilgrim's Progress*.

The lives Oliphant mourned were not heroic: a husband who left her unprovided for in Rome, two sons, full of potential, whose lives came to nothing; a daughter who died before reaching adulthood; a promising nephew felled by typhoid in India; brothers who drank and were feckless. The experience of bereavement for Oliphant was exacerbated by bafflement as to why she alone had been spared. When Judith Butler asks in *Precarious Life* (2004) "Whose lives count as lives?" and "What makes for a grievable life?" she is thinking of a very different context from Oliphant's Victorian England: *Precarious Life* is a set of essays written in response to post 9/11 American foreign policy in Iraq and Palestine. Nevertheless, the notion of a "grievable life" (which should be all lives, valued equally with our own) and how we handle our "vulnerability to loss and the task of mourning that follows," may be useful in providing a framework for discussing Oliphant's increasing preoccupation with death, and the rationalization of its meaning for her as a survivor (Butler, 2004: 20). "Loss and vulnerability seem to follow from our being socially constructed bodies, attached to others," Butler argues, "at risk of losing those attachments, exposed to others" (2004: 20). Her suggestion of the "transformative effect of loss" (2004: 21) was not something Oliphant experienced, however hard she tried to substitute new attachments (for example her two nieces, Madge and Denny) for those she had lost, but Butler's theory of "relationality" (2004: 24) (the way grief brings to the fore our relations with others) is something that can be reconfigured to suit Oliphant's circumstances. "Relationality," for Butler, leads to "a way of thinking about how we are not only constituted by our relations but also dispossessed of them as well" (2004: 24). What this means is that her and our "primary others" live on in our own being but, for Butler, "they also haunt the way I am, as it were, periodically undone and open to becoming unbounded" (28). Butler sees this as a bodily experience as well as an emotional or psychological condition, and writes in terms of "being a bodily being, already given over, beyond ourselves, implicated in lives that are not our own" (28).

For Butler this form of relationality, afflicted by grief in the post 9/11 context is liable to result in violent political action. Instead, she counsels, in effect, rechannelling grief towards a recognition of human vulnerability and our collective responsibility for protecting it. Then, she argues, "we might critically evaluate and oppose the conditions under which certain human lives are more vulnerable than others, and thus certain human lives are more grievable than others" (Butler, 2004: 30). Applied to Oliphant, living in a very different world which had not yet experienced nuclear war or global terrorism (though political anarchy, often in the form of assassination attempts on prominent figures, was increasing across Europe), Butler's ideas may appear mismatched; but we can, I think, extract from her theorizing of the relationship between grief and political violence a set of ideas which associate grief and mourning with human vulnerability, bodily undoing, psychological haunting, and the desire for political action or reparation.

While loss in Oliphant's writing rarely leads to acts of reprisal, it does enforce readers' awareness of the overlooked and forgotten in society, especially women and children, but also ordinary, average young men at a turning-point in their lives. A common feature of Oliphant's supernatural tales is their attention to lives that were vulnerable in the past, or are standing still in the present, for want of any impetus. The fleeting collisions between the dead and the living in these stories usually refocus the living and placate the dead, but there are instances where they merely exacerbate the state of impasse, or drive the haunted into worse collapse. While it may be odd to find an author like Oliphant, best known for witty and ironic social observation, turning, relatively late in her career, to a literary genre requiring mastery of suspense and sensationalism, these tales allowed her space to explore the different facets of bereavement, ranging from antagonism between the living and the dead, to insatiable desire for meaningful connection. They also allowed her to explore what might be called "the curse of the family": not just in the sense that they concern ancestral ghosts, but also because many of the living are immobilised by continuing commitments to the family, and unable to move forward in their lives. The family in these tales both re-enacts previous patterns of obstructive behaviour, and warns its survivors to break that pattern. For a woman, especially, trapped by the repercussions of historical events (as we see, for example, in 'The Library Window'), the curse is especially disabling, but men too are doomed to confront demanding ancestors who are still attempting to redirect their choices.

In attempting supernatural fiction Oliphant was entering a well-populated field, which, as the century progressed, came under increasingly varied influences, including interest in popular superstition, as promulgated by servants, the alleged discoveries of Spiritualists and mediums, and full-blown occultism. Both theology and psychology, along with the beginnings of psychoanalysis, prompted curiosity about receptive states of mind, and obsessive "hauntings" by the vulnerable, while familiarity with Dante's *Divine Comedy* (well-known to Oliphant) allowed speculation about a tangible afterlife as a physical location. Oliphant was more or less open to all these Victorian versions of the unseen and the unknowable, as testified by her literary experiments, whether in terms of narrators, style and language, didactic content, or overall purpose, though she has little apparent sympathy with purely scientific explanations. In an overview of her religious beliefs towards the end of her life, 'The Fancies of a Believer' (1895), she characterises the age as "at once more believing and more unbelieving than many of the ages that have preceded it." So far as her own place in this spectrum of belief is concerned, she sounds unenthusiastic about the available standpoints, but "can only claim to be one of the people whose nature it is to believe rather than to doubt." God's way of "accounting for the universe" seemed to her still the best option (Oliphant, 1895b: 237). As she prepared this article, she asked William Blackwood "whether the Believer should be a man or woman? Naturally I should say the first, but the tendency of the day is so much (apparently) in the other direction that I hesitate" (Oliphant, 1974: 404). The article went out unsigned, and gender-neutral, but some of its thoughts obliquely reflect recent experiences with her sons: as, for example, when she insists: "We cannot turn the will or change the career of those who are most dear and precious to us" (Oliphant, 1895b: 246). Ultimately, she writes for those who, like her, are searching for explanations of unaccountable loss. It seems to be no coincidence that most of her ghostly figures are young.

Oliphant was like her contemporaries in publishing many of her ghost stories in periodicals: usually *Blackwood's*, but occasionally elsewhere. 'Earthbound' appeared in *Fraser's Magazine* (1880), while an abridged version of *A Beleaguered City* was published in the *New Quarterly Magazine* in 1879. The umbrella title of *Stories of the Seen and the Unseen* neatly divides her supernatural writings into two types: those recounting the visitations of ghosts to family homes, and those detailing the travels of the recently dead into the unknown territories of the afterlife. While the latter sound the more ground-breaking, Oliphant was by no means the first nineteenth-century author to speculate about the physical terrain and organisation of Heaven. In 1871 she had reviewed one such novel by Elizabeth Stuart Phelps, *The Gates Ajar* (1868), whose heroine, Mary Cabot, devastated by the death of her only brother, questions her Aunt Winifred at length about what exactly she can expect to find through the open gates of the afterlife. At this point, Oliphant was unimpressed by this kind of writing, and, while conceding its popularity, rated it as "not very good" (Oliphant, 1871: 436). Nevertheless, she found it increasingly necessary to imagine not just a tangible home for the dead, but also a process of arrival, information-gathering, and integration into a kindly collective of people like herself, resting after a lifetime of toil.

Critical Reception

Critical response to Oliphant's supernatural stories has been mixed, ranging from Q.D. Leavis's view that they are "over-rated" and self-indulgent (Leavis, 1974: 22), to Esther H. Schor's that they are "incisive essays in the cultural practice of interpretation" (Schor 1993: 385). M. R. James claimed in 1929 that "The religious ghost story, as it may be called, was never done better than by Mrs. Oliphant in 'The Open Door' and 'A Beleaguered City'" (1929: 171). 'The Open Door' he further praised as one of only two "really good ghost stories I know in the language wherein the elements of beauty and pity dominate terror" (the other was Lanoe Falconer's [Mary Elizabeth Hawker's] *Cecilia de Noel* 1891) (James 17 April 1931). Melissa Edmundson, in pairing Oliphant with her near-contemporary Charlotte Riddell (1832–1906), sees her, like Riddell, as a creator of "uncomfortable houses," in which living characters form relationships with spectral figures, resulting in what Edmundson fittingly designates "psychological appeasement" (Edmundson, 2010: 51–2). Jenni Calder has persuasively demonstrated how two of Oliphant's finest novels, *Miss Marjoribanks* (1866) and *Hester* (1883), illuminate emotional tensions between characters via metaphors of darkness and light, and open and closed doors and windows, much as her supernatural tales do, to explore the frustrations of women's lives and degrees of perception (Calder, 2003: 485–502).

The five "Little Pilgrim" stories, however, have found less favour with modern readers. Their format, of journeys taken through the landscape of the afterlife, by bewildered new arrivals asking questions, is alien to a sceptical age suspicious of didactic dialogues with angels. Rarely too are her stories genuinely spine-chilling. Oliphant's supernatural tales are largely about attempted communication by the dead with the living, often in an advisory capacity, or as "unfinished business." While characters who encounter her restless spirits are sometimes frightened, others are more concerned to discover scientific explanations or to settle family problems. Some even want to establish romantic relationships with the revenants. The nameless narrator's cry in 'The Library Window' (1896) of "What did it mean? Oh, what did it mean?" might be the epigraph for any one of her stories, though some are successfully resolved by marriage and the resumption of a disrupted family life (Oliphant, 2000: 391). Most of her ghost seers, however, are very slow to understand and act on what these spectral messengers are asking them to do, and the spirits themselves often strangely ineffective and limited in their arsenal of resources. The most frustrated of all is the eponymous Old Lady Mary, who has hidden her will in the secret drawer of an Italian cabinet where no one thinks of looking, and she is unable to direct them.

Beginnings and Themes

While her first serious attempt in the genre is usually regarded as 'The Secret Chamber' (1876), later expanded into her novel, *The Wizard's Son* (1884), Oliphant had published a Christmas ghost story, 'A Christmas Tale,' in *Blackwood's* as early as 1857. As Elisabeth Jay indicates, however, this is something of a tease: partly because the mysterious father and son with whom her narrator takes supper, turn out to be figures in the narrator's dream, but also because his anxiety to halt an apparently imminent parricide is "an allegory demonstrating that the New Year can only come of age at the expense of the death of the Old Year" (Jay, 1995: 158–9). Nevertheless, the narrator meets a family configuration typical of Oliphant, and of the mid-Victorian ghost story more generally, in terms of its generational misunderstandings, moody son, and lonely manor house.

The themes of her most successful stories are essentially domestic, focused on the haunting of houses and gardens by spectral figures who make repeated visits until they have been understood, and actions taken to mend past wrongs or reposition survivors towards a happier or fairer future. As many critics have observed, it is not only the troubled inhabitants of these houses that form the focus of Victorian ghost stories, but also the architecture or fabric of their houses and gardens that provide a landscape of opportunity for unnatural encounters. The sheer domesticity of Oliphant's supernatural tales is evident just from their titles, with all their references to windows, doors, chambers and portraits, and most of the ghosts are women or children who once lived in these houses. Doors and windows provide a hinge between two worlds: not just of the living and the dead, but, as Melissa Edmundson suggests, between two social classes, "the wealthy and the working classes" (Edmundson, 2010: 61), to which one could add, men and women. Jay observes that the door found in Oliphant's most successful tales, "both is and is not there," its intermittent access to a liminal world allowing the "unseen to find a point of entry" (Jay, 1995: 170). The unreliability of the window peaks in 'The Library Window', in which the female narrator is the only person who can see a window opposite her Aunt Mary's house with increasing clarity, while her Aunt's friends merely argue about whether the window ever existed or was blocked in to evade the Window Tax.

Oliphant's self-consciousness about the conventions of the ghost story is evident in her story 'Earthbound', not only in the mysterious apparition of a woman in white apprehended by a nervous man — Oliphant admired Wilkie Collins's *Woman in White* (1860) —but also in the family's discussion of supernatural stories (a trope also used by Henry James in *The Turn of the Screw*, 1898).[1] Following the death of their son and brother, the Beresfords of 'Earthbound' are in a subdued mood on Christmas night, and reject the traditional ghost story as unsuitable entertainment in their circumstances. They do, however, discuss supernatural matters, exposing a generational divide between the bereaved parents, who ponder "those sensations and presentiments that seem sometimes to convey a kind of prophecy, only understood after the event, of sorrow on the way," and the "young ones," who amuse themselves with talk of "spiritualism" and other such phenomena, "which we are all half glad to think cannot be explained" (Oliphant, 2000: 140). What is interesting about this passage is the way a house party in mourning both critiques the very subgenre which is supposed to reflect their feelings and experiences, and also subdivides along generational and gendered lines. Sir Robert expresses complete scepticism about the existence of a family ghost, while his wife believes "there is something — very vague" (Oliphant, 2000: 140). The family ghost is not in fact their son, as one would expect, but a woman, and her existence is first mentioned (oddly enough) by the old rector, Mr. Lightfoot, further complicating the theology of the afterlife in this story.

Oliphant's Ghosts and Their Seers

As Srdjan Smajić notes, the ghost seer is a crucial element of any supernatural tale, in the context of "contemporary debates about the relationship between vision and knowledge, seeing and believing" (2010: 17). Both ghost and seer are also products of their time and place, either culturally misaligned, or temporally out of kilter, the spectre having left life at an earlier point. As in *A Christmas Carol* (1843), arguably the most famous Victorian ghost story, the more didactic spirits target a particular person in order to change their behaviour or rectify a wrong. By Dickens's time, as Louise Henson argues, there was already a substantial body of work on what she calls "the philosophy of apparitions", a mixture of psychological and physiological theory associated with medical case studies, designed to find a rational explanation for spectral visitations: "Sensations from the present are interwoven with ideas from a remembered past which temporarily became dominant, and are closely related to apprehensions about the future," resulting in the playing out of a "drama of the self" (Henson, 2004: 47). In Oliphant's supernatural tales, within these dramas, certain patterns recur. These include a troubled family history, generational disagreements, susceptible, but sometimes nameless, seers, who may or may not have any connection with the apparition, and subthemes of gendered expectations. Spectral presences in Oliphant's short fiction repeatedly test the "manliness" of male seers, without applying such harsh tests to the women who see ghosts. In this respect her preoccupation with the failings of men, discussed in the previous chapter, is taken to new levels.

In Oliphant's stories, like Dickens's, the spectral presence is invisible to most people, except those for whom it has a message, and targets male characters (adults and occasionally children) more often than female. This pattern implies that men have more to learn about what has gone wrong in the past, especially in relation to their treatment of women and children, whose sense of injustice remains as powerful in death as in life. While several of her stories involve young men puzzling out the message of a dead woman, 'The Library Window' is the only one of Oliphant's stories in which a susceptible young woman has to decipher the meaning of a male spirit, which more directly threatens her long-term wellbeing than many of the female spectres do their male seers. On the other hand, living female characters are implicated in many of the male seers' experiences, whether as victims of social or familial neglect (as in 'The Portrait'), or as taken-for-granted mother-substitutes (as in 'The Lady's Walk'). The doubling and duplicating of female identities in many of Oliphant's supernatural tales implies that, for some (the male seers and their families), women are seen as interchangeable.

In comparison with these weightier issues of family history, naming of both seer and ghost seems to have been almost a perfunctory matter for Oliphant, given the frequency with which such details are left blank. While the male narrator's named identity is perhaps less important in 'The Land of Darkness' (a bleak version of the afterlife full of aggressive strangers), the absence of names seems especially odd in 'The Library Window,' where neither key character is named (the female narrator is always addressed as "Honey" by her Aunt Mary). In 'The Lady's Walk,' the named male narrator, Mr. Temple, hears the footsteps of an unidentified female ghost, while in this, and a similar story, 'Earthbound', the ghost is doubled with a female character (Maud, in 'Earthbound', Charlotte in 'The Lady's Walk'). Similarly, the portrait of Philip Canning's mother, the subject of 'A Portrait,' is assumed by their friends to be of Philip's wife, Agnes, his mother's cousin, who bears the same name as his mother, as well as resembling her physically. The density of these doublings intensifies the relevance to the seer's psychological history, besides pointing to additional anxieties about "relationality," in the sense of family histories and marriages. Philip's father's response, for example, to seeing the portrait of his long-dead wife, is to think of their physical incompatibility in their present forms. "'How am I to meet that young creature [...] But what—what am I to say to her, Phil, when I meet her again, that —that angel?'" (Oliphant, 2000: 288) Mr. Canning, at seventy, is as daunted by the image of his wife as a twenty-year-old woman in a white dress, as Philip is by the ludicrousness of this innocent-looking creature, to him "no more than a child," being his mother (287). In other words, she looks too young to be either a wife or a mother, and yet she has been both, leaving both men with a burden of guilt and regret for the harm they have unwittingly caused her, through the risks of marriage and childbirth. The apparent interchangeability of dead women with living namesakes seemingly gives the men an opportunity to correct past wrongs, but may hint at the risk of repeating them, through the inevitability of women's loss of freedom in marriage.

While the male seer may confer greater credibility and rationality on the story, the men themselves are often more nervous and susceptible than their female companions, in keeping, perhaps, with Oliphant's tendency to portray men as lacking self-mastery. 'The Portrait's' hero, Philip Canning, for example, overcome by violent "leaps of the heart," senses that an extraordinary "occurrence" is taking place, without actually seeing a ghost, but only feeling a presence; that he is being made "a helpless instrument without any will of mine, in an operation of which I knew nothing" (Oliphant, 2000: 306). The ghosts themselves divide about equally into male and female, as do the recently dead travellers to the afterlife, who constitute a second strand of "supernatural" tales in the Oliphant oeuvre.

Risky Relationships: Expanding Possibilities

As Steven Connor suggests, for many Victorians, "The 'supernatural' was no alternative or other world, but rather an image, annex or extension of the imposing, ceaselessly volatile real world of the nineteenth century" (Connor 2004: 258) While this "extension" may largely refer to the material aspects of people's lives, for Oliphant it is also a space where they can experiment with alternative relationships. Unexpectedly, perhaps, these possibilities are needed and sought by men more than women in her supernatural stories, many of them (like the men in her novels), caught in a state of impasse in their lives. Edmund Coventry of 'Earthbound', for example, is described in the blandest of terms as an average-looking twenty-seven-year-old, with "a very nice estate, and a house in town, and no relations to speak of." Lady Beresford has already identified him as a suitable match for her second daughter, Maud (Oliphant, 2000: 139), whose company he enjoys, but more in the manner of a substitute brother than a would-be husband. There is far more life in his relationship with the ghostly woman he meets in the garden than with the innocuous Maud, a girl as pleasant and unremarkable as himself.

Perhaps the explanation is that Edmund's "woman in white" is essentially that: a woman, whose half-smile and pretty wave suggest the perfect combination of discreet sexual confidence, as well as the gentleness and purity on which the narrative insists. Her clothes, unlike Maud's, are distinctive, if ambiguous in their symbolism: "a white dress, with a black mantle round the shoulders, and a large hat: not unlike the kind of costume which people in aesthetic circles begin to affect, but far more real and natural, it seemed to him" (Oliphant, 2000:144). His stream-of-consciousness accretes clause upon clause, as he tries to pinpoint her social position. Here Oliphant's knowledge of dress is crucial, as the woman's black upon white means something very different from the keeper's niece's "black, with the usual white collar" (149). While the keeper's niece wears the practical uniform of a humble woman who needs to work for her living, the sheer impracticality of the lady's white dress outdoors in winter suggests she is somehow displaced from a protected life at home. Like Collins's Woman in White, her incongruousness in the otherwise deserted landscape stops his breath.

While a raised heart rate is Oliphant's usual way of recording a character's vulnerability, and "bodily undoing" (to use Butler's term), she here makes clear its sexual significance for Edmund: "He had the same feeling which a man sometimes has," the narrator explains, "when he suddenly meets a lovely face and says to himself that, please God, this woman is the one woman for him" (144). Esther Schor succinctly notes that this woman in white is "simultaneously a woman to be possessed and a text to be interpreted" (Schor, 1993: 374) – though in fact she possesses him, and after their third meeting, he appears at breakfast the next morning "silent as a ghost at the cheerful breakfast table" (157), and after the final visitation "pale as a ghost, but asleep" (p. 170). Vampire-like, she seems to be turning him into her kind, while inducting him, first via encouraging gestures, and then through enigmatic speech, into a state of sexual arousal thus far uninspired by Maud. Though only nineteen, the woman is more experienced than he is, and indeed finally confesses she is 'Earthbound' as a punishment for too much loving the earth (155). In effect Edmund and the mysterious woman form a relationship where, though he repeatedly offers to "see her home," he is steadily "unmanned" by his leaping, plunging heartbeat, dreaminess, and even "tears" (157). Through his ghostly encounters, Edmund's sexuality is unlocked, and a marriage proposal rehearsed to the ghostly Maud (for that is the woman's name) before he is ready to propose to her living double.

All is explained by the presence of a portrait, another favourite device of the Victorian ghost story. In this case, the lady obligingly makes one final appearance, standing next to her own image, as her infatuated lover repeatedly cries "I do not understand" (168). A figure from the eighteenth century (her portrait is dated 1777—reminding us perhaps of the 1698 portrait of Mircalla, Countess Karnstein, in Sheridan Le Fanu's *Carmilla*, 1872), she finally convinces him there can be no further relationship between them. She has no message for the family or any kind of request. Her invisibility and silence are her punishment, and there is no clarity as to why Edmund, of all people in the house, should be the one to see her. Ghost stories, however, seem by their very nature, to demand an interpretation, which in this case weighs the living man's needs with the dead woman's. The story works both to warn against overvaluing earthly relationships, and against missed opportunities for quiet domestic happiness. Above all, it educates the man more than the woman to reassess his life, and outgrow a chivalrous fantasy in favour of the realities of middle-class marriage.

It is easy to confuse 'Earthbound' with 'The Lady's Walk', as the two share similar features. Once again, a young man (Mr. Temple), seemingly with little to do, is the guest of a bereaved family (again, mourning a son and brother). He has feelings for the eldest sister,

Charlotte Campbell (known as "Chatty"), but is unable to act on them, instead being drawn to a spectral female figure he first hears and then sees: "tall and slight, and wrapped apparently in a long cloak, a dress usual enough in those rainy regions" (Oliphant, 1882: 242). Again, all the family are baffled as to who she can be, though they know they have a family ghost, whose continued presence protects them, and it is obvious to the reader that she has materialised in this form. The differences are that this time the man narrates his own story, and the ghost has a clear warning for the family, that the eldest son, Colin, is in danger. "Colin had 'gone wrong' in every way that a young man could do," the narrator explains, and in his father's and sister's presence, Colin shoots himself (Oliphant, 1882–83: 344). The story increasingly teases the reader with the spectral lady's similarity to Charlotte. Both wring their hands and sigh, both take a motherly responsibility for the family's welfare, and Charlotte's appearance grows steadily more ghostlike: for example when she comes downstairs one night, "like a ghost through the dim-coming shadows." Temple starts to think the spectre "might be Charlotte herself in an unconscious shadow-shape," a motherly earlier Charlotte, "her very kin and prototype" (Oliphant, 1882–83: 357–8). Either way, an invisible barrier stops Temple reaching an understanding with the prototype or her descendant, other than that by the end of the story he has assumed guardianship of the family from the ghostly lady. The overall "message" of the tale remains ambiguous. While Elisabeth Jay suggests the ghost is exorcised for attempting to play Providence (Jay, 1995: 168), the material acts of self-sacrifice performed by both Temple and Charlotte (Temple by using an inheritance to buy Ellermore, the family home) produce only a state of resigned impasse at the end of the story, as Temple tries to convince himself that being good friends with Charlotte and knowing each other's secrets is better than marriage, given her insistence that marriage is impossible, because of her promise to her mother to look after her siblings. When she tells Temple that the members may change, but "the family never goes away" (1882–83: 237) she seems to be speaking for all women, Oliphant included, whose opportunities have been restricted by a stubborn, self-denying commitment to their domestic responsibilities. The futility, for both the ghost and Chatty, of trying to protect them is meanwhile borne out by the series of disasters the family experiences in the course of a short tale.

Both these stories trace the efforts at communication by a wistful female domestic spectre made doubly redundant, both by being dead, and not the person the family are mourning. Her needs, like those of her living doubles, seem unimportant, so that there is little to choose between the spectre and the cypher-woman in the home where a son is being mourned. 'The Portrait' and 'Old Lady Mary' similarly exile a woman from her former life, helpless to influence the material needs of those who come after, but these stories differ from the two previously discussed, in that the family context broadens, to include more realistic social issues. In 'The Portrait', Philip Canning, another son, unemployed until he becomes his father's agent, is waylaid alternately by his mother's force-field (for want of a better word), and his father's tenant, Mary Jordan, whose path he crosses in much the same random way as his male counterparts in the other stories encounter spectral female figures. The story implicitly asks the reader to make some connection between Mary Jordan, the destitute mother outside the house, and the ghostly portrait of the dead mother within, both women having suffered at the hands of the Canning men. Oliphant helps the reader to perceive a connection between them when she has the father blame his son's faintness on "that woman Jordan" (Oliphant, 2000: 303). Mrs. Jordan does indeed seem like a petitioning ghost in the way she responds to his "What do you want with me?" with "Oh, sir, I want to speak to you!" (281). She also has a clear message for his father: "Tell him to think what he's doing, driving poor creatures to despair" (282). Together, the living woman and the dead raise Philip's awareness of women's suffering in the tight-lipped respectable world in which he lives with his father. His pity for his mother is the stronger as he views her portrait, unable at first to see her in the right relationship to himself: "Poor child I said to myself; so sweet a creature: poor little tender soul! as if she had been a little sister, a child of mine,—" (287). Like the other male narrators of the ghost stories, Philip has a shallow experience of the opposite sex, and the narrowest of emotional ranges. Before he can marry, he needs to understand more of the hidden lives of women suffering acutely at the hands of men. In infantilising his own mother, as a "little sister" or "child" of his own, he is refusing to acknowledge the sexual life she had with his father: a kind of adolescent denial of his parents' physical relationship. Mrs. Jordan's sleeping baby, however, is a reminder of the adult life he has so far avoided in his own person. Soon afterwards he finds in his father's drawing-room a "bit of knitting [...] something for an infant," which his mother had evidently been making for him before she died (289). As with Oliphant's other ghost stories, the plot develops through a series of clues which gradually connect the family history with the crises of the present time.

In this case, however, there is no mystery about the ghostly presence: only about what Philip should do to lay his mother's restless spirit, and give his own life some meaning. From this point his future is inseparable from the needs of the women who depend on the Cannings, father and son, for their survival. Mrs. Jordan's presence proliferates, in the form of numerous "open-mouthed" petitioners at their front door (298), all wanting him to intervene with his father to reduce their rents. The final petitioner is Agnes, the poor relation in mourning, his mother's cousin, whose servant visits his father, beseeching his support. As in 'Earthbound' a suitable bride quickly appears from within the family, to reset the faulty patterns of the past, but in the process Philip has outgrown his romantic sorrow for his young mother, and announced himself to his father as "a man, with a right to speak my mind" (303). It is by re-educating their men away from unrealistic conceptions of women, that several of Oliphant's ghost stories repair the damage done by unthinking ancestors or, more generally, by the patriarchal present. Attraction to a beautiful, but forbidden, woman, in the meantime, awakens their dormant sexuality, and enables some of them, at least, to redirect their feelings towards a realistic marriage closer to hand.

'Old Lady Mary' is one of Oliphant's quirkiest supernatural tales, and perhaps her least frightening, maintaining an ironic humour, despite its underlying social criticism, from the paradoxical opening line: "She was very old, and therefore it was hard for her to make up her mind to die" (Oliphant, 2000: 211). The tale's autobiographical allusions both prefigure Oliphant's growing sense that she seemed destined to live for ever, while the younger people died, and also reflect the bereavements she had already suffered. For example we hear that Lady Mary "did not forget the dark day when her first-born was laid in the grave" (212), perhaps a reminder of Maggie Oliphant's death in Rome in 1864. Lady Mary also looks back over her life, both before and after death, in what reads like an autobiographical impulse. Indeed, when she enters the afterlife, she is told by a male friend: "You are going to think about your life, and all that was imperfect in it, and which might have been done better" (226). As Jenni Calder suggests, 'Old Lady Mary' is a transitional text "between those supernatural stories which take place on earth, and those which tell of the voyages of spirits in the world beyond the grave" (Calder, 2000: 409). In this story, the predominant theme is the invisibility of women, both dead and alive. While Lady Mary feels powerless to help her goddaughter and the servants, whom she unthinkingly neglected when she was alive, all the women in the story are struggling in different ways to be heard and heeded. The story oscillates between Lady Mary's anxieties in the afterlife and her goddaughter's in real life, where "little" Mary actually feels stimulated by the poverty that has suddenly come upon her. The story anticipates aspects of Henry

James's *The Turn of the Screw* (1898) in that little Mary's main charge, Connie Turner, in asking too many pointed questions about Lady Mary, causes her governess to react hysterically, seizing the child "with a pressure that hurt Connie" (269–70). Connie in turn points to the door and cries out: "'The lady! The lady! […] There, there! don't you see her? she is going in'" (270). While in Oliphant's story it is the child, rather than the governess who sees the ghost, tension nevertheless escalates between the adult and the child over the presence that only one of them can sense. The spell is broken when the governess begs God to tell Lady Mary that she never blamed her for apparently doing nothing to provide for her. By this time, however, ghost-seeing in Lady Mary's old house has been so vulgarised that other seers include the servant Betsy, who claims to have heard a "hollow and terrible voice" (265), and even Fido, the dog— but never little Mary herself until the end of the story.

As R.H. Hutton observed in an 1896 review of Oliphant's "Seen and Unseen" stories, the predominant feature is the way her disembodied spirits manoeuvre awkwardly in the afterlife to achieve "much the same sort of things as they had been accustomed to do with their embodied spirits […] in the seen world" (Hutton, 1896: 131). There can seem something petty and mundane about these ghostly activities: in this case Lady Mary behaves like someone who has lost something, and is now racking her brains to remember where she put it. Her irresponsible treatment of her goddaughter, however —"the prettiest object of all" among her collection of self-indulgent "paraphernalia" (221) — opens up a significant debate about the plight of middle-class single women, which remained one of Oliphant's primary concerns in her fiction. In 'Lady Mary,' even the servants are aware of how difficult it will be, compared with themselves, for little Mary to find work, given that "the poor little thing […] is left on the charity of folks she don't belong to" (241). Oliphant further probes this question by playing on the notion of "kindness," a word which, with its variants, reverberates through the story, reminding readers of its social nuances, in terms of who shows (or owes) kindness to whom. While little Mary protests that her godmother was "more kind to me than a mother" (250), her well-wishers equate "kindness" more directly with financial support. To Mrs. Turner, the woman who rents what used to be Lady Mary's house, the goddaughter has been treated "so unkindly" (247), that she quickly offers her a chance to stay in the house by working for them as a governess. As the story progresses the notion of "kindness" has been so extensively unpacked and repurposed, that from having begun as a simple offer of a home and companionship by her godmother, it becomes loaded with all the discomforts of being patronised by a family little Mary knows are her social inferiors. Even Mrs. Turner cheerfully acknowledges this as she tells the doctor, "'We're not fine people, doctor, but we're kind people'" (255). Whether as unpaid companion or paid governess Mary is a woman confined to a house on someone else's terms, like Lady Mary herself, now baffled by life in Heaven as she tries to understand its house rules. Moreover, what happens to little Mary in the end is unclear. We know that she collapses into serious illness after forgiving her godmother, but the last word is with Lady Mary herself, returning gratefully to Heaven, with a cry of "how well one is in one's own place! how blessed to be at home!" (273). This strangely insensitive conclusion leaves little Mary's situation unresolved, as if once again Lady Mary's complacency has further displaced the child she wanted to protect.

'The Library Window' (1896)

This late ghost story, the last of Oliphant's set in a realist environment, is often regarded as one of her finest. For Tamar Heller, this "brilliantly eerie tale" is especially significant because of its haunting "by images of reading and writing" (1997: 23). The dominant image is of a male scholar seen working in a college library window, observed by the narrator, a young unnamed girl spending the summer with her Aunt Mary in "St

Rule's" (assumed to be St. Andrews in Scotland). This in itself is a highly resonant image, implying as it does that writing and scholarship are masculine preserves, a view gradually confirmed by the release of more information about the narrator. Her father, for example, is a "great writer," and the man's study reminds her of her father's, but she is baffled by the man's complete absorption in his work, and especially his failure to notice her (Oliphant, 2000: 380). Oliphant had used a similar image in 'The Little Pilgrim Goes Up Higher' (1882), where the female Pilgrim visits a vast library in the afterlife, full of male historians working on "all the records of the world" (Oliphant, 1883b: 91). Throughout 'The Library Window,' however, Oliphant sustains what Heller acknowledges as an inversion of the voyeuristic "male gaze" of a woman.[2] Jonathan Schroeder (1998) further summarizes that "to gaze implies more than to look at — it signifies a psychological relationship of power, in which the gazer is superior to the object of the gaze" (Schroeder, 1998: 208). While this is generally assumed to be the case in gaze theory, Oliphant's story unsettles the reader's assumptions, not only by inverting the usual relationship between male gazer and his female object, but also by driving the narrator towards an obsessive hysterical state, which, as with little Mary of 'Old Lady Mary' finally curtails her engagement with the spectral figure. Only the narrator can see the male scholar, who becomes increasingly visible to her the more she gazes at the window, as if, in her neediness, she is creating him.

The narrator herself is a keen reader, hence a passive consumer in the profession of literature which the doubly male figure of the writer — literally patriarchal when her father's image is recalled — so resolutely represents. At the same time, her increasingly emotional interest in the man and her frustration at being ignored, extend the meaning of her obsession in ways that even her elders begin to notice. As she tries to make the man look at her, Oliphant adds a further element: a sexually-charged "wicked fairy," her aunt's friend, Lady Carnbee, who wears a diamond ring with "a sharp malignant prick, oh full of meaning" (Oliphant 2000: 381). In a home where her aunt is continually sewing, and the girl is assumed to be an adolescent, the "Sleeping Beauty" symbolism of induction into sexuality is familiar, and when the man in the library finally faces her and opens the window, the girl's language enacts a process of bodily evisceration. Feeling "as if my heart were being drawn out of me," she leans against the glass, "drawn to him as if I could have gone out of myself, my heart out of my bosom, my eyes out of my head" (395). By the end of this encounter, she is "in a kind of rapture, yet stupor too" (395), again, like the sensations Bram Stoker's or Sheridan Le Fanu's vampires induce in their victims. He has even waved at her like the woman who hails the male narrator of 'Earthbound,' but his wave is ambiguous: it may be a "salutation—yet not exactly that either, for I thought he waved me away" (395).

As with many of Oliphant's other supernatural stories, the ending, when it finally comes, is almost perfunctory, abandoning the central figure to an unknown fate. Stung by Lady Carnbee's "sharp wicked stone" (401), recalling the vampire's sting in Le Fanu's *Carmilla* (1872), the narrator becomes the watched, not the watcher: "Aunt Mary watched me, every movement I made, her eyes shining, often wet, with a pity in them that almost made me cry" (399). Moreover she learns that Aunt Mary has also seen the man in her time: he wreaks revenge on "the women of our blood" (399), because of a female ancestor who waved to a male scholar, and the sharp-edged diamond ring was the "token" (400). The narrator admits at the end of the story that she never knew what her aunt meant by this phrase, but for the reader it is likely to function both as pledge of connection between them (like an engagement ring), and perhaps as a kind of curse. Elisabeth Jay sees it as representing "the double-edged gift of a woman writer's imagination" (Jay 1995: 265), which in this case clearly destroyed the narrator's peace of mind. As for her ancestor, when the scholar refused to respond, her brothers killed him (like the brothers in Keats's 'Isabella' (1818)). Has the narrator seen him since? She is vague about this, but thinks she saw him in a crowd at the dockside when she returned, a widow from India, many years later.[3] Either way, the underlying resonances of the fatal relationship between the male scholar and the girl, the crushing of her first sexual feelings, and banishment back home like a child, make this last major story of Oliphant's an indictment of the limited choices open to women of imagination yearning for something beyond the peaceful domestic round of their elders.

Open Doors and Male Hauntings

If the majority of Oliphant's spectral figures seem to be women in white with a healing message, their male equivalents are more aggressive and demanding, of whom the most mysterious and terrifying is undoubtedly the warlock-lord of Kinloch-houran in *The Wizard's Son*, prefigured by the "wicked Earl" in 'The Secret Chamber'. Where her spectral encounters involve mixed genders — men seeing women, women seeing men— they usually become emotionally involved, to the extent that falling in love with a ghost implicitly acknowledges her protagonists' frustrated romanticism. Apart from 'The Library Widow', these are relatively benign hauntings where conversations with troubled revenants help to resolve earthbound situations, often for both parties, living and dead. Where men meet men, however, there is a more violent undercurrent, alongside more pressure to find a rational explanation for the unscientific phenomenon of a ghostly haunting. Two such tales, 'The Secret Chamber' and 'The Open Door', both set in Scotland, bear the hallmarks of a typical Oliphant supernatural story, embedded in a troubled family history, with the equally familiar reports of vanishing doors and chambers, thudding heartbeats, and debates about whether ghosts can really exist; but they go further than this in tightening the pressure on the seer to act in order to save lives. As Elisabeth Jay notes, however, "within a particular tale two stories often compete for our attention," and in these two the ghostly mystery runs alongside (or reflects on) a father-son generational plot (Jay, 1995: 157). While the story more obviously foregrounds a crisis in the son's life, it also forces the father to confront repressed aspects of his own past and present anxieties. Women are marginalised in both stories, apart from 'The Open Door', where the revenant child Willie's plangent cry of "'Oh mother, let me in!'" (177), recalls the petitioning ghost of the first Catherine in *Wuthering Heights* and the little ghost girl in Elizabeth Gaskell's 'The Old Nurse's Story' (1852).

It is often these masculine inter-generational subtexts that provide the most significant challenges. Whereas in 'The Open Door', the narrator-father, Henry Mortimer, is glad of time away from his family, in London, in 'The Secret Chamber', the father, Lord Gowrie, is clearly relieved to be able to share with his son on his coming of age the ordeal through which he has been living since he too had to meet his ancestor, "the wicked Earl." 'The Open Door', meanwhile, forces Mortimer to accept responsibility, both for his fragile son, and for the ghost of the former housekeeper's son, Willie, by developing a more empathetic side to his much vaunted masculinity. In these two stories Oliphant explores very different father-son relationships. Mortimer's habit of taking his family for granted and mentioning them with affectionate detachment, is abruptly broken by his only son Roland's rapid decline after "hearing voices among the ruins" (Oliphant, 2000: 177). Their first dialogue on Mortimer's return, establishes the father's concept of masculinity as being about self-control. The first thing his frail son—frail from the Indian climate endured because of his father's career— must do is to "be quite quiet, and not excite yourself' […] He was quiet directly, like a man, as if he quite understood" (178). The father then urges: "tell it all out like a man" (178). Significantly, Roland hears the mysterious sounds more clearly after his father has left for London, perhaps indicating the father's repressive effect not just on his son, but also on Willie, the revenant. Mortimer's confusion about what to make of this story partly hinges on his shame that his son "should be a ghost-seer; for that generally means a hysterical temperament and weak health, and all that men most hate and fear for their children" (181). Roland's simple conviction, that in this extreme situation his father will know what to do, is far from certain, until Mortimer realizes that his own son will die unless he helps the "the poor suffering human creature that moaned and pleaded so" (204).

In 'The Secret Chamber', the son's exposure to the "wicked Earl" brings father and son closer together. Indeed the son has come through the ordeal more successfully than his father did, by resisting the temptation to take the Earl's proffered hand. We have already seen the importance of touch in Oliphant's realist fiction: it is equally so in her supernatural tales, where the touch of a spectre's hand is potentially all the more ambiguous, besides confirming its claim on the seer. Lindores,[4] indeed, initially welcomes this confrontation as an opportunity to settle the issue of the "unseen," "the final settlement of a hundred questions," but unexpectedly the Earl presents himself as a "benevolent venerable patriarch," an ancestral father-figure (Oliphant, 2000: 120–1). The tale can therefore be read, like 'The Open Door', as exploring the nuances and meaning of fatherhood through the vehicle of a supernatural encounter. For Lindores, his immediate problem is to understand why his own father was so terrified of the man who invites him forward with the simple statement: "I am your father" (121), followed (when Lindores confronts him with the cross-shaped handle of his sword), with "my son! Lindores!" (123). In the mental struggle that follows, the strain on his body and mind, as shown by Oliphant, results in a similar kind of evisceration to that experienced by the girl in 'The Library Widow', and again the protagonist is locked in a double gaze with the spectre, which "seemed to drag his eyes out of their sockets, his heart out of his bosom" (126). Escaping the ghost's (literal) clutches, Lindores instead exchanges touches and kisses with his real father, Gowrie, but at a point when the reader feels all must be well, Lindores both sees a portrait of the Earl invisible to his guests, and fails to rediscover the secret chamber where he met the ghost of his ancestor. Even after standing up to the wicked Earl, Lindores has been tainted by the coming-of-age ordeal, his initiation into ancestral manhood.

As in *The Wizard's Son,* this coming of age test bears all the characteristics of a male initiation rite, but in both texts Oliphant adds her own particular concerns about male inertia, and the inescapable curse of the family. Like the father in *A Country Gentleman and His Family* (1886), Gowrie is "honest" and "dull," while his son Lindores is fresh out of university and full of ambition, specifically rejecting the "country gentleman" lifestyle he is due to inherit. Instead he means to travel and stand for Parliament. After his shattering experience with Earl Robert, whose hand he refuses, his future is just as uncertain as little Mary's, or the unnamed narrator of 'The Library Window.' The narrator's foresight, like a tantalizing ghost's, fails just at the point when it is most needed, with the comment: "I cannot tell the reader what young Lindores has done to carry out his pledged word and redeem his family" (135). There is more hope in *The Wizard's Son,* but only after Walter Methven has endured several confrontations with his spectral ancestor, who may, or may not, be an aspect of his own psyche. Elisabeth Jay, in her introduction to this novel in Pickering and Chatto's *Selected Works,* argues that Walter's extreme experience with the "Wizard" is used by Oliphant to "suggest the apocalyptic dimensions of the shock it will take to shatter and remake the easy habits into which a young man like Walter Methven has fallen" (Oliphant, 2015b: xxiii). For her, therefore, the novel is an intense "psychodrama," which nevertheless leaves the reader uncertain whether the warlock-lord is "an inner voice of spiritual temptation" or "a spectral presence," who is occasionally seen by other people in Walter's circle (Oliphant, 2015b: xvii). While this is by no means Oliphant's final statement on ghostly encounters, it is her most significant on the relationship between drifting young men and the shock needed to re-energise them. Even Walter's dissolute friend Captain Underwood, in telling what he knows of the previous lord's experience, when he was out shooting, wonders whether it might have been "a call to him" (2015b: 55). Mrs. Methven, adopting the vocabulary of 'The Open Door', thinks her son will be "'man enough, I hope, to meet an emergency'" (55).

What we know about the warlock-lord is that as his death was never proven, his son declined to take the title, and forbade his son to do so, but this deference to a past mystery ceased with subsequent generations. Walter is therefore, at one level, dealing with a resentful ancestor safeguarding his own supremacy, a father refusing to let his sons inherit his title. If this is a psychodrama, as Jay proposes, the situation could also reflect his sense of unworthiness to inherit the title and property, but his encounters with the warlock-lord suggest other possibilities. The ongoing story of masculinity, and its disabling lack of choices, which courses through Oliphant's oeuvre, aligns him straightaway with her more positively portrayed heroes, Arthur Vincent and Frank Wentworth (discussed in chapter Four), in being thrust into situations not of their own making. The first question put to him by the warlock-lord on his first appearance, just after Walter has refused to evict his tenant crofters, is "'Is there anything special in you to disqualify you for doing a disagreeable duty?'" (Oliphant, 2015b: 109). If nothing else, the mysterious man forces him to think more profoundly about almost everything in his life, including the identity of his tormentor, whom he suspects of being "a monomaniac" (167). It is not only Walter who is teased in this way by the compulsion to explain these recurrent visitations, but the reader too. The novel offers, if anything, too many possible explanations, many of them given by the warlock-lord himself, as he tells Walter half way through the novel that he is looking for a worthy opponent to be his conqueror. This discussion hinges on the disparity between the estate's growth and prosperity over centuries, and the undistinguished nature of its title-holders. Pointedly, the wizard tells Walter he has been as "'good for nothing'" as his predecessor: "'consuming your mother's means, opposing her wishes, faithful to no one'" (256). This is essentially a father-son relationship, with the warlock-lord asking him searching questions about his choice of bride as well as his work for the estate. He is perversely enough the father-figure Walter never had alongside his widowed mother, and at times he sounds to be also channelling his mother's accusations about his spendthrift ways.

Increasingly the wizard becomes Walter's mentor, a kind of supernatural life-coach, urging him to adapt his plans and marry Katie Williamson, the Glasgow heiress, rather than the more idealistic Oona Forrester. Tauntingly, he suggests: "'Your ideal has always been impossible, for you have never had heart or will to keep to it'" (266). Walter could very easily marry Katie and consolidate his position. He even proposes to her, and instantly regrets it, bringing on a final physical trial when he and Oona nearly die in an explosion in the tower, and their spiritual union of "[t]wo that made up one" (405) is finally endorsed — though not before she too has had an interview with the worldly ancestor, and, like Lindores in 'The Secret Chamber', is unsure whether or not to take his hand (368). The novel ends with all happily resolved, but on a note of lingering doubt as to what exactly happened, and "whether the terrible conflicts which he had gone through were not conflicts between the better and worse parts of his own nature, without any external influence" (401).

Afterlives: The Unseen

While Oliphant's ghosts usually seek out individuals to address, her best-known supernatural story, 'A Beleaguered City' (1879), explores the multi-faceted impact of the supernatural on a whole community of people living together, and exposes them to questions of where their loved ones might have gone, and whether they can still see those they have left behind. This story embodies in effect a collective discussion of the afterlife, and with so many witnesses to the emptying of the city by command of the dead, there is no shortage of people to exchange opinions on what really happened. Set in France, in the real town of Semur, with the additional doctrinal and spiritual pressures of Catholicism, this story is often anthologized as one of Oliphant's most successful. The community is split in all directions between the worldly and the sceptical, and along gender lines between male rationalism and female reverence for the wishes of the "grievable" dead. The extraordinary events they experience, separately and together, bring out both the best and the worst in people's behaviour for a few hours, forcing them to speculate about what they actually believe. The tale's principal narrator, Martin Dupin, the city's mayor, tells his story carefully and rationally, setting up the pervasive imagery of doors into the unseen, gates and portals letting in the cold air of the dead, and expelling the inhabitants from their homes. While Dupin's steadfastness crumbles in the face of this mass expulsion, his wife, Agnès volunteers to confront this supernatural force, which includes their dead daughter, Marie, and parley with them. Significantly, she would ask "what is their meaning: and if no way can be found — no act of penitence" (Oliphant, 2000: 42). Although her offer is declined, the great symbolic moment of the story is indeed the discovery of an olive branch laid over an unveiled picture of Marie in his wife's room (Oliphant, 2000: 64). Far from refining the material prejudices and religious superstitions of the city as a whole, however, this climactic discovery is where the mayor's spirituality peaks, before he, along with the rest of his community, falls back into his old habits as normality returns to the city. While for Diana Basham the story "deals explicitly with the exclusion of women," required as they are to wait on the sidelines while the men consult over what to do, it can also be read as a satire of local officialdom (Basham 1992: 169). The language of the men's self-important bureaucracy, with all its circumlocutions and references to the dignity of office — "A man does what is his duty" (61); "I took it upon myself to speak" (45) — contrasts sharply with the women's collective spirituality, and that of Paul Lecamus, the one man with visionary powers. When all the excitement is over and the citizens are allowed back into their homes, Dupin summarizes the limited impact even of a shared experience on this scale: his rational materialism tells him that "everything goes on as if it would endure for ever. We know this cannot be, yet it does not move us" (100). His wife takes what appears to be the opposite view, but hers too is based on a kind of resignation: "My wife does not question, she believes much; and in respect to that which she cannot acquiesce in, she is silent" (100). They are both aware that within a relatively short time they too will "be as they are—as shadows, and unseen" (100).

What exactly happens when we join the "Unseen" increasingly preoccupied Oliphant in the final years of her career. Although the travels of her 'Little Pilgrim' and the young woman of 'Dies Irae' (1895) through the landscapes of the afterlife have attracted little interest from modern critics, they were popular in her own time in terms of visualising a tangible landscape of rest and quiet companionship where the fortunate dead, after proving their worth, are reunited with those who were dear to them. *A Little Pilgrim in the Unseen* (1882) reads at times like a feminist utopia, and it is surprising to think this was written immediately before the worldly late, great novels such as *Hester* (1883) and *The Ladies Lindores* (1883). In the Pilgrim's afterlife, tired women are allowed to rest, and to welcome newcomers. They progress gradually through the system until they are permitted to meet their parents and other close relatives. The Pilgrim (based on a Windsor neighbour, Nelly Clifford) clearly finds it easier to relate to other women (with whom she often holds hands) than, for example, a man who stumbles in, and, trying not to look lost, asks for directions. Her strength gone from her, the little Pilgrim "had no word to say to him" (Oliphant, 1883b: 61). Later, she discovers that couples work together, "and it is no longer needful that one should sit at home while the other goes forth" (128). The second tale ends with the Pilgrim (who was unmarried in real life) reverting to a blissful childhood, with her parents teaching her the language of those peacefully at rest in Heaven.

This is only one side of the picture, however, as Oliphant also presents apocalyptic versions of the afterlife, as in 'The Land of Darkness', where newcomers meet with a barrage of rudeness, indifference and physical violence as they try to make sense of what has happened to them. It appears to be no coincidence that this violent scenario afflicts men, rather than women, her hero often bruised, beaten and bleeding after brawling his way through a Dantean Purgatory. An authorial note informs the reader that this story has come from the historians' archives, visited in *The Little Pilgrim* (Oliphant, 2000: 313). Her final tale, 'The Land of Suspense' (1897), while gentler in tone, charts a journey taken by a thinly-disguised version of her elder son, Cyril. As his father, brothers and sisters deny him entry through the heavenly gateway, the nameless young man, who never intended any harm, and always meant to do better, recalls how often he was welcomed back home by his forgiving mother, who would, he is sure, have let him in: "She would have torn me from these stones, and brought me in had she been here" (Oliphant, 1897: 136). We see, too, in this story, hints of the long-past, scarcely-begun history of Cyril's relationship with his father, who died when the boy was only three. "If my father had been here!" (146) is recalled as something he often said to himself in the past. If Cyril dreamt of any special favours from his father, however, his redemption can be achieved now only by praying for his mother, the sole survivor of their family. Having at last prayed sincerely in a natural woodland cathedral of arched trees, the young man feels "the soft touch upon his forehead like the hand of his mother" (157), and is reunited with all the family, including his younger brother Cecco: "two fair young men," as Oliphant characterises them for the last time, "—fairer than they had been on earth" (157).

If "[a] ghost is a sign of importance not to be despised," as the narrator claims in 'The Secret Chamber' (Oliphant, 2000: 109), Oliphant's female and child ghosts were generally unimportant people when they were living; "ungrievable" in Butler's sense of never counting for much, but with the power to haunt even those who never knew them. Although their work is often little more than unfinished family business which requires several attempts to be understood by baffled seers or sceptical communities, it reflects similar concerns to her realist fiction. These ghosts mainly right the wrongs of the vulnerable, especially mothers; they stand up for those who were overlooked in their lifetimes, and force the living to halt in their business and ponder the morality of their own or their ancestors' actions. Her male spectres, by contrast, seek to control their descendants and fight them to the death. They act as vengeful fathers of modern aimless sons who shirk their inheritance, and must be prompted to take responsibility. The *Little Pilgrim* and other stories of the afterlife, which all describe journeys through tangible landscapes, similarly focus on the ways in which individuals, both men and women, are afforded one last chance to rethink their assumptions, review their lives, and learn how to support others, with women being treated more forgivingly than men, as they are largely the victims. As her own life drew to a close it was perhaps inevitable that Oliphant would personalise the afterlife as the home of her errant sons. When Cyril died in 1890, she regarded his as a "failed" life: "Oh, if I could but follow my boy in thought where he is yours," she confided in God, "if I could but feel how it is, if not where he is" (Jay, 1990: 44). In Butler's terms, this was still, for her, a "grievable" life, if an undistinguished one, and she needed to know where he had gone. For all her lifelong concern for taken-for-granted mothers, it was a son who failed to fulfil the bright promise of his childhood that inspired her final word on the world of the dead, and on the haunted vulnerability of those who mourn.

Conclusion

"I have done very well for a woman, and a friendless
woman with no one to make the best of me"
(Oliphant 1990: 91)

In December 2013 Jenni Murray, presenting a BBC Radio 4
Woman's Hour discussion of Mrs. Oliphant asked: "Why do we
know so little of her?" The answer was that she was "not a very
conventional great novelist." The occasion was the launch of *Hester*
(1883) as a "15 Minute Drama" series in five episodes, adapted by
Kate Clanchy and Zena Forster, with Penelope Wilton voicing
Mrs. Oliphant as narrator. While the *Woman's Hour* website in
2018 was still describing Oliphant as "an unjustly-neglected British
writer," it also called her "the feminist Trollope," and praised the
novel's "deliciously written and sardonic narration." When asked
how good a writer they thought Oliphant was, the creators of this
"radical dramatization" said the "best bits" were "just brilliant,"
and compared her with Dickens, Flaubert and Chekhov.[1]

Oliphant herself was not so sure. The phrase "not a very
conventional great novelist" might well have intrigued her, with
its ambiguous word order and uncertain emphasis. Does it mean
that she *was* a great novelist, only not very conventional? Or "not
a great novelist," as judged by our usual standards? Throughout
her critical history Oliphant has always been discussed in terms of
falling short, of not being quite good enough: a view she herself

promulgated. While feeling she had "done very well for a woman," she also confesses in her *Autobiography* to feeling "rather a failure all round" (Oliphant, 1990: 17). Her claim that "No one even will mention me in the same breath with George Eliot" is often cited (Oliphant, 1990: 16–17). As this study indicated from the start, however, people did mention her in the same breath as George Eliot, and if she has not since enjoyed a reputation like Eliot's, Eliot too was in the critical doldrums for a while as literary tastes changed. Contrary to her own expectations, however, Oliphant weathered the fashions of the twentieth century to be first reclaimed as a "forgotten" and "anti-feminist" woman writer, and then, over the last fifty years, not only remembered, but her supposed anti-feminism reappraised, her periodical articles rediscovered, her best novels salvaged and republished, her anniversaries observed, her *Autobiography* celebrated, and plaques unveiled in her honour.[2] John Stock Clarke marked her mid-twentieth century revival with a new Bibliography, subtitled *The Rise, Decline and Recovery of a Reputation. A Secondary Bibliography 1949–2005*, the contention of which is that while "The story of the fifty-one years from 1849 to 1900 has been very complex; the story of the next century is of a classic simplicity, a narrative of a reputation suddenly entirely extinguished, and then, slowly at first, rediscovered and eventually revalued at roughly its true estimate" (Clarke online 35).

In 1999, the journal *Women's Writing* published a special issue commemorating her *Autobiography*'s centenary (Jay and O'Gorman, 1999); and now twenty years on, it is salutary to look back and see how the new themes identified by contributors, including the supernatural as social commentary, "motherhood and melodrama," her position in the (anti-) feminist debates of the time, and her relationship with Queen Victoria, have remained important, while others, such as Claire Pettitt's exploration of Oliphant's "Self-help, and Industrial Success Literature," have the potential to be more fully explored (Pettitt, 1999: 163–179). Oliphant, in other words, has defied her own predictions. She rewards both close reading and topical updating, while her distinctive voice— the favourite critical term is "ironic," but she can be bleakly self-denigrating — repays the close attention often withheld from such prolific Victorians.

The ambiguity and richness of her writing, and the availability of many of her shorter texts, especially the ghost stories, make Oliphant especially rewarding to teach. As noted by Elisabeth Rose Gruner and referenced in Chapter 2, 'The Story of a Wedding Tour' (1893), with its bold start and guilty ending, remains a provocative and gripping feminist text, as do many of the ghost stories. Broadview's scholarly edition (2019) of *Queen Eleanor and Fair Rosamond* (1886) makes available a short bigamy novel, while the many twists and turns of the *Autobiography* record Oliphant's alternating passages of self-doubt and self-assertion as a Victorian female novelist comparing herself with George Eliot and the other great names of the period. As Philip Davis puts it, in a sensitive analysis of the passage in her *Autobiography* recounting her mother's death, and her attempts to bear it alone (Oliphant, 1990: 37–8), "It is as though you were having to read ordinary life itself, passing by with its meanings half-hidden and its questions already fading" (Davis, 2008: 67). Laurie Langbauer's study of *Novels of Everyday Life* (1999) also captures this aspect of Oliphant's appeal. Being able to write movingly and comically about the mundanity of daily life, which was something also admired in George Eliot, was perhaps Oliphant's most sustained achievement.

There is an unrushed quality about her best novels, which record conversations in all their natural ebb and flow, like the easy movements of a film script. Whether this is Ellen Merridew of *Hester* (1883) upbraiding her new husband Algernon for being "'such an old Redborough person,'" because he has an inborn respect for Aunt Catherine (Oliphant, 2015a: 139), or Mrs. Tozer of *Salem Chapel* (1863) declaring "'We never can be took wrong of an evening, Tozer and me; there's always a bit of something comfortable for supper'" (Oliphant, 1986: 37), there is an air of authenticity about even her secondary characters which enriches her writing. The Tozers are never anything but warmly hospitable, yet Oliphant conveys Arthur's feeling of utter despair that they have claimed him as theirs, when he feels his natural place is with the dazzling Lady Western. Parties and dinners are indeed Oliphant's forté, whether Dissenting suppers at the cheesemonger's, or Ellen Merridew's "reckless young dinners, where there was no solemnity at all, and perhaps not much wit" (Oliphant, 2015a: 178). Under cover of multiple conversations there is plenty of opportunity at these gatherings to exchange snide remarks at the expense of the unaware: so when Ellen boasts of all she has learnt about social fashions "Abroad," Roland Ashton asks "'Where is Abroad?'" in "an undertone which was so confidential and intimate" that even one of the spiteful old ladies, Matilda Vernon-Ridgway, is charmed (Oliphant, 2015a: 142). A similar kind of teasing arises from Emma Ashton's insistence on "having her chance," which the mischievous pretend not to understand: "What was your chance?' said Hester with a set countenance" (Oliphant, 2015: 195). In these exchanges men and women are alike ridiculed, but moderately. Each sex has its flaws and susceptibilities, and if women are more often the victims, men too are entangled in social networks that spoil their plans.

Oliphant's ear for a euphemistic phrase bandied about in company by worldly people modulates into a more earnest dwelling on phrases which prefigures the modernist techniques of Henry James, T.S. Eliot and Virginia Woolf. James's playing with apparently innocent, but loaded words such as "advantage" and "value" (which have both moral and material nuances) is intellectually more rigorous than Oliphant's games with lazy colloquialisms, but James also rings the changes on "chance." In a long, exploratory dialogue between Lambert Strether and Maria Gostrey in *The Ambassadors* (1903) for example, over Strether's mission to separate Chad Newsome from an unsuitable alliance in Paris, the word is passed back and forth between them, without being explicitly defined. "'I'm thinking of his mother,'" says Strether in discussion with Miss Gostrey, in a way one suspects Oliphant would have approved, "'He has darkened her admirable life.'" In the meantime, if Chad separates from the unsuitable woman in Paris, says Strether, "'he'll come in for a particular chance—a chance that any properly constituted young man would jump at'" (James, 1976: 47). For both James and Oliphant "chance" means more than just an opportunity. It means manipulating a situation so that personal advantage can be gained from it, but it also requires the other person in the dialogue to decode what is being said, just as we have to guess what Oliphant means by "the Wentworth complaint" in *The Perpetual Curate*, or the "token" in 'The Library Window,' or James by the mysterious small article at Woollett. This is not to suggest that Oliphant is an incipient modernist, or that she is the only Victorian realist novelist who plays with such phrases: only that her techniques look forward into the twentieth century as well as backward into the mid-nineteenth, and in that respect she narrows the gap between mature Victorianism and early modernism. In the inconclusive endings of her supernatural stories, too, Oliphant seems to be departing from the tight narrative structures of the typical Victorian ghost narrative, and gesturing towards more of a Jamesian style. Penny Fielding, in her contribution to the 1999 special issue of *Women's Writing*, is intrigued by the doubling and substitutions of characters and ghosts with the same names, and the introduction of other characters who seem significant, but are not the haunting spectres of the recently dead, and indeed disappear from the narrative. 'Earthbound,' she proposes, "in its refusal of narrative structure or exegesis, looks not only at the modern, but also forward to modernism" (Fielding, 1999: 212). It is not only the short stories that distrust the full disclosure of a high Victorian ending, but also several of her novels, where the fates of key characters, such as Hester Vernon, or Cicely St. John are left for readers to work out for themselves.

Even so, it is unnecessary to defend Oliphant's importance by downplaying what makes her a stolid Victorian realist, and reconfiguring her as a transitional bridge into the new century she narrowly missed entering. She stands or falls on her own merits, which this study has argued make her both traditional and innovative, cautious and outspoken, representative of her age, and yet always distinctive, individual, and opinionated. If Oliphant stops short of being an outright feminist, imagining other futures for women trapped in domestic roles, and recoils from the sexual frankness of the 1890s, she makes a lifelong protest against taking women for granted and assuming men are the stronger sex. It is indeed more appropriate now to discuss Oliphant more widely in terms of gender, rather than anti/feminism, but the picture is constantly changing. Such is the richness of her realism, and the multifaceted nature of her fictional communities that if her "true estimate" (to borrow Clarke's terminology), is unlikely to reach consensus any time soon, it will at least remain the subject of critical debate for decades to come.

Notes

Abbreviations

MOWO   Margaret Oliphant Wilson Oliphant
NLS   The National Library of Scotland

Introduction

1. For example *Sharpe's London Journal* found it "religious without cant" (January 1850, p. 120), while *The Spectator* compared it with Jane Austen and John Galt (22 December 1849, p. 1212).
2. MOWO to William Blackwood, 9 March 1882, Blackwood MS 4437, NLS.
3. MOWO to William Blackwood, 31 January 1882, Blackwood MS 4437, NLS.
4. MOWO to William Blackwood, 16 February 1884, Blackwood MS 4462, NLS.
5. 'The Death of Mrs. Oliphant. A Well-Known Novelist,' *The Pall Mall Gazette*, 28 June 1897.
6. For information on who read Oliphant, and what she read, see the Open University/AHRC database *UK Red: "the experience of reading in Britain, from 1450–1945"* http://www.open.ac.uk/Arts/reading/UK/search.php.[accessed on 28 April 2018].
7. In private Carlyle was less fulsome about the Irving biography, telling his brother John there was little "likeness of man or work" in it (p. 87).
8. See also Jay's Introduction and 'A Note on the Text' to her 1990 edition of the *Autobiography*.
9. Woolf used the title 'Moments of Being' as the title for a short story of 1928, subtitled 'Slater's pins have no points.' The term refers to moments of illumination or understanding, similar to James Joyce's "epiphanies." In Woolf's story, like Oliphant's, the realization concerns the wrongness of a possible marriage and the preference for independence.
10. The *Autobiography* was republished in 1974 by Leicester University Press, and has since been edited by Laurie Langbauer (Chicago University Press 1988) and Elisabeth Jay (Oxford University Press, 1990 and Broadview Press, 2002).
11. *Kirsteen* was reissued, with an introduction by Merryn Williams, by Everyman, in 1984a, and as Volume 22 in Pickering and Chatto's *Selected Works of Margaret Oliphant*, introduced and edited by Gail Marshall (2015).

12. *A Widow's Tale And Other Stories by Mrs. Oliphant*, With an Introductory Note by J.M. Barrie (Edinburgh and London: William Blackwood and Sons, 1898). On the St Giles plaque see Jay (1995), p. 1.
13. For example, *Salem Chapel* (1975) and *The Perpetual Curate* (1976), edited by R.L. Wolff.
14. 'Margaret Oliphant in Context,' 6 July 2015 at the University of Leicester.
15. *Manful Assertions: Masculinities in Britain since 1800*, ed. Michael Roper and John Tosh (London: Routledge, 1991); R.W. Connell, *Masculinities* (Cambridge: Polity Press, 1995, reprinted 2005); Herbert Sussman, *Victorian Masculinities: Manhood and Masculine Poetics in Early Victorian Literature and Art* (Cambridge: Cambridge University Press, 1995); *Performing Masculinity*, ed. Rainer Emig and Antony Rowland (Basingstoke and New York: Palgrave Macmillan, 2010); and Phillip Mallett, *The Victorian Novel and Masculinity* (Basingstoke and New York: Palgrave Macmillan, 2015). See also *Victorian Masculinities*, a special issue of *Critical Survey*, edited by Graeme Smart and Amelia Yeates 20:3 (2008).

Chapter 1

1. MOWO to John Blackwood, 30 March [1877], Blackwood MS 4364, NLS.
2. MOWO to John Blackwood, 28 March 1877, Blackwood MS 4364, NLS.
3. John Blackwood to MOWO, 6 March 1877, Letter Book May 1874–March 1877, Blackwood MS 30365. p. 561.
4. Although Oliphant proposed the 'Old Saloon' series of opinion pieces in *Blackwood's*, she was not the sole contributor. Other instalments were written by Alexander Allardyce and Jane Emily Gerard (among others), while contributors to the 'Brown Owl' column in *Atalanta*, included L.B Walford, Sarah Tytler, and Charlotte M. Mason.
5. 'Thomas Carlyle,' *Macmillan's Magazine* 43 (April 1881), pp. 482–96.
6. MOWO to John Blackwood, n.d. Blackwood MS 4103, NLS, cited by Joanne Shattock in *Selected Works* I (2011), p. 17.
7. See Joanne Shattock, *Selected Works* 1 (2011), p. 509, note 4; cf p. 141, for the married women's property petition of 1856, which MOWO was asked to sign. See also "The Great Unrepresented" (Oliphant 1866: 368). George Eliot also declined to sign the suffrage petition.
8. Oliphant's 'The Anti-Marriage League' appeared in *Blackwood's Magazine* in January 1896. Hardy's response is given in his 'Postscript' to the 1912 Wessex edition of *Jude*.
9. The title of this series evolved in 1890 to 'A Commentary in an Easy-Chair.'
10. Oliphant refers here to "the daughters who revolt, and demand latch-keys, and to go to music-halls of an evening" (1894: 290). Oliphant writes similarly in 'Things in General,' *Atalanta* (1894: 416).
11. See for example 'The Female Bachelor,' *Saturday Review* (2 June 1894) [author unknown], pp. 582–3, which states that "The female bachelor has a latchkey; that is an essential" (582).

12. Oliphant to John Blackwood, n.d. [1855] MS 4111, NLS.

13. Oliphant widely reviewed European literature for *Blackwood's* in the 1880s, including 'A Few French Novels' (1881), and a round-up of French novels for "The Old Saloon" (September 1888c)

Chapter 2

1. Confusingly Oliphant recycles the same names for entirely different characters in her fiction: hence this Mr. Cavendish does not reappear as Dick Cavendish in *A Country Gentlemen*. Hester Southcote is different from Hester Vernon, and there are several Mildmays and Chattys in her fiction.

2. *Census of England and Wales for the Year 1871. General Report, Volume IV* (London: Eyre and Spottiswoode, 1873), p. xviii.

3. 1,227,669 widows reduce to 879,173 by remarriage. For comparison the number of widowers (noticeably fewer) reduces from 1,024,769 to 398,202 (Census, 1871, p. xviii).

4. See for example, 'History and "literary value": *Adam Bede* and *Salem Chapel*,' by Peter Brooker, Paul Stigant and Peter Widdowson in *Popular Fictions: Essays in Literature and History*, ed. Peter Humm, Paul Stigant, and Peter Widdowson (1986) rpt (London and New York: Routledge, 2013), pp. 68–93; and Wagner, *Antifeminism and the Victorian Novel*.

Chapter 3

1. For example, Marlene Tromp in *The Private Rod: Marital Violence, Sensation and the Law in Victorian Britain* (2000), and Heather Milton in 'The Female Confessor, Confession, and Domains of Discourse in Margaret Oliphant's *Salem Chapel*', in Tamara S. Wagner (ed.), 2009, pp. 197–216.

2. Few of Oliphant's novels were illustrated, not least because *Blackwood's Magazine*, in which several were serialised, did not carry illustrations. I have found a curious image of Lucilla Marjoribanks, in 1890s dress, looking tall, but slim, with Mr. Ashburton, with the caption "Miss Marjoribanks put her hand to her breast," but this is a rare instance of such textual illustration [http://www.oliphantfiction. com/x0200_single_title.php?titlecode=msmarj: accessed on 25 February 2018].

3. See, for example, her 'Fireside Commentaries' for the *St James's Gazette* for 28 May 1888 and 8 June 1888.

4. Henry Tilney claims to "understand muslins […] particularly well" in Chapter 3 of *Northanger Abbey* (Austen, 1972, p. 49).

Chapter 4

1. http://www.victorianweb.org/history/census.html [accessed 5 May 2018].

2. https://www.le.ac.uk/eh/teach/ug/modules/eh3107/occupations.pdf [accessed 5 May 2018].

3. Though see Clare Pettitt, '"Every man for himself, and God for us all!": Mrs. Oliphant, Self-Help, and Industrial Success Literature' (1999).

4. The contrasting careers of fathers and sons are summarised in Chapter X of *Lady Car*.

Chapter 5

1. Oliphant told John Blackwood in 1862, "I must say I think the 'Woman in White' a marvel of workmanship," *Autobiography and Letters* (1974: 186). She also reviewed the novel for *Blackwood's* in "Sensation Novels" (May 1862), pp. 564–84.

2. See Laura Mulvey, 'Visual Pleasure and Narrative Cinema'.

3. The Indian link of course evokes echoes of Wilkie Collins's *The Moonstone* (1868), and wider literary associations between diamonds and India, with the diamond symbolising imperial exploitation as well as superstition and mystery. See Chapter 2 of John Plotz's *Portable Property: Victorian Culture on the Move* (Princeton and Oxford: Princeton University Press, 2008).

4. Confusingly, Oliphant recycled the name of "Lindores" for *The Ladies Lindores*, rather than for *The Wizard's Son*, for which 'The Secret Chamber' was a kind of rehearsal.

Conclusion

1. The 5 episode "15 Minute Drama" series of *Hester* (1883) started on 30 December 2013, and was made available on Radio 4 Extra in August 2017. A discussion of the novel was held with Clanchy and Forster on *Woman's Hour* on 31 December 2013. https://www.bbc.co.uk/programmes/b03mcmx3. Accessed 10 May 2018.

2. A plaque was unveiled in St Giles's Kirk, Edinburgh, in 1908, and in 1997 a blue plaque on 9, Clarence Crescent, Windsor, the house where she lived from 1872–1896.

Bibliography

Primary Archives

Blackwood Papers, National Library of Scotland (NLS). Correspondence of Margaret Oliphant with John Blackwood and other members of the publishing house.

MOWO to John Blackwood, n.d. [1855] MS 4111, NLS.

MOWO, 6 March 1877, Letter Book May 1874–March 1877, Blackwood MS 30365.

MOWO to John Blackwood, 28 March 1877, Blackwood MS 4364, NLS.

MOWO to John Blackwood, 30 March [1877], Blackwood MS 4364, NLS.

MOWO to William Blackwood, 31 January 1882, Blackwood MS 4437, NLS.

MOWO to William Blackwood, 9 March 1882, Blackwood MS 4437, NLS.

MOWO to William Blackwood, 16 February 1884, Blackwood MS 4462, NLS.

Correspondence of Margaret Oliphant with Alexander Macmillan and other members of the publishing house 1858–95. Macmillan Archive, The British Library.

Works by Margaret Oliphant

Fiction

1851. *John Drayton, Being A History of the Early Life and Development of a Liverpool Engineer.* 2 vols. London: Richard Bentley.

1853. *Harry Muir: A Story of Scottish Life.* 3 vols. London: Hurst and Blackett.

1857. *The Days of My Life: An Autobiography.* 3 vols, London: Hurst and Blackett.

1861. 'The Rector', *Blackwood's Edinburgh Magazine* 90 (September), pp. 284–301.

1863. 'Mrs. Clifford's Marriage', *Blackwood's Edinburgh Magazine* 93 (March) pp. 284–300; (April), pp. 414–436.

1882–3. 'The Lady's Walk', *Longman's Magazine,* Vol I, December – January, pp. 229–252; pp. 341–364.

1882 (rpt.1883). 'The Little Pilgrim Goes Up Higher', in *A Little Pilgrim in the Unseen.* London: Macmillan and Co.

1883a. *The Ladies Lindores.* 3 Vols. London and Edinburgh: William Blackwood and Sons.

1883b. *A Little Pilgrim in the Unseen.* London: Macmillan and Co.

1886. *A Country Gentleman and His Family.* 3 vols. London: Macmillan and Co.

1887. *The Son of His Father.* 3 vols. London: Hurst and Blackett.

1889. 'The Mystery of Mrs. Blencarrow'. London: Spencer Blackett.

1891a. *Janet.* 3 vols. London: Hurst and Blackett.

1895a. *Dies Irae: The Story of a Spirit in Prison.* Edinburgh and London: William Blackwood and Sons.

1897b. 'The Land of Suspense'. Edinburgh: Blackwood and Son.

1984a. *Kirsteen: The Story of a Scotch Family Seventy Years Ago.* Dent: London and Melbourne.

1984d. *Hester.* Jenny Uglow (ed.). London: Virago.

1986a. *Salem Chapel.* Penelope Fitzgerald, (ed.), 3 vols, London: Virago.

1986b. *The Rector, and the Doctor's Family.* Penelope Fitzgerald (ed.). London: Virago.

1987a. *The Perpetual Curate.* Penelope Fitzgerald, (ed.). London: Virago.

1987b. *The Curate in Charge.* Merryn Williams, (ed.). Gloucester: Alan Sutton Publishing.

1988. *Miss Marjoribanks.* Penelope Fitzgerald, (ed.). London: Virago.

1989. *Phoebe, Junior*. Penelope Fitzgerald, (ed.). London: Virago.
2000. *A Beleaguered City and Other Tales of the Seen and the Unseen*. Jenni Calder (ed.). London: Canongate Classics.
_____. 'Earthbound', pp. 137–170.
_____. 'The Land of Darkness', pp. 313–361.
_____. 'Old Lady Mary', pp. 211–273.
_____. 'The Library Window', pp. 363–402.
_____. 'The Open Door', pp. 171–210.
_____.'The Secret Chamber', pp.107–135.
_____. 'The Portrait', pp. 275–312.
2002. *Phoebe, Junior*. Elizabeth Langland (ed.). Peterborough Ontario: Broadview Press.
2003. *Hester*. Philip Davis and Brian Nellist (ed.). Oxford: Oxford University Press.
2013a. *Lady Car: The Sequel of a Life*, in Josie Billington (ed.), *The Selected Works of Margaret Oliphant*. Vol 10, *Novellas*, London: Pickering and Chatto.
2013b. 'Mr. Sandford', in Muireann O'Cinneide (ed.), *The Selected Works of Margaret Oliphant*. Vol 11. London: Pickering and Chatto. pp. 153–199.
2013c. 'A Story of a Wedding Tour', in Muireann O'Cinneide (ed.), *The Selected Works of Margaret Oliphant*. Vol 11. London: Pickering and Chatto, pp.253–269.
2013d. 'A Widow's Tale', in Muireann O'Cinneide, (ed.), *The Selected Works of Margaret Oliphant*. Vol 11. London: Pickering and Chatto, pp.203–249.
2015a. *Hester*. Valerie Sanders (ed.). *The Selected Works of Margaret Oliphant*. Vol 20. London, Pickering and Chatto.
2015b. *The Wizard's Son*. Elisabeth Jay, (ed.), *The Selected Works of Margaret Oliphant*. London, Pickering and Chatto, Vol 21.
2019. *Queen Eleanor and Fair Rosamond*. Pamela Perkins (ed.), Peterborough, Ontario: Broadview Press.

Miscellaneous Works by Oliphant

1862. *The Life of Edward Irving*. 2 vols. 5th edition London: Hurst and Blackett,
1868. 'Historical Sketches of the Reign of George II. No. 1 -The Queen', *Blackwood's Magazine* 103 (February), pp.195–221.
1891b. *Memoir of the Life of Laurence Oliphant and of Alice Oliphant, his Wife*. 2 vols, Edinburgh and London: William Blackwood.
1897a. *Annals of a Publishing House: William Blackwood and his Sons. Their Magazine and Friends. By Mrs. Oliphant*. 2 vols. Edinburgh and London.
1974. *Autobiography and Letters of Mrs. Margaret Oliphant*. Mrs. Harry Coghill (ed.), with an Introduction by Q. D. Leavis. Leicester: Leicester University Press.
1990. *The Autobiography of Margaret Oliphant: The Complete Text*. Jay, Elisabeth (ed.). Oxford and New York: Oxford University Press.
2005. *Dress*. London: Elibron Classics.

Periodical Articles by Oliphant

1854. 'Mary Russel [sic] Mitford,' June. *Blackwood's Edinburgh Magazine*, 75 pp. 658–70.

1855. 'Modern Novelists – Great and Small,' May. *Blackwood's Edinburgh Magazine*, 77, pp. 554–68.

1856. 'The Laws Concerning Women,' April. *Blackwood's Edinburgh Magazine*, 79, pp. 379–87.

1858. 'The Condition of Women,' February. *Blackwood's Edinburgh Magazine*, 83, pp. 138–54.

1862. 'Sensation Novels,' May. *Blackwood's Edinburgh Magazine*, 91, pp. 564–84.

1866. 'The Great Unrepresented,' September. *Blackwood's Edinburgh Magazine*, 100, pp. 367–79.

1867. 'Novels,' September. *Blackwood's Edinburgh Magazine*, 102, pp. 257–280.

1868. 'The Queen of the Highlands,' February. *Blackwood's Edinburgh Magazine* 103, pp. 242–50.

1869a. 'Charles Reade's Novels,' October. *Blackwood's Edinburgh Magazine*, 106, pp. 488–514.

1869b. '*The Subjection of Women*', October. *Edinburgh Review* 130, pp.572–602.

1870. 'New Books', August. *Blackwood's Edinburgh Magazine*, 108, pp.166–188.

1871. 'American Books', October. *Blackwood's Edinburgh Magazine*, 110, pp. 422–442.

1874. 'The Rights of Women,' 7 March. *The Spectator*, pp. 301–2.

1879. 'Two Ladies,' February. *Blackwood's Edinburgh Magazine* 125, pp. 206–24.

1880. 'The Grievances of Women,' May. *Fraser's Magazine*, 101, pp. 698–710.

1881. 'A Few French Novels', December. *Blackwood's Edinburgh Magazine* 130, pp. 703–23.

1887. 'In Maga's Library: The Old Saloon,' January. *Blackwood's Edinburgh Magazine,* 141 pp. 126–53.

1888a. 'A Fireside Commentary',11 January. *St. James's Gazette*, pp. 5–6.

1888b. 'A Fireside Commentary', 30 January. *St. James's Gazette*, pp. 5–6.

1888c. 'The Old Saloon,' September. *Blackwood's Edinburgh Magazine*, 44, pp. 419–43.

1889a. 'A Commentary from My Chair', 7 December. *The Spectator*, pp. 804–5.

1889b. 'A Commentary from an Easy-Chair', 14 December. *The Spectator*, pp. 804–5.

1890a. 'A Commentary in an Easy-Chair', 9 August. *The Spectator*, pp. 177–8.

1890b. 'A Commentary in an Easy-Chair', 20 September. *The Spectator*, pp. 374–5.

1890c. 'A Commentary in an Easy-Chair', 18 October *The Spectator*, p. 521.

1893. 'Things in General,' December. *Atalanta*, pp. 220–3.

1894a. 'The Looker-on,' August. *Blackwood's Edinburgh Magazine*, 156, pp. 285–308.

1894b. 'Things in General,' August. *Atalanta*, pp. 732–4.

1895b. 'The Fancies of a Believer,' February. *Blackwood's Edinburgh Magazine*, 157, pp.237–55.

1895c. 'The Looker-on,' December. *Blackwood's Edinburgh*, 158, pp. 905–27.

1896a. 'The Anti-Marriage League,' January. *Blackwood's Edinburgh Magazine*, 159, pp. 135–49.

1896b. 'The Looker-on,' October. *Blackwood's Edinburgh Magazine*, 160, pp.481–507.

Secondary

Aindow, Rosy, 2016. *Dress and Identity in British Literary Culture 1870–1914*. London and New York: Routledge.

Anon., December 1849. 'Passages in the Life of Mrs. Margaret Maitland,' *Tait's Edinburgh Magazine* 16, pp. 759–766.

Anon., 12 November 1864. 'Chronicles of Carlingford,' *The Athenaeum*, p. 629.

Anon., 7 July 1866. 'Chronicles of Carlingford: Miss Marjoribanks,' *The Athenaeum*, pp. 12–13.

Anon., 23 July 1887. 'Novels,' *The Saturday Review*, p. 125.

Anon., 2 June 1894. 'The Female Bachelor,' *The Saturday Review*, pp. 582–3.

Anon., 28 June 1897. 'The Death of Mrs. Oliphant. A Well-Known Novelist,' *The Pall Mall Gazette*, p. 8.

Atkinson, Juliette, 2010. *Victorian Biography Revisited*. Oxford: Oxford University Press.

Austen, Jane, 1972. *Northanger Abbey.* (ed.), Anne Ehrenpreis. Harmondsworth: Penguin.

Barrie, J. M., 1898, *A Widow's Tale and Other Stories by Mrs. Oliphant*, With an Introductory Note by J. M. Barrie. Edinburgh and London: William Blackwood and Sons.

Basham, Diana, 1992. *The Trial of Woman: Feminism and the Occult Sciences in Victorian Literature and Society*. Basingstoke and London: Macmillan.

Brooker, Peter, Paul Stigant and Peter Widdowson, 2013. 'History and "literary value": *Adam Bede* and *Salem Chapel*,' in *Popular Fictions: Essays in Literature and History* (ed.), Peter Humm, Paul Stigant, and Peter Widdowson. London and New York: Routledge.

Bourdieu, Pierre, 1979/1984. *Distinction: A Social Critique of the Judgement of Taste*. Trans. Richard Nice. Harvard: Cambridge, Mass.

Bourdieu, Pierre, 1991. *Language and Symbolic Power*, (ed.), John B. Thompson. Cambridge: Polity Press.

Bourdieu, Pierre, and Pierre Bourdieu and Loic Wacquant, 1992. *An Invitation to Reflexive Sociology*. Chicago: University of Chicago Press.

Bown, Nicola, Carolyn Burdett and Pamela Thurschwell (eds.), 2004. *The Victorian Supernatural*. Cambridge: Cambridge University Press.

Brontë, Charlottte, 2000. *The Letters of Charlotte Brontë*, ed. Margaret Smith, 3 vols, Vol II, Oxford: The Clarendon Press.

———, 1849. 'Passages in the Life of Mrs. Margaret Maitland,' *The Spectator* (22 December), pp. 1212–1213.

_____, 1979. *Villette*, Tony Tanner (ed.). Harmondsworth: Penguin.

Browning, Robert, 1989. *Robert Browning: Selected Poetry*, Daniel Karlin (ed.). London: Penguin.

Butler, Judith, 2006. *Gender Trouble: Feminism and the Subversion of Identity*. New York and Abingdon: Routledge.

_____, 2004. *Precarious Life: The Powers of Mourning and* Violence. London and New York: Verso.

Calder, Jenni 2003. 'Through Mrs. Oliphant's Library Window,' *Women's Writing*, 10:3, pp. 485–502.

Campbell, Ian, Aileen Christianson, and David R. Sorenson (eds.), 2010. *The Collected Letters of Thomas and Jane Welsh Carlyle*, Vol 38. Duke-Edinburgh edition. Durham, NC: Duke University Press.

Census of England and Wales for the Year 1871. General Report, Volume IV. London: Eyre and Spottiswoode, 1873

Clarke, John Stock, 1986. *Margaret Oliphant*. Victorian Fiction Research Guides University of Queensland.

Clarke, John Stock. *Mrs. Oliphant, 1828–1897. The Rise, Decline and Recovery of a Reputation. A Secondary Bibliography 1949–2005* [online]. http://www.victoriansecrets.co.uk/wordpress/wp-content/uploads/2012/05/33-Margaret-Oliphant.pdf. Accessed: 11 May 2018.

Cobbe, Frances Power, 1889. 'Excess of Widows over Widowers,' *The Westminster Review*, 131 (January). pp. 501–5.

Colón, Susan E., 2012. *Victorian Parables*. London and New York: Continuum.

Coleridge, Christabel, 1903. *Charlotte Mary Yonge: Her Life and Letters*. London: Macmillan and Co.

Connell, R. W., 1995/2005. *Masculinities*. Cambridge: Polity Press.

Connor, Steven, 2004. 'Afterword', in Bown et, al. (eds.), *The Victorian Supernatural*. Cambridge: Cambridge University Press, pp.258–77.

Curran, Cynthia, 1993. 'Private Women, Public Needs: Middle-Class Widows in Victorian England,' *Albion*, 25:2 (Summer) pp. 217–236.

Dabby, Benjamin, 2017. *Women as Public Moralists in Britain: From the Bluestockings to Virginia Woolf.* The Boydell Press and Royal Historical Society.

D'Albertis, Deirdre, 1997. 'The Domestic Drone: Margaret Oliphant and a Political History of the Novel,' *Studies in English Literature, 1500–1900,* 37:4, *Nineteenth Century* (Autumn), pp. 805–829.

Darwin, Charles, 1872. *The Expression of the Emotions in Man and Animals*. London: John Murray.

Davidoff, Leonore, and Catherine Hall, 1997. *Family Fortunes: Men and Women of the English Middle Class 1780–1850*. London: Routledge.

Davis, Philip, 2008. *Why Victorian Literature Still Matters*. Chichester, Malden, Oxford: Wiley-Blackwell.

Dingle, Deliverance, 1887. 'Clothes from the Novelist's Point of View,' *The Lady's World* (June).

Edmundson, Melissa, 2010. 'The "Uncomfortable Houses" of Charlotte Riddell and Margaret Oliphant,' *Gothic Studies*, 12:1 (May), pp. 51–67.

Eliot, Simon, 1992. *A Measure of Popularity: Public Library Holdings of Twenty-four Popular Authors 1883–1912*. Oxford and Bristol: History of the Book- On Demand series.

Emig, Rainer, and Antony Rowland, (eds.), 2010. *Performing Masculinity*. Basingstoke and New York: Palgrave Macmillan.

Fielding, Penny, 1999. 'Other Worlds: Oliphant's Spectralisation of the Modern,' *Women's Writing*, 6:2, pp. 201–213.

Finkelstein, David, 2002; rpt 2010. *The House of Blackwood: Author-Publisher Relations in the Victorian Era*. University Park, Pennsylvania: Pennsylvania University Press.

Finlayson, Ian, 2004. *Browning: A Private Life*. London: HarperCollins.

Fraser, Hilary, Stephanie Green and Judith Johnston, (eds.), 2003. *Gender and the Victorian Periodical*. Cambridge: Cambridge University Press.

Garland-Thomson, Rosemarie, 2005. 'Feminist Disability Studies,' *Signs: Journal of Women in Culture and Society*, 30:2 (Winter), pp. 1557–1587.

Garland-Thomson, Rosemarie, 2011. 'Integrating Disability, Transforming Feminist Theory,' in Kim Q. Hall (ed.), *Feminist Disability Studies*. Bloomington and Indianapolis: Indiana University Press, pp. 13–47.

Gruner, Elisabeth Rose, 2005. 'Short Fiction by Women in the Victorian Literature Survey,' in Jeanne Moskal and Shannon R. Wooden, (eds.), *Teaching British Women Writers 1750–1900*. New York: Peter Lang, pp. 101–109.

[Gwynn, Stephen], 1899. 'The Life and Writings of Mrs. Oliphant,' *Edinburgh Review* 190 (1 July), 26–47.

Haight, Gordon S., (ed.), 1954–78. *The George Eliot Letters*. 9 Vols. New Haven: Yale University Press.

Hamilton, Susan (ed.), 2004. *Criminals, Idiots, Women, and Minors: Victorian Writing By Women on Women*, 2nd edition. Peterborough, Ontario: Broadview Press.

Harman, Barbara Leah, and Susan Meyer, (eds.), 1996. *The New Nineteenth Century: Feminist Readings of Underread Victorian Fiction*. New York and Abingdon: Taylor and Francis.

Heller, Tamar, 1997. 'Textual Seductions: Women's Reading and Writing in Margaret Oliphant's "The Library Widow",' *Victorian Literature and Culture*, 25:1. pp. 23–37.

Henley, W. E., 1884a. 'New Novels,' *The Academy*, (5 January), pp. 5–6.

Henson, Louise, 2004. 'Investigations and fictions: Charles Dickens and ghosts,' in Nicola Bown, Carolyn Burdett and Pamela Thurschwell (eds.), *The Victorian Supernatural*. Cambridge: Cambridge University Press, pp. 44–63.

Hillman, David, and Ulrika Maude (eds.), 2015. *The Cambridge Companion to the Body in Literature*. Cambridge: Cambridge University Press.

Hollander, Anne, 1993. *Seeing Through Clothes*. Berkeley, Los Angeles, London: University of California Press.

Houston, Gail Turley, 1999. *Royalties: The Queen and Victorian Writers*. Charlottesville and London: University Press of Virginia.

Hughes, Clair, 2006. *Dressed in Fiction*. London: Berg.

_____, 2001. *Henry James and the Art of Dress*. Basingstoke and New York: Palgrave.

[Hutton, R. H.], 1896. 'The Seen and the Unseen,' *The Spectator* (25 January), pp. 130–1.

James, Henry, 1984b. 'New Novels,' in Leon Edel with Mark Wilson (eds.), *Henry James, Literary Criticism: Essays, American and English Writers*. New York: The Library of America, pp. 26–33.

_____, 1984b. 'London Notes, August 1897,' in Leon Edel with Mark Wilson (eds.), *Henry James, Literary Criticism: Essays, American and English Writers*. New York: The Library of America, pp. 1406–1413.

_____, 1976. *The Ambassadors*. Harmondsworth: Penguin.

James, M.R., 1931. 'Ghosts – Treat Them Gently!' *The Evening News* (17 April). https://mrjamesarchive.wordpress.com/read/ghosts-treat-them-gently/ [accessed 25 November 2018]

James, M.R., 1929. 'Some Remarks on Ghost Stories,' *The Bookman*, 77 (December) pp. 169–172.

Jameson, Fredric, 2013. *The Antinomies of Realism*. London: Verso.

Jay, Elisabeth, and Francis O'Gorman (eds.), 1999. 'Margaret Oliphant,' *Special Number: Women's Writing*: 6:2.

Jay, Elisabeth, 1995. *Mrs. Oliphant: A Fiction to Herself: A Literary Life*. Oxford: The Clarendon Press.

Jones, Wendy S. 2005. *Consensual Fictions: Women, Liberalism, and the English Novel*. Toronto, Buffalo, London: University of Toronto Press.

Karlin, Daniel, 2002. 'Having the Whip-Hand in *Middlemarch*,' in *Rereading Victorian Fiction*, (ed.), Alice Jenkins and Juliet John. Houndmills, Basingstoke: Palgrave, pp. 29–43.

Korte, Barbara, 1997. *Body Language in Literature*. Toronto, Buffalo, London: University of Toronto Press.

Kortsch, Christine Bayles, 2016. *Dress Culture in Late Victorian Women's Fiction: Literacy, Textiles, and Activism*. London and New York: Routledge.

Langbauer, Laurie, 1999. *Novels of Everyday Life: The Series in English Fiction, 1850–1930*. Ithaca and London: Cornell University Press.

Langland, Elizabeth, 1995. *Nobody's Angels: Middle-Class Women and Domestic Ideology in Victorian Culture*. Ithaca and London: Cornell University Press.

Lawler, Steph, 2008. *Identity: Sociological Perspectives*. Cambridge and Malden: Polity Press.

Leavis, Q.D. 1989. 'Mrs. Oliphant: *Miss Marjoribanks* (Introduction) [1969],' in *Collected, Essays* (1989) G. Singh (ed.), 3 Vols. Cambridge: Cambridge University Press. III, pp. 135–158.

_____, 1989. 'Mrs. Oliphant: *The Autobiography and Letters*' (Introduction) in *Collected Essays* III, pp.159–181.

Lee, Hermione, 2013. *Penelope Fitzgerald: A Life.* London: Chatto & Windus.

Levine, George, 2016. 'Taking Oliphant Seriously: *A Country Gentleman and His Family,*' *ELH*, 83, pp. 233–258.

Litchfield, H. E. (ed.), 2010 *Emma Darwin, Wife of Charles Darwin: A Century of Family Letters by H. E. Litchfield,* 2 Vols, 1904, rpt. Cambridge: Cambridge University Press.

Lobban, John Hay, 1897. 'Mrs. Oliphant,' *Blackwood's Magazine* 162 (July), pp. 161–4.

Loftus, Donna, 2012, 'Entrepreneurialism or Gentlemanly Capitalism,' in Martin Hewitt (ed.), *The Victorian World.* Abingdon and New York: Routledge, pp. 193–208.

Logan, Deborah Anna (ed.), 2007. *The Collected Letters of Harriet Martineau,* 5 Vols. London: Pickering and Chatto.

Mallett, Phillip, 2015. *The Victorian Novel and Masculinity.* Basingstoke and New York: Palgrave Macmillan.

Mansfield, Katherine, 1915. 'The Little Governess,' in *Katherine Mansfield: Selected Stories,* (ed.), Angela Smith (2002). Oxford: Oxford University Press, pp. 47–59.

Marcus, Sharon, 1999. *Apartment Stories: City and Home in Nineteenth-Century Paris and London.* Berkeley, Los Angeles and London: University of California Press.

Merleau-Ponty, Maurice, 2005. *Phenomenology of Perception,* trans. Colin Smith. London and New York.

Michie, Elise B., 2011. *The Vulgar Question of Money. Heiresses, Materialism, and the Novel of Manners from Jane Austen to Henry James.* Baltimore: The Johns Hopkins University Press.

Milton, Heather, 2009. 'The Female Confessor, Confession, and Domains of Discourse in Margaret Oliphant's *Salem Chapel,*' in Tamara S. Wagner (ed.), *Antifeminism and the Victorian Novel: Re-reading Nineteenth-Century Women Writers,* Amherst, New York: Cambria Press, pp. 197–216.

Mulvey, Laura, 1975. 'Visual Pleasure and Narrative Cinema,' *Screen*, 16:3 (1 October), pp. 6–18.

O'Mealy, Joseph H. O., 2012. 'Mrs. Oliphant, *Miss Marjoribanks* (1866), and the Victorian Canon,' in Barbara Leah Harmon and Susan Meyer (eds.), *The New Nineteenth Century: Feminist Readings of Underread Victorian Fiction,* pp. 63–76.

Ofek, Galia, 2009. *Representations of Hair in Victorian Literature and Culture.* Farnham and Burlington: Ashgate Publishing.

Onslow, Barbara, 2000. *Women of the Press in Nineteenth-Century Britain.* Basingstoke: Palgrave Macmillan.

Oosterom, Judith van, 2010. *The Whirligig of Time: Margaret Oliphant in her Later Years.* Bern: Peter Lang.

Pettitt, Clare, 1999. '"Every man for himself, and God for us all": Mrs. Oliphant, Self-Help, and Industrial Success Literature,' *Women's Writing*, 6:2, pp. 163–179.

Plotz, John, 2008. *Portable Property: Victorian Culture on the Move.* Princeton and Oxford: Princeton University Press.

Reynolds, Kimberley, and Nicola Humble, 1993. *Victorian Heroines: Representations of Femininity in Nineteenth-Century Literature and Art*. Hemel Hempstead: Harvester Wheatsheaf.

Robinson, Amy, 2009. '"An original and unlooked-for ending?" Irony, the Marriage Plot, and the Antifeminism Debate in Oliphant's *Miss Marjoribanks*,' in Tamara S. Wagner, *Antifeminism and the Victorian Novel*, pp. 159–176.

Robinson, Solveig C., 2005. '"Expanding a 'Limited Orbit'": Margaret Oliphant, *Blackwood's Edinburgh Magazine*, and the Development of a Critical Voice,' *Victorian Periodicals Review*, 38:2 (Summer), pp. 199–220.

Roper, Michael, and John Tosh (eds.), 1991. *Manful Assertions: Masculinities in Britain since 1800*. London: Routledge.

Rose, Jonathan, 2007. 'Modernity and Print I: Britain 1890–1970,' in *A Companion to the History of the Book*, (eds.), Simon Eliot and Jonathan Rose. Malden, Oxford, and Victoria: Blackwell Publishing.

Rubik, Margarete, 1994. *The Novels of Mrs. Oliphant: A Subversive View of Traditional Themes*. Bern: Peter Lang.

———, 1995. 'The Subversion of Literary Clichés in Oliphant's Fiction,' in D. J. Trela, (ed.), *Margaret Oliphant: Critical Essays on A Gentle Subversive*. Selinsgrove: Susquehanna University Press, and London: Associated University Presses, pp. 49–65.

Sanders, Valerie, 1996. *Eve's Renegades: Victorian Anti-Feminist Women Novelists*. Houndmills, London and New York: Macmillan.

———, (ed.), 2012. *The Selected Works of Margaret Oliphant*, Part II: Vol 5, *Literary Criticism 1887–97*. London: Pickering and Chatto.

Schor, Esther H., 1993. 'The Haunted Interpreter in Margaret Oliphant's Supernatural Fiction,' *Women's Studies: An Interdisciplinary Journal*, 22:3 (1 June), pp. 371–388.

Schroeder, Jonathan, 1998. 'Consuming representation: a visual approach to consumer research,' in Barbara B. Stern (ed.), *Representing Consumers: Voices, Views and Visions*. London and New York: Routledge, pp. 193–230.

Sharpe's London Journal (1850). 'Mrs. Margaret Maitland,' (January), 115–120.

Shattock, Joanne, 2018. 'Margaret Oliphant on Marriage and Its Discontents,' in Carolyn Lambert and Marion Shaw (eds.), *For Better, For Worse: Marriage in Victorian Novels*. New York and Abingdon: Routledge, pp. 101–15.

———, 2010. 'The culture of criticism.' In *The Cambridge Companion to English Literature 1830–1914*. (ed.), Joanne Shattock. Cambridge: Cambridge University Press, pp. 71–90.

———, 2011. *The Selected Works of Margaret Oliphant: Part I: Literary Criticism and Literary History:* Vol I, *Literary Criticism, 1854–69*. London: Pickering and Chatto.

———, 2000. 'Work for Women: Margaret Oliphant's Journalism.' In L. Brake, B. Bell, and D. Finkelstein (eds.), *Nineteenth-Century Media and the Construction of Identities*. New York: Palgrave, pp. 165–177.

[Skelton, John], 1883. 'A Little Chat about Mrs. Oliphant,' *Blackwood's Magazine* (January), pp. 73–91.

Smajić, Srdjan, 2010. *Ghost-Seers, Detectives, and Science*. Cambridge: Cambridge University Press.

Smart, Graeme, and Amelia Yeates, (eds.), 2008. *Victorian Masculinities, Critical Survey*, 20:3.

Speller, John R.W., 2011. *Bourdieu and Literature*. Cambridge: Open Book Publishers.

[Stephen, Leslie], 1899. 'Studies of a Biographer – Southey's Letters,' *The National Review* (July), 740–57.

Stern, Kimberly J., 2016. *The Social Life of Criticism: Gender, Critical Writing, and the Politics of Belonging*. Ann Arbor: University of Michigan Press.

Stewart, Clare, 2001. '"Weird Fascination": The Response to Victorian Women's Ghost Stories,' in Emma Liggins and Daniel Duffy (eds.), *Feminist Readings of Victorian Popular Texts: Divergent Femininities*. Aldershot, Burlington, Singapore, Sydney: Ashgate, pp. 108–125.

Stoddard Holmes, Martha, 2004. *Fictions of Affliction: Physical Disability in Victorian Culture*. Ann Arbor: The University of Michigan Press.

Sussman, Herbert, 1995. *Victorian Masculinities: Manhood and Masculine Poetics in Early Victorian Literature and Art*. Cambridge: Cambridge University Press.

Thaden, Barbara Z., 1997. *The Maternal Voice in Victorian Fiction: Rewriting the Patriarchal Family*. New York: Garland Publishing, and London: Taylor and Francis.

Trela, D. J., (ed.), 1995. *Margaret Oliphant: Critical Essays on a Gentle Subversive*. Selinsgrove: Susquehanna University Press, and London: Associated University Presses.

Trollope, Anthony, 1986 (1864–5), *Can You Forgive Her?* (ed.), Stephen Wall. London: Penguin.

Tromp, Marlene, 2000. *The Private Rod: Marital Violence, Sensation, and the Law in Victorian Britain*. Charlottesville and London: University of Virginia Press.

Tuchman, Gaye, with Nina E. Fortin, 1989. *Edging Women Out: Victorian Novelists, Publishers, and Social Change*. London: Routledge.

Wagner, Tamara S. (ed.), 2009. *Antifeminism and the Victorian Novel: Rereading Nineteenth-Century Women Writers*. Amherst, New York: Cambria Press.

Wilkes, Joanne (ed.), 2012. *The Selected Works of Margaret Oliphant*, Part II: Vol 5, *Literary Criticism 1887–97*. London: Pickering and Chatto.

————, 2010. *Women Reviewing Women in Nineteenth-Century Britain: The Critical Reception of Jane Austen, Charlotte Brontë and George Eliot*. Farnham and Burlington: Ashgate Publishing.

Williams, Merryn, 1986. *Margaret Oliphant: A Critical Biography*. Basingstoke and London: Macmillan.

Wilson, Elizabeth, 2003. *Adorned in Dreams: Fashion and Modernity*. London: Virago 1985 rpt. Rutgers University Press, New Brunswick.

Woolf, Virginia, 1944. 'Moments of Being,' in *A Haunted House, and Other Stories*. London: The Hogarth Press.

Zakreski, Patricia, 2016. 'Fashioning the Domestic Novel: Rewriting Narrative Patterns in Margaret Oliphant's *Phoebe, Junior* and *Dress*,' *Journal of Victorian Culture*, 21:1, pp. 56–73.

Websites

https://www.bbc.co.uk/programmes/b03mcmx3. Accessed 10 May 2018.

https://www.le.ac.uk/eh/teach/ug/modules/eh3107/occupations.pdf. Accessed 5 May 2018.

http://www.oliphantfiction.com/ Accessed 18 May 2018.

http://www.oliphantfiction.com/x0200_single_title.php?titlecode=msmarj. Accessed 25 February 2018

http://www.open.ac.uk/Arts/reading/UK/search.php. Accessed 28 April 2018.

http://www.victorianweb.org/history/census.html. Accessed, 5 May 2018.

Index

Anti-feminism, 2, 19, 20, 88, 188, 196
Austen, Jane, 5, 26, 50, 63, 112, 193, 212; *Northanger Abbey*, 118, 197, 206

Barrie, J.M., 11, 24, 194, 206
Blackwood, John, 3, 8, 29, 34, 40, 129, 150, 195, 196, 197, 199
Blackwood, William, 7, 159, 193
Blackwood's Edinburgh Magazine, 22, 23, 30, 107, 195, 197, 203, 212, 214; 'general utility woman' for, 30; history of, Chapter 1; 32–4; masculinity of, 32, 50; 'The Looker-on', 31, 45, 47–9 'Old Saloon,' 31–33, 193, 195, 205
body, the, 14, 26, 27, 62, 68, 90, 112, 116–17, 119, 121, 145, 179, 210, 211; beards, 27, 89, 94, 98, 103, 109, 110, 138, 153; hands, 96–102; disabled, 105–111; *The Doctor's Family*, 95–8; *Miss Marjoribanks*, 100–105; *Salem Chapel*, 78–9; theories of, 91–5
Bourdieu, Pierre, cultural capital, 113, 116; embodiment, 92–4; habitus, 93; hexis, 93; literary field, 13, 33–4; symbolic power, 61; 79, 96, 133, 206, 214
Braddon, Mary Elizabeth, sales 22; 36, 52, 59; *Lady Audley's Secret*, 49, 55

Brontë, Charlotte, 2,3, 5, 6, 9, 12, 50, 52, 86, 94, 207, 216; *Jane Eyre*, 36, 50; *Shirley*, 3; *Villette*, 111; on *Margaret Maitland*, 3
Butler, Judith, 27, 207; 'grievable' lives, 156–7, 'relationality', 156, 165

Carlyle, Jane, 9, 11; Thomas, 9, 34, 72, 111, 135, 194, 195, 207
Clarke, John Stock, 16, 23, 188
clothes, 27, 47, 78, 80, 89–95, 100, 110–122, 167, 208, 210; men's clothes, 119–122
Collins, Wilkie, 22, 23, 30, 50, 52, 106; *The Woman in White*, 30, 52
critical approaches, 26–7; theory of the body, 91–5; masculinities, 132–6

dresses, black, 28, 78–9, 90, 114–15, 120; white, 27, 79, 90, 104, 113–18, 120, 162, 165, 167, 177

Eliot, George, 2,3, 5, 6, 10,11, 15, 23,38–9, 58, 112,126, 146, 167, 195, 209, 216; Compared with MOWO, 12, 24, 26, 33, 86, 188–9; on *Carlingford Chronicles*, 3, *The Rector*, 3; sales 8; *Adam Bede*, 3, 135, 147; *Daniel*